Campbell's®

RECIPE-A-DAY
Calendar

Notes

Pictured on the front cover: One-Dish Chicken & Rice Bake *(March 13)*

ISBN: 978-1-4508-8148-7

Manufactured in China.

8 7 6 5 4 3 2 1

Microwave Cooking: Microwave ovens vary in wattage. Use the cooking times as guidelines and check for doneness before adding more time.

Preparation/Cooking Times: Preparation times are based on the approximate amount of time required to assemble the recipe before cooking, baking, chilling or serving. These times include preparation steps such as measuring, chopping and mixing. The fact that some preparations and cooking can be done simultaneously is taken into account. Preparation of optional ingredients and serving suggestions is not included.

Notes

You've known for years now how reliable and delicious *Campbell's* recipes are—after all, it's just not a holiday without Green Bean Casserole on the table! But there's no reason to wait for a special occasion to enjoy the many kitchen-tested recipes *Campbell's* has to offer. No matter what type of meal you're preparing, *Campbell's* and their trusted family of brands has something that will fit the bill perfectly.

To help you discover an entire year of delicious dishes, we've put together this *Campbell's* **Recipe-A-Day Calendar** so that every day can reach its full flavor potential! Kick off your new year with comforting slow-cooker favorites, then head into the warmer months with plenty of great grilling ideas and inspiration for using fresh, seasonal spring and summer produce. Hearty fall dishes and holiday classics round out the year, but sprinkled throughout the weeks and months are easy-to-make recipes for busy nights, kid-friendly family favorites, and terrific options for entertaining like scrumptious spreads, dips, and decadent desserts.

Let *Campbell's* join you on your year of deliciousness!
We can't wait to see what you cook up!

Notes

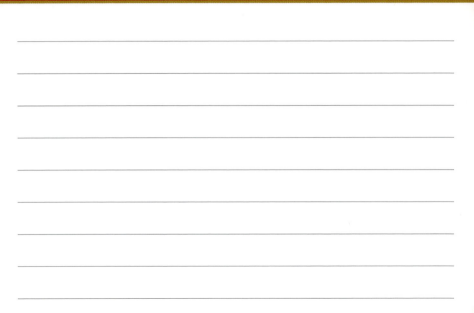

Buffalo Chicken Dip

prep 10 minutes | **bake** 20 minutes | **makes** 32 servings (about 4 cups)

- **1 package (8 ounces) cream cheese, softened**
- **½ cup blue cheese salad dressing**
- **½ cup hot pepper sauce**
- **2 ounces crumbled blue cheese or shredded mozzarella cheese (about ½ cup)**
- **2 cans (12.5 ounces each) Swanson® Premium White Chunk Chicken Breast in Water, drained**
- **Assorted fresh vegetables and Pepperidge Farm® crackers**

1. Heat the oven to 350°F.

2. Stir the cream cheese in a 9-inch deep-dish pie plate with a fork or whisk until smooth. Stir in the dressing, hot sauce and blue cheese. Stir in the chicken.

3. Bake for 20 minutes or until the chicken mixture is hot and bubbling. Stir the chicken mixture before serving. Serve with the vegetables and crackers for dipping.

To make in the microwave: Use a microwavable 9-inch deep-dish pie plate. Prepare the dip as directed above in step 2. Microwave, uncovered, on HIGH for 5 minutes or until the chicken mixture is hot, stirring halfway through the cook time.

Tip: This dip can be kept warm in a small slow cooker or fondue pot on the buffet table.

To reduce the fat: Use Neufchâtel or light cream cheese and reduced-fat blue cheese salad dressing.

Bacon Potato Chowder

prep 15 minutes | **cook** 3 hours | **makes** 8 servings

- 4 **slices bacon, cooked and crumbled**
- 1 **large onion, chopped (about 1 cup)**
- 4 **cans (10¾ ounces each) Campbell's® Condensed Cream of Potato Soup**
- 4 **soup cans milk**
- ¼ **teaspoon ground black pepper**
- 2 **large russet potatoes, cut into ½-inch pieces (about 3 cups)**
- ½ **cup chopped fresh chives**
- 2 **cups shredded Cheddar cheese (about 8 ounces)**

1. Stir the bacon, onion, soup, milk, black pepper, potatoes and ¼ **cup** chives in a 6-quart slow cooker.

2. Cover and cook on HIGH for 3 to 4 hours or until the potatoes are tender.

3. Add the cheese and stir until the cheese is melted. Serve with the remaining chives.

Barley and Lentil Soup

prep 10 minutes | **cook** 8 hours | **makes** 8 servings

- 8 cups Swanson® Beef Broth (Regular, 50% Less Sodium **or** Certified Organic)
- 2 cloves garlic, minced
- 1 teaspoon dried oregano leaves, crushed
- 4 large carrots, sliced (about 3 cups)
- 1 large onion, chopped (about 1 cup)
- ½ cup **uncooked** dried lentils
- ½ cup **uncooked** pearl barley

1. Stir the broth, garlic, oregano, carrots, onion, lentils and barley in a 3½- to 6-quart slow cooker.

2. Cover and cook on LOW for 8 to 9 hours* or until the lentils and barley are tender.

Or on HIGH for 4 to 5 hours.

Top It Off!

- Buttery, golden brown bread crumbs are a popular choice when it comes to topping a casserole. Making your own bread crumbs is a great way to use up a leftover loaf of bread.

- To make bread crumbs, preheat oven to 300°F. Place a single layer of bread slices on a baking sheet and bake 5 to 8 minutes or until completely dry and lightly browned. Cool completely. Process in food processor or crumble in resealable plastic food storage bag until very fine.

- For additional flavor, season with salt, pepper and a small amount of dried herbs, ground spices or grated cheese as desired. Generally, 1 slice of bread equals ⅓ cup bread crumbs.

Beef Teriyaki

prep 10 minutes | **cook** 15 minutes | **makes** 4 servings

- 2 **tablespoons cornstarch**
- 1¾ **cups Swanson® Beef Stock**
- 2 **tablespoons soy sauce**
- 1 **tablespoon packed brown sugar**
- ½ **teaspoon garlic powder**
- 1 **boneless beef sirloin steak**
- 4 **cups fresh or frozen broccoli florets**
  Hot cooked rice

1. Stir the cornstarch, stock, soy sauce, brown sugar and garlic powder in a small bowl until the mixture is smooth.

2. Stir-fry the beef in a 10-inch nonstick skillet over medium-high heat until well browned, stirring often. Pour off any fat.

3. Add the broccoli to the skillet and cook for 1 minute. Stir in the cornstarch mixture. Cook and stir until the mixture boils and thickens. Serve the beef mixture over the rice.

Tip: To make slicing easier, freeze the beef for 1 hour before slicing.

Casserole Tips

- Casserole cookware comes in a variety of shapes, sizes and materials that fall into 2 general descriptions. They can be either deep, round containers with handles and tight-fitting lids or square and rectangular baking dishes. Casseroles are made out of glass, ceramic or metal. When preparing a casserole, it's important to bake the casserole in the proper size dish so that the ingredients cook evenly in the time specified.

- If the size of the casserole or baking dish isn't marked on the bottom of the dish, it can be measured to determine the size.

  Round and oval casseroles are measured by volume, not inches, and are always listed by quart capacity. Fill a measuring cup with water and pour it into an empty casserole. Repeat until the casserole is filled with water, keeping track of the amount of water added. The amount of water is equivalent to the size of the dish.

  Square and rectangular baking dishes are usually measured in inches. If the dimensions aren't marked on the bottom of a square or rectangular baking dish, use a ruler to measure on top from the inside of one edge to the inside of the opposite edge.

Beefy Taco Dip

prep 5 minutes | **cook** 15 minutes | **makes** 2 servings

- ½ **pound ground beef**
- 1½ **teaspoons chili powder**
- 1 **cup Pace® Chunky Salsa**
- ½ **of an 8-ounce package cream cheese, cut into pieces**
- ½ **cup shredded Cheddar cheese**
  - *Assorted Toppings* (optional)
  - **Sour cream** (optional)
  - **Tortilla chips**

1. Cook the beef and chili powder in a 10-inch skillet over medium-high heat until the beef is well browned, stirring often. Pour off any fat.

2. Stir the salsa, cream cheese and Cheddar cheese in the skillet. Cook and stir until the cheese is melted. Sprinkle with the *Assorted Toppings* and top with the sour cream, if desired. Serve with the tortilla chips.

Assorted Toppings: Chopped tomatoes, sliced green onions, sliced pitted ripe olives.

Measuring Liquid Ingredients

- Use clear glass or plastic measuring cups with calibrations marked on the side when measuring liquid ingredients. An ideal set of liquid measures include 1 cup, 2 cup and 4 cup measures.

- To measure liquid accurately, place the measuring cup on the counter so it is level. Fill to the desired mark. Compare the ingredient amount with the cup calibration at eye level. Do not pick up the cup because you may not hold it level, resulting in an error in measuring. Small amounts of liquid (under ¼ cup) can be measured with measuring spoons by filling the spoon to the rim.

Berry Rum Toddies

prep 5 minutes | **cook** 5 minutes | **makes** 2 servings

- 1   bottle (16 ounces) V8 Splash® Berry Blend Juice Drink (2 cups)
- ¼   cup dark spiced **or** regular rum
- ½   teaspoon ground cinnamon
- ¼   teaspoon ground ginger
- 2   cinnamon sticks

1. Heat the juice drink, rum, cinnamon and ginger in a 1-quart saucepan to a boil over medium heat and cook for 5 minutes, stirring occasionally.

2. Pour the juice mixture into **2** mugs.

3. Serve immediately with the cinnamon sticks.

Measuring Dry Ingredients

- The tools needed for measuring dry ingredients include a set of four metal or plastic dry measures (1 cup, ½ cup, ⅓ cup and ¼ cup) and a set of measuring spoons (1 tablespoon, 1 teaspoon, ½ teaspoon, ¼ teaspoon and sometimes ⅛ teaspoon).

- To measure accurately, fill the measure to overflowing and with a straight edge of a metal spatula, sweep across the top of the measure to level the ingredient. Flour should be spooned into the cup. Do not dip the measuring cup into the flour, because this will compact the flour and result in an inaccurate measure.

Braised Short Ribs with Red Wine Tomato Sauce

prep 10 minutes | **cook** 7 hours | **makes** 8 servings

- 4 **pounds beef short ribs, cut into serving-sized pieces**
- 2⅔ **cups Prego® Fresh Mushroom Italian Sauce**
- 1 **cup dry red wine**
- 1 **bag fresh or frozen whole baby carrots**
- 1 **large onion, chopped (about 1 cup)**
  Hot cooked rice

1. Season the ribs as desired.

2. Stir the Italian sauce, wine, carrots and onion in a 3½-quart slow cooker. Add the ribs and turn to coat.

3. Cover and cook on LOW for 7 to 8 hours* or until the ribs are fork-tender. Serve with the rice.

Or on HIGH for 4 to 5 hours.

Tips

Time Savers

- Save time by preparing your casserole in a baking dish that doubles as a serving dish—less cleanup!

- Salted water takes longer to boil. To save time, don't salt water until after it is boiling.

- To defrost meat quickly and safely use your microwave! (Be sure to follow the manufacturer's instructions for defrosting.)

- When a recipe calls for chicken strips, don't spend time slicing chicken breasts—buy chicken tenders instead.

- Save on cleanup time by portioning food right from the pot onto dinner plates. Call it restaurant-style!

Cheesy Chicken Pizza

prep 15 minutes | **bake** 15 minutes | **makes** 4 servings

- 1 package (about 13 ounces) refrigerated pizza dough
- ½ cup Pace® Picante Sauce
- ½ cup Prego® Traditional Italian Sauce **or** Roasted Garlic & Herb Italian Sauce
- 1 cup chopped cooked chicken **or** turkey
- ½ cup sliced pitted ripe olives
- 2 green onions, sliced (about ¼ cup)
- 4 ounces shredded mozzarella cheese (about 1 cup)

1. Heat the oven to 425°F.

2. Unroll the dough onto a greased 12-inch pizza pan. Press the dough into a 12-inch circle. Pinch up the edge to form a rim.

3. Stir the picante sauce and Italian sauce in a small bowl. Spread the picante sauce mixture over the crust to the rim. Top with the chicken, olives, onions and cheese.

4. Bake for 15 minutes or until the cheese is melted and the crust is golden brown.

Tip: For a crispier crust, prepare the dough as directed in step 2. Bake the dough for 5 minutes. Remove the dough from the oven and proceed as directed in steps 3 and 4.

Campbell's

Vegetables

- No time to chop fresh produce? Buy bags of pre-cut vegetables—they work great in many recipes!

- For side dishes and mix-ins, keep frozen vegetables on hand instead of fresh—they cook faster and keep longer!

- To quick-thaw frozen vegetables, remove from the packaging and place in a microwavable bowl. Cover with waxed paper and microwave on HIGH 2 to 3 minutes, breaking apart with a fork every 30 seconds until easily separated but not cooked.

Chili Mac

prep 15 minutes | **cook** 30 minutes | **makes** 4 servings

- 1   pound ground beef
- 1   cup Pace® Picante Sauce
- 1   tablespoon chili powder
- 1   can (14.5 ounces) whole peeled tomatoes, drained and cut up
- 1   cup frozen whole kernel corn
- 1½ cups elbow pasta, cooked and drained (about 3 cups)
- ½   cup shredded Cheddar cheese
    Sliced avocado **and** sour cream

1. Cook the beef in a 10-inch skillet over medium-high heat until well browned, stirring often to separate the meat. Pour off any fat.

2. Stir the picante sauce, chili powder, tomatoes and corn in the skillet and heat to a boil. Reduce the heat to low. Cook for 10 minutes.

3. Stir in the pasta. Top with the cheese. Cover and cook until the cheese is melted. Garnish with the avocado and sour cream.

Cooking Pasta

- For every pound of pasta, bring 4 to 6 quarts of water to a rolling boil. Gradually add pasta, allowing water to return to a boil. Stir frequently to prevent the pasta from sticking together.

- Pasta is finished cooking when it is tender but still firm to the bite, or al dente. The pasta continues to cook when the casserole is placed in the oven so it is important that the pasta be slightly undercooked. Otherwise, the more the pasta cooks, the softer it becomes and, eventually, it will fall apart.

- Immediately drain pasta to prevent overcooking. For best results, combine pasta with other ingredients immediately after draining.

- If a recipe calls for cooked pasta and time is short, use faster cooking pastas, such as angel hair and spaghettini.

Dripping Roast Beef Sandwiches with Melted Provolone

prep 5 minutes | **cook** 5 minutes | **bake** 3 minutes | **makes** 4 servings

- 1 can (10½ ounces) Campbell's® Condensed French Onion Soup
- 1 tablespoon reduced-sodium Worcestershire sauce
- ¾ pound thinly sliced deli roast beef
- 4 Pepperidge Farm® Classic Soft Hoagie Rolls with Sesame Seeds
- 4 slices deli provolone cheese, cut in half
- ¼ cup drained hot **or** mild pickled banana pepper rings

1. Heat the oven to 400°F.

2. Heat the soup and Worcestershire in a 2-quart saucepan over medium-high heat to a boil. Add the beef and heat through, stirring occasionally.

3. Divide the beef evenly among the rolls. Top the beef with the cheese slices and place the sandwiches onto a baking sheet.

4. Bake for 3 minutes or until the sandwiches are toasted and the cheese is melted. Spoon the soup mixture onto the sandwiches. Top **each** sandwich with 1 **tablespoon** pepper rings.

Tip: You may substitute ½ of a 11.25-ounce package Pepperidge Farm® Texas Toast (4 slices), prepared according to package directions, for the rolls in this recipe. Serve the sandwiches open-faced.

Tips

Cooking Rice

- Different types of rice require different amounts of water and cooking times. Follow the package instructions for the best results.

- When a recipe will be served over rice, save time by heating the cooking water while you're preparing the recipe. It'll be ready when you are!

- To test rice for doneness, bite into a grain or squeeze a grain between your thumb and index finger. The rice is done when it is tender and the center is not hard.

Easy Chicken & Biscuits

prep 10 minutes | **bake** 35 minutes | **makes** 4 servings

- 1 can (10¾ ounces) Campbell's® Condensed Cream of Broccoli Soup (Regular **or** 98% Fat Free)
- 1 can (10¾ ounces) Campbell's® Condensed Cream of Potato Soup
- ⅔ cup milk
- ½ teaspoon poultry seasoning
- ⅛ teaspoon ground black pepper
- 2 cups frozen mixed vegetables
- 2 cups cubed cooked chicken **or** turkey
- 1 package (7.5 ounces) refrigerated biscuits

1. Stir the soups, milk, poultry seasoning, black pepper, vegetables and chicken in a 2-quart shallow baking dish.

2. Bake at 400°F. for 20 minutes or until the chicken mixture is hot and bubbling. Stir the chicken mixture. Top with the biscuits.

3. Bake for 15 minutes or until the biscuits are golden brown.

Tip: Substitute Campbell's® Condensed Cream of Celery Soup for the Cream of Broccoli.

Slow Cookers

- Manufacturers recommend that slow cookers should be one-half to three-quarters full for best results.

- Keep a lid on it! The slow cooker can take as long as twenty minutes to regain the heat lost when the cover is removed. If the recipe calls for stirring or checking the dish near the end of the cooking time, replace the lid as quickly as you can.

- As with conventional cooking recipes, slow cooker recipe time ranges are provided to account for variables such as temperature of ingredients before cooking, how full the slow cooker is, and even altitude. Once you become familiar with your slow cooker you'll have a good idea which end of the time range to use.

- To clean your slow cooker, follow the manufacturer's instructions. To make cleanup even easier, spray with nonstick cooking spray before adding food.

Easy Chicken & Cheese Enchiladas

prep 15 minutes | **bake** 40 minutes | **makes** 6 servings

- 1 **can (10¾ ounces) Campbell's® Condensed Cream of Chicken Soup (Regular or 98% Fat Free)**
- ½ **cup sour cream**
- 1 **cup Pace® Picante Sauce**
- 2 **teaspoons chili powder**
- 2 **cups chopped cooked chicken**
- ½ **cup shredded Monterey Jack cheese**
- 6 **flour tortillas (6-inch), warmed**
- 1 **small tomato, chopped (about ½ cup)**
- 1 **green onion, sliced (about 2 tablespoons)**

1. Heat the oven to 350°F. Stir the soup, sour cream, picante sauce and chili powder in a medium bowl.

2. Stir 1 **cup** soup mixture, chicken and cheese in a large bowl.

3. Divide the chicken mixture among the tortillas. Roll up the tortillas and place seam-side up in a 2-quart shallow baking dish. Pour the remaining soup mixture over the filled tortillas. Cover the baking dish.

4. Bake for 40 minutes or until the enchiladas are hot and bubbling. Top with the tomato and onion.

Tip: Stir ½ **cup** canned black beans, rinsed and drained, into the chicken mixture before filling the tortillas.

Herbs and Spices

- When purchasing fresh herbs, look for brightly colored, fresh-looking leaves without any brown spots or signs of wilting.

- Fresh herbs are very perishable, so purchase them in small amounts. For short-term storage, place the herb stems in water. Cover leaves loosely with a plastic bag or plastic wrap and store in the refrigerator. They will last from two days (basil, chives, dill, mint, oregano) to five days (rosemary, sage, tarragon, thyme).

- When purchasing dried herbs or spices, mark each container with the purchase date and discard any remaining after six months. Buy small quantities of infrequently used herbs and spices. Store in a cool, dry place in tightly covered lightproof containers. Do not place above the range as heat and moisture will cause the flavor to deteriorate more quickly.

Easy Party Meatballs

prep 5 minutes | **cook** 6 hours | **makes** 8 servings

- **3** **cups (1 pound 10 ounces) Prego® Marinara Italian Sauce**
- **1** **jar (12 ounces) grape jelly**
- **½** **cup prepared chili sauce**
- **2½** **pounds frozen fully-cooked meatballs, cocktail size**

1. Stir the Italian sauce, jelly, chili sauce and meatballs in a 4½-quart slow cooker.

2. Cover and cook on LOW for 6 to 7 hours* or until the meatballs are cooked through. Serve the meatballs on a serving plate with toothpicks.

Or on HIGH for 3 to 4 hours.

Tips: Larger-size **or** turkey meatballs can also be used, if desired. For a special touch, serve with cranberry chutney for dipping.

Best Measurement Equivalents

1 tablespoon	=	3 teaspoons
1 cup	=	16 tablespoons
1 cup	=	8 fluid ounces
1 pint	=	2 cups
1 pint	=	16 fluid ounces
1 quart	=	4 cups (2 pints)
1 quart	=	32 fluid ounces
1 gallon	=	16 cups (8 pints or 4 quarts)

Garlic Chicken, Vegetable & Rice Skillet

prep 5 minutes | **cook** 40 minutes | **makes** 4 servings

Vegetable cooking spray
1¼ **pounds skinless, boneless chicken breast halves**
2 **cloves garlic, minced**
1¾ **cups Swanson® Chicken Stock**
¾ **cup uncooked regular long-grain white rice**
1 **bag (16 ounces) frozen vegetable combination**
   (broccoli, cauliflower, carrots)
⅓ **cup grated Parmesan cheese**
Paprika

1. Spray a 12-inch skillet with the cooking spray and heat over medium-high heat for 1 minute. Add the chicken and garlic and cook for 10 minutes or until the chicken is well browned on both sides. Remove the chicken from the skillet.

2. Stir the stock, rice and vegetables in the skillet and heat to a boil. Reduce the heat to low. Cover and cook for 15 minutes. Stir in the cheese.

3. Return the chicken to the skillet. Sprinkle the chicken with the paprika. Cover and cook for 10 minutes or until the chicken is cooked through and the rice is tender.

I'm Dreamy for a White Chocolate Fondue

prep 5 minutes | **cook** 10 minutes | **makes** 12 servings

- ⅓ **cup heavy cream**
- 1 **tablespoon orange-flavored liqueur or ½ teaspoon orange extract**
- 1 **package (about 12 ounces) white chocolate pieces**
  Assorted Dippers: **Assorted Pepperidge Farm® Cookies, whole strawberries, banana chunks, dried pineapple pieces and/or fresh pineapple chunks**

1. Heat the heavy cream, liqueur and chocolate in a 1-quart heavy saucepan over low heat until the mixture is melted and smooth, stirring occasionally.

2. Pour the mixture into a fondue pot or slow cooker. Serve warm with the *Assorted Dippers*.

Hearty Vegetarian Chili

prep 10 minutes | **cook** 20 minutes | **makes** 4 servings

- 2 **tablespoons vegetable oil**
- 1 **large onion, chopped (about 1 cup)**
- 1 **small green pepper, chopped (about ½ cup)**
- ¼ **teaspoon garlic powder or 2 small garlic cloves, minced**
- 1 **tablespoon chili powder**
- ½ **teaspoon ground cumin**
- 2½ **cups V8® 100% Vegetable Juice**
- 1 **can (about 15 ounces) black beans or red kidney beans, rinsed and drained**
- 1 **can (about 15 ounces) pinto beans, rinsed and drained**

1. Heat the oil in a 2-quart saucepan over medium heat. Add the onion, pepper, garlic powder, chili powder and cumin and cook until the vegetables are tender, stirring occasionally.

2. Stir the vegetable juice in the saucepan and heat to a boil. Reduce the heat to low. Cook for 5 minutes.

3. Stir in the beans and cook until the mixture is hot and bubbling.

Stuffed Clams

prep 20 minutes | **cook** 15 minutes | **bake** 20 minutes | **makes** 24 appetizers

- **24 cherrystone clams, scrubbed**
- **2 slices bacon, diced**
- **3 tablespoons butter**
- **1 medium onion, chopped (about ½ cup)**
- **¼ teaspoon garlic powder or 1 clove garlic, minced**
- **1½ cups Pepperidge Farm® Herb Seasoned Stuffing**
- **2 tablespoons grated Parmesan cheese**
- **2 tablespoons chopped fresh parsley or 2 teaspoons dried parsley flakes**

1. Heat the oven to 400°F.

2. Open the clams. Remove and discard the top shells. Arrange the clams in a 3-quart shallow baking dish.

3. Cook the bacon in a 10-inch skillet over medium-high heat until crisp. Remove the bacon from the skillet and drain on paper towels.

4. Add the butter, onion and garlic powder to the hot bacon drippings and cook until the onion is tender. Stir the stuffing, cheese, parsley and cooked bacon in the skillet and mix lightly. Divide the stuffing mixture evenly among the clams.

5. Bake for 20 minutes or until the clams are cooked through.

Lighter Chicken Cheesesteaks

prep 10 minutes | **cook** 20 minutes | **makes** 2 servings

Vegetable cooking spray
1   medium onion, sliced (about ½ cup)
1   tablespoon water
2   portions frozen chicken sandwich steaks
2   slices fat-free American pasteurized process cheese product
4   slices Pepperidge Farm® 100% Natural 100% Whole Wheat Bread
Sliced hot cherry pepper

1. Spray a 10-inch skillet with the cooking spray and heat over medium heat for 1 minute. Add the onion and water. Cover and cook for 5 minutes or until the onion is tender. Remove the onion from the skillet and keep warm.

2. Increase the heat to medium-high. Add the sandwich steaks and cook until well browned and cooked through. Top with the cheese and cook until the cheese is melted.

3. Divide the steak mixture between **2** bread slices. Top with the onions, hot peppers and remaining bread slices.

Roasted Garlic Mashed Potatoes

prep 10 minutes | **bake** 1 hour | **cook** 15 minutes | **makes** 6 servings

- 1   **whole bulb garlic**
- 2⅔ **cups Swanson® Chicken Broth (Regular, Natural Goodness® or Certified Organic)**
- 5   **large potatoes, cut into 1-inch pieces (about 7½ cups)**
- 2   **tablespoons chopped chives or green onion tops (optional)**

1. Cut off the top of the garlic bulb. Drizzle with **about 2 tablespoons** of the broth. Wrap the bulb in aluminum foil and bake at 350°F. for 1 hour or until softened.

2. Place the broth and potatoes in a 3-quart saucepan and heat to a boil over medium-high heat. Reduce the heat to medium. Cover and cook for 10 minutes or until the potatoes are tender. Drain, reserving the broth.

3. Mash the potatoes with **1¼ cups** of the broth, **2 or 3 cloves** of roasted garlic* and chives, if desired. Add additional broth, if needed, until desired consistency is reached.

Leftover roasted garlic is perfect for garlic toast, meat gravy, soups, etc.

Lighter Skillet Beef & Vegetables

prep 10 minutes | **cook** 30 minutes | **makes** 4 servings

- ¾ **pound extra lean ground beef**
- 1 **medium onion, chopped (about ½ cup)**
- 1 **teaspoon dried basil leaves, crushed**
- ½ **teaspoon garlic powder or 2 cloves garlic, minced**
- 1 **can (10½ ounces) Campbell's® Fat Free Beef Gravy**
- 1 **package (about 9 ounces) frozen mixed vegetables**
- 1½ **cups rotini pasta, cooked according to package directions without salt (about 2 cups)**

1. Cook the beef, onion, basil and garlic powder in a 10-inch skillet over medium-high heat, until the beef is well browned, stirring often to separate the meat. Pour off any fat.

2. Stir the gravy and vegetables in the skillet and heat to a boil. Reduce the heat to low. Cover and cook for 10 minutes or until the vegetables are tender-crisp. Stir in the rotini and cook until the beef mixture is hot and bubbling.

Beef Wellington

thaw 40 minutes | **prep** 15 minutes | **cook** 40 minutes | **chill** 1 hour | **bake** 25 minutes | **makes** 10 servings

1 (2- to 2½-pound) beef tenderloin
   Ground black pepper (optional)
1 egg
1 tablespoon water
1 tablespoon butter

2 cups finely chopped mushrooms
1 medium onion, finely chopped (about ½ cup)
½ of a 17.3-ounce package Pepperidge Farm® Puff Pastry Sheets (1 sheet), thawed

1. Heat the oven to 425°F. Place beef into a lightly greased roasting pan. Season with pepper. Roast for 30 minutes or until a meat thermometer reads 130°F. Cover pan and chill for 1 hour.

2. Reheat the oven to 425°F. Beat the egg and water in a small bowl with a fork or whisk.

3. Heat the butter in a 10-inch skillet over medium-high heat. Add the mushrooms and onion and cook until the mushrooms are tender and all the liquid is evaporated, stirring often.

4. Unfold the pastry sheet on a lightly floured surface. Roll the pastry sheet into a rectangle 4 inches longer and 6 inches wider than the beef. Brush the pastry sheet with the egg mixture. Spoon the mushroom mixture onto the pastry sheet to within 1 inch of the edges. Place the beef in the center of the mushroom mixture. Fold the pastry over the beef and press to seal. Place seam-side down onto a baking sheet. Tuck the ends under to seal. Brush the pastry with the egg mixture.

5. Bake for 25 minutes or until the pastry is golden brown and a meat thermometer reads 140°F.

Mediterranean Chicken Casserole

prep 20 minutes | **bake** 30 minutes | **makes** 4 servings

- 1 **can (10¾ ounces) Campbell's® Condensed Cream of Celery Soup (Regular or 98% Fat Free)**
- ½ **cup water**
- ½ **teaspoon dried oregano leaves, crushed**
- ¼ **teaspoon ground black pepper**
- 1 **package (10 ounces) frozen chopped spinach, thawed and well drained**
- 2 **cups cubed cooked chicken**
- ⅔ **cup orzo pasta, cooked and drained**
- ½ **cup shredded Italian cheese blend**

1. Stir the soup, water, oregano, black pepper, spinach, chicken and pasta in a 2-quart shallow baking dish. Cover the baking dish.

2. Bake at 375°F. for 30 minutes or until the chicken mixture is hot and bubbling. Sprinkle with the cheese.

Tip: You can substitute 3 cans (4.5 ounces **each**) Swanson® Premium White Chunk Chicken Breast in Water, drained, for the cubed cooked chicken.

Gingerbread with Dried Cherries

prep 15 minutes | **cook** 2 hours | **makes** 6 servings

Vegetable cooking spray
3 cups all-purpose flour
1 teaspoon baking powder
1 teaspoon baking soda
1 teaspoon ground cinnamon
1 teaspoon ground ginger
¼ teaspoon salt
¼ teaspoon allspice

1 cup (2 sticks) butter, softened
½ cup packed brown sugar
4 eggs
¾ cup molasses
1 cup V8® 100% Vegetable Juice
1 cup dried cherries
Whipped cream (optional)

1. Spray the inside of a 4-quart slow cooker with the cooking spray.

2. Stir the flour, baking powder, baking soda, cinnamon, ginger, salt and allspice in a medium bowl.

3. Place the butter and brown sugar into a large bowl. Beat with an electric mixer on medium speed until creamy. Beat in the eggs and molasses.

4. Reduce the speed to low. Alternately beat in the flour mixture and the vegetable juice. Stir in the cherries. Pour the batter into the cooker.

5. Cover and cook on HIGH for 2 to 3 hours or until a toothpick inserted in the center comes out with moist crumbs. Spoon the gingerbread into bowls. Top with the whipped cream, if desired.

Melt-in-Your-Mouth Short Ribs

prep 10 minutes | **cook** 8 hours | **makes** 6 servings

- 6 serving-sized pieces beef short ribs (about 3 pounds)
- 2 tablespoons packed brown sugar
- 3 cloves garlic, minced
- 1 teaspoon dried thyme leaves, crushed
- ¼ cup all-purpose flour
- 1 can (10½ ounces) Campbell's® Condensed French Onion Soup
- 1 bottle (12 fluid ounces) dark ale **or** beer
  Hot mashed potatoes **or** egg noodles

1. Place the beef into a 5-quart slow cooker. Add the brown sugar, garlic, thyme and flour and toss to coat.

2. Stir the soup and ale in a small bowl. Pour over the beef.

3. Cover and cook on LOW for 8 to 9 hours* or until the beef is fork-tender. Serve with the mashed potatoes.

Or on HIGH for 4 to 5 hours.

Prosciutto Asparagus Spirals

thaw 40 minutes | **prep** 15 minutes | **bake** 15 minutes | **makes** 30 servings

- **1** package (17.3 ounces) Pepperidge Farm® Puff Pastry Sheets, thawed
- **6** tablespoons garlic & herb spreadable cheese, softened
- **8** slices prosciutto **or** thinly sliced ham
- **30** medium asparagus spears, trimmed

1. Heat the oven to 400°F. Unfold the pastry sheets on a lightly floured surface. Spread **3 tablespoons** cheese on **each** pastry sheet. Top each with **4 slices** prosciutto. Cut **each** into **15** strips crosswise, making **30** in all.

2. Tightly wrap **1** pastry strip around **each** asparagus spear, prosciutto-side in. Place the pastries seam-side down onto 2 baking sheets.

3. Bake for 15 minutes or until the pastries are golden brown.

January 20

Mozzarella Meatball Sandwiches

prep 15 minutes | **bake** 10 minutes | **cook** 20 minutes | **makes** 4 servings

- 1 loaf (11.75 ounces) Pepperidge Farm® Frozen Mozzarella Garlic Cheese Bread
- ½ cup Prego® Traditional Italian Sauce **or** Organic Tomato & Basil Italian Sauce
- 12 (½ ounce **each**) **or** 6 (1 ounce **each**) frozen meatballs

1. Heat the oven to 400°F. Remove the bread from the bag. Carefully separate the bread halves with a fork. Place the **2** bread halves, cut-side up, onto a baking sheet.

2. Bake for 10 minutes or until the bread is heated through.

3. Heat the Italian sauce and meatballs in a 2-quart saucepan over low heat. Cook and stir for 20 minutes or until the meatballs are heated through. Spoon the meatball mixture onto the bottom bread half. Top with the top bread half. Cut into quarters.

December 25

Classic Standing Rib Roast

prep 15 minutes | **roast** 2 hours 20 minutes | **stand** 20 minutes | **makes** 8 servings

- 1 **(7- to 8-pound) beef standing rib roast**
- ¼ **teaspoon ground black pepper**
- ½ **cup Swanson® Beef Stock (Regular or Unsalted)**
- 3 **tablespoons red wine**

1. Heat the oven to 325°F. Season the beef with the black pepper. Place the beef into a roasting pan, rib-side down.

2. Roast for 2 hours 20 minutes for medium-rare or until desired doneness. Remove the beef to a cutting board and let stand for 20 minutes.

3. Spoon off any fat from the pan drippings. Stir the stock and wine, if desired, in the pan. Cook and stir over medium-high heat until the sauce is reduced slightly, scraping up the browned bits from the bottom of the pan. Season with additional black pepper, if desired. Serve the stock mixture with the beef.

Pomegranate Blueberry Granita

prep 10 minutes | **freeze** 5 hours 30 minutes | **makes** 6 servings

- 4 **cups V8 V-Fusion® Pomegranate Blueberry Juice**
- 2 **cups fresh blueberries and/or strawberries**
- 2 **tablespoons honey**
- 2 **tablespoons lemon juice**

1. Place the juice, blueberries, honey and lemon juice into a blender container. Cover and blend until smooth. Pour the mixture into an 11×7-inch baking pan. Cover the pan tightly with plastic wrap.

2. Freeze for 45 minutes or until the edges of the mixture become icy. Stir the mixture with a whisk. Cover and freeze for 45 minutes. Stir the mixture again with the whisk.

3. Cover the pan and freeze for 3 hours or until the mixture is frozen solid.

4. Scrape the frozen mixture with a fork to form icy flakes. Cover and freeze for 1 hour.

5. Spoon the granita into goblets or parfait glasses. Garnish with mint leaves and serve with additional fresh fruit.

Tip: Using a metal baking pan is best for this recipe. The metal conducts the cold better which facilitates freezing.

Cranberry Apple Bread Pudding

prep 10 minutes | **stand** 20 minutes | **bake** 40 minutes | **makes** 6 servings

Vegetable cooking spray
4 cups Pepperidge Farm® Cubed Herb Seasoned Stuffing **or** Herb Seasoned Stuffing
¾ cup dried cranberries
4 eggs
2½ cups milk
½ cup sugar
½ cup chunky sweetened applesauce
1 teaspoon vanilla extract
Brandied Butter Sauce

1. Heat the oven to 350°F. Spray a 2-quart shallow baking dish with the cooking spray. Place the stuffing into the dish. Sprinkle the cranberries over the stuffing.

2. Beat the eggs, milk, sugar, applesauce and vanilla extract in a medium bowl with a fork or whisk. Pour the milk mixture over the stuffing mixture. Stir and press the stuffing mixture into the milk mixture to coat. Let stand for 20 minutes.

3. Bake for 40 minutes or until a knife inserted in the center comes out clean. Serve warm with the *Brandied Butter Sauce*.

Brandied Butter Sauce: Heat ½ **cup** (1 stick) butter in a 1-quart saucepan over medium heat until the butter is melted. Add ½ **cup** packed light brown sugar. Cook and stir until the sugar dissolves and the mixture is hot and bubbling. Remove the saucepan from the heat. Whisk in **2 tablespoons** brandy. Makes 1 cup.

Quick Skillet Ziti

prep 5 minutes | **cook** 20 minutes | **makes** 4 servings

- **1 pound ground beef**
- **1 jar (24 ounces) Prego® Traditional Italian Sauce or Marinara Italian Sauce**
- **5 cups tube-shaped pasta (ziti), cooked and drained**
- **Grated Parmesan cheese**

1. Cook the beef in a 10-inch skillet until well browned, stirring often to separate the meat. Pour off any fat.

2. Stir the Italian sauce and pasta in the skillet and heat through. Sprinkle with the cheese.

Sweet Potato Pie

prep 15 minutes | **bake** 1 hour | **cool** 3 hours | **makes** 8 servings

- **3 large sweet potatoes, peeled and cut into cubes (about 3 cups)**
- **¼ cup heavy cream**
- **1 can (10¾ ounces) Campbell's® Condensed Tomato Soup**
- **1 cup packed brown sugar**
- **3 eggs**
- **1 teaspoon vanilla extract**
- **½ teaspoon ground cinnamon**
- **½ teaspoon ground nutmeg**
- **1 (9-inch) frozen pie crust**

1. Heat the oven to 350°F.

2. Place potatoes into a 3-quart saucepan and add water to cover. Heat over medium-high heat to a boil. Reduce the heat to low. Cover and cook for 10 minutes or until the potatoes are tender. Drain the potatoes well in a colander.

3. Place the potatoes and heavy cream into a large bowl. Beat with an electric mixer on medium speed until the mixture is fluffy. Beat in the soup, brown sugar, eggs, vanilla extract, cinnamon and nutmeg. Pour the potato mixture into the pie crust and place onto a baking sheet.

4. Bake for 1 hour or until set. Cool the pie in the pan on a wire rack about 3 hours.

Savory Sausage with Onions and Peppers

prep 15 minutes | **cook** 7 hours | **makes** 8 servings

- 2 jars (1 pound 10 ounces **each**) Prego® Traditional Italian Sauce
- 3 large onions, sliced (about 3 cups)
- 3 large green **and/or** red peppers, cut into 2-inch-long strips (about 6 cups)
- 3 pounds sweet **or** hot Italian pork sausages, cut into 4-inch-long pieces
- 8 long hard rolls, split **or** hot cooked spaghetti
  Grated Parmesan cheese

1. Stir the Italian sauce, onions, peppers and sausage in a 6-quart slow cooker.

2. Cover and cook on LOW for 7 to 8 hours* or until the sausage is cooked through. Spoon the sausage mixture into the rolls or serve it over the spaghetti. Top with the cheese.

Or on HIGH for 4 to 5 hours.

Tip: For more overall flavor and color, brown the sausage before adding to the slow cooker.

Puff Pastry Christmas Trees

thaw 40 minutes | **prep** 30 minutes | **bake** 10 minutes |
cool 10 minutes | **makes** 8 pastries

- **1** package (17.3 ounces) Pepperidge Farm® Puff Pastry Sheets (2 sheets)
- **⅓** cup prepared vanilla pudding **or** lemon curd
- **⅓** cup honey, warmed
  Green decorating sugar
- **8** raspberries **or** maraschino cherry halves

1. Heat the oven to 400°F.

2. Unfold **1** pastry sheet on a lightly floured surface. Cut **4** stars of **each** size, using **3** star cookie cutters in graduated sizes. Repeat with the remaining pastry sheet. Place the **24** stars on baking sheets.

3. Bake for 10 minutes or until golden. Remove from baking sheets and cool on wire rack.

4. Top **1** large star pastry with **about 1 teaspoon** pudding. Top with **1** medium star pastry, turning star so points do not line up. Top with **about 1 teaspoon** pudding and place **1** small star pastry on top, turning so points do not line up. Repeat with remaining star pastries, making **8** "trees." Drizzle "trees" with honey. Sprinkle with green sugar and top **each** with a raspberry.

Scalloped Potatoes

prep 15 minutes | **cook** 4 hours | **stand** 5 minutes | **makes** 6 servings

Vegetable cooking spray
- 3 **pounds Yukon Gold or Eastern potatoes, thinly sliced (about 9 cups)**
- 1 **large onion, thinly sliced (about 1 cup)**
- 1 **can (10¾ ounces) Campbell's® Condensed Cream of Mushroom Soup (Regular or 98% Fat Free)**
- ½ **cup Campbell's® Condensed Chicken Broth**
- 1 **cup shredded Cheddar or crumbled blue cheese (about 4 ounces)**

1. Spray the inside of a 6-quart slow cooker with the cooking spray. Layer **one third** of the potatoes and **half** of the onion in the cooker. Repeat the layers. Top with the remaining potatoes.

2. Stir the soup and broth in a small bowl. Pour over the potatoes. Cover and cook on HIGH for 4 to 5 hours or until the potatoes are tender.

3. Top the potatoes with the cheese. Cover and let stand for 5 minutes or until the cheese is melted.

Spicy Mary Martini

prep 5 minutes | **makes** 2 servings

2 cans (5.5 ounces **each**) Spicy Hot V8® Vegetable Juice
6 tablespoons pepper-flavored vodka
  Dash chipotle hot pepper sauce **or** to taste
2 cups ice cubes
  Seasoned salt
2 stalks celery

1. Put the vegetable juice, vodka, pepper sauce and ice in a cocktail shaker. Cover and shake until blended.
2. Strain into **2** chilled tall glasses rimmed with seasoned salt, if desired.
3. Serve with the celery.

Slow Cooked Chicken & Bean Burritos

prep 10 minutes | **cook** 6 hours | **makes** 12 servings

- 1 **can (10¾ ounces) Campbell's® Condensed Cheddar Cheese Soup**
- 1 **teaspoon garlic powder**
- 2 **tablespoons chili powder**
- 2 **pounds skinless, boneless chicken thighs, cut into 1-inch pieces**
- 1 **can (about 14 ounces) black beans, rinsed and drained**
- 1 **can (about 14 ounces) pinto beans, rinsed and drained**
- 12 **flour tortillas (8- to 10-inch), warmed**
  Chopped lettuce
  Chopped tomato

1. Stir the soup, garlic powder, chili powder and chicken in a 3½– to 4-quart slow cooker.

2. Cover and cook on LOW for 6 to 7 hours* or until the chicken is cooked through.

3. Mash the black and pinto beans with a fork in a medium bowl. Stir into the chicken mixture. Spoon **about ½ cup** of the chicken mixture down the center of **each** tortilla. Top with the lettuce and tomato. Fold the tortillas around the filling.

Or on HIGH for 3 to 4 hours.

Snow Kids in Puff Pastry Shells

prep 20 minutes | **cook** 20 minutes | **makes** 6 servings

1	**package (10 ounces) Pepperidge Farm® Puff Pastry Shells**
1½	**cups prepared chocolate pudding**
	Whipped topping
	Green decorating sugar
	Colored fruit strips
1	**package (5 ounces) Pepperidge Farm® Gingerman Homestyle Cookies**

1. Prepare the pastry shells according to the package directions.

2. Spoon the pudding into the pastry shells. Top with the whipped topping and sprinkle with the green sugar. Refrigerate until serving time. Press the Snow Kids into the filled pastry shells. Serve immediately.

For Snow Kids: Use the colored fruit strips to make hats and scarves to "dress" the cookies. For the eyes, roll bits of the fruit strips into balls.

Slow-Cooked Pulled Pork Sandwiches

prep 15 minutes | **cook** 8 hours | **stand** 10 minutes | **makes** 12 servings

1.   tablespoon vegetable oil
1.   boneless pork shoulder roast (3½ to 4 pounds), netted **or** tied
1.   can (10½ ounces) Campbell's® Condensed French Onion Soup
1.   cup ketchup
¼   cup cider vinegar
3   tablespoons packed brown sugar
12 Pepperidge Farm® Sandwich Rolls

1. Heat the oil in a 10-inch skillet over medium-high heat. Add the pork and cook until well browned on all sides.

2. Stir the soup, ketchup, vinegar and brown sugar in a 5-quart slow cooker. Add the pork and turn to coat.

3. Cover and cook on LOW for 8 to 9 hours* or until the pork is fork-tender.

4. Remove the pork from the cooker to a cutting board and let stand for 10 minutes. Using 2 forks, shred the pork. Return the pork to the cooker.

5. Spoon the pork and sauce mixture on the rolls.

Or on HIGH for 4 to 5 hours.

Twice-Baked Squash Medley

prep 30 minutes | **bake** 1 hour 30 minutes | **makes** 8 servings

- 3 **spaghetti squash** (about 1½ pounds **each**)
- ½ teaspoon ground black pepper
- 2 cups chopped pecans
- 1 cup raisins
- ¼ cup packed brown sugar
- 1 tablespoon pumpkin pie spice
- 8 **acorn squash** (about 1 pound **each**)
- 24 Pepperidge Farm® Golden Butter Distinctive Crackers, crushed (about 1 cup)
- 4 tablespoons (½ stick) butter, melted

1. Heat oven to 350°F. Cut **each** spaghetti squash in half lengthwise. Scoop out and discard seeds. Sprinkle the inside cavity of **each** with pepper and place cut-side down in a 17×11-inch roasting pan. Bake for 45 minutes or until fork-tender. Scrape squash with a fork to separate spaghetti-like strands and place in a large bowl. Stir in pecans, raisins, brown sugar and pumpkin pie spice.

2. Cut off "tops" of the the acorn squash, about 1 inch from stem end and reserve. Scoop out the seeds and discard. Cut a small portion off the bottom of **each** squash to make a flat base. Place the squash shells in the roasting pan.

3. Spoon the spaghetti squash mixture evenly into cavities of **each** acorn squash. Stir the cracker crumbs and butter in a small bowl. Sprinkle the crumbs evenly over the squash mixture. Bake for 45 minutes or until heated through. Place reserved squash "tops" on baking sheet and bake for the last 5 minutes of baking time. Top **each** squash with an acorn "top."

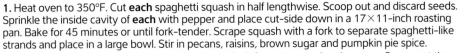

Spiced Pot Roast

prep 5 minutes | **marinate** 12 hours | **bake** 3 hours |
stand 10 minutes | **makes** 8 servings

- 3 tablespoons packed brown sugar
- 2 teaspoons ground cloves
- 2 teaspoons ground allspice
- 2 teaspoons ground cinnamon
- 1 teaspoon cracked black pepper
- 1 boneless beef bottom round roast **or** beef chuck pot roast (about 4 pounds)
- 2 cups Swanson® Beef Stock
- 1 bottle (12 ounces) dark beer **or** stout
  Hot boiled potatoes
  Chopped fresh parsley (optional)

1. Stir the brown sugar, cloves, allspice, cinnamon and black pepper in a large bowl. Add the beef and turn to coat. Cover the bowl and refrigerate for 12 hours or overnight.

2. Place the beef in a 6-quart oven-safe saucepot. Pour the stock and beer over the beef. Cover the saucepot.

3. Bake at 350°F. for 3 hours or until the beef is fork-tender. Remove the beef from the saucepot and let stand for 10 minutes. Thinly slice the beef. Serve with the stock mixture and the potatoes. Sprinkle with the parsley, if desired.

Turkey Sweet Potato Casserole

prep 15 minutes | **cook** 10 minutes | **bake** 30 minutes | **makes** 6 servings

- 2 cups mashed, cooked sweet potatoes
- 2 tablespoons packed brown sugar
- ½ teaspoon ground cinnamon
- ⅛ teaspoon ground nutmeg
- ⅓ cup evaporated milk
- ¼ cup Swanson® Chicken Stock
- 1 small onion, minced (about ¼ cup)
- 1 can (10¾ ounces) Campbell's® Condensed Cream of Chicken Soup (Regular **or** 98% Fat Free)
- 3 cups cubed cooked turkey
- 3 tablespoons water
- ¼ cup chopped walnuts (optional)
- Chopped fresh parsley (optional)

1. Stir the sweet potatoes, brown sugar, cinnamon, nutmeg and milk in a medium bowl. Spoon the sweet potato mixture around the inside edge of a 10-inch round casserole, forming a ring.

2. Heat the stock and onion in a 10-inch skillet over medium-high heat to a boil. Reduce the heat to low. Cook until the onion is tender, stirring occasionally. Stir in the soup, turkey and water. Cook until the mixture is hot and bubbling. Spoon the turkey mixture into the center of the sweet potato ring.

3. Bake at 350°F. for 30 minutes or until the turkey mixture is hot and bubbling. Sprinkle with the walnuts and parsley, if desired.

Super Simple Nacho Pasta

prep 15 minutes | **cook** 5 minutes | **makes** 4 servings

- 1 can (10¾ ounces) Campbell's® Condensed Fiesta Nacho Cheese Soup
- ½ cup milk
- 4 cups corkscrew-shaped pasta (rotini), cooked and drained

Stir the soup, milk and pasta in a 3-quart saucepan. Heat through over medium heat.

Spicy Corn Bread Stuffing

prep 10 minutes | **cook** 15 minutes | **makes** 6 servings

- ½   **pound bulk pork sausage**
- 2   **stalks celery, chopped (about 1 cup)**
- 1   **large onion, chopped (about 1 cup)**
- 1¾   **cups Swanson® Chicken Broth (Regular, Natural Goodness® or Certified Organic)**
- 5   **cups Pepperidge Farm® Cornbread Stuffing**
- ¼   **cup seeded and chopped cherry pepper**

1. Cook the sausage, celery and onion in a 4-quart saucepot over medium-high heat until the sausage is browned and the vegetables are tender. Pour off any fat.

2. Stir the broth in the saucepot and heat to a boil. Remove the saucepot from the heat. Add the stuffing and peppers and mix lightly.

Turkey Fajita Wraps

prep 10 minutes | **cook** 6 hours | **makes** 8 servings

- 2 cups Pace® Picante Sauce
- 2 large green **or** red peppers, cut into 2-inch-long strips (about 4 cups)
- 1½ cups frozen whole kernel corn, thawed
- 1 tablespoon chili powder
- 2 tablespoons lime juice
- 3 cloves garlic, minced
- 2 pounds turkey breast cutlets, cut into 4-inch-long strips
- 16 flour tortillas (8-inch), warmed
  Shredded Mexican cheese blend

1. Stir the picante sauce, peppers, corn, chili powder, lime juice, garlic and turkey in a 4-quart slow cooker.

2. Cover and cook on LOW for 6 to 7 hours* or until the turkey is cooked through.

3. Spoon **about** ½ cup of the turkey mixture down the center of **each** tortilla. Top with the cheese. Fold the tortillas around the filling.

Or on HIGH for 3 to 4 hours.

Tip: Delicious served with an assortment of additional toppers: sliced green onions, sliced ripe olives, shredded lettuce, sliced jalapeño peppers, sour cream **and/or** chopped fresh cilantro.

Veal Spiedini

prep 30 minutes | **cook** 20 minutes | **makes** 6 servings

- ½ **cup Italian-seasoned dry bread crumbs**
- ¼ **cup toasted pine nuts**
- 6 **slices prosciutto, cut into thirds**
- 1¼ **pounds veal scalloppine, cut into 18 pieces and pounded thin**
- ¼ **pound mozzarella cheese, cut into matchstick-thin strips**
- ¼ **cup olive oil**
- 3 **cups Prego® Traditional Italian Sauce or Heart Smart Traditional Italian Sauce**
- 1 **package (10 ounces) Pepperidge Farm® Mozzarella Garlic Bread Grated Parmesan cheese (optional)**

1. Heat the oven to 400°F. Stir the bread crumbs and pine nuts in a small bowl.

2. Divide the prosciutto among the veal pieces. Top **each** with **1 tablespoon** bread crumb mixture. Divide the mozzarella cheese among the veal pieces. Roll up the veal pieces around the filling. Thread **3** veal rolls onto **each** of **6** (6-inch) skewers.

3. Heat the oil in a 12-inch skillet over medium heat. Add the skewers and cook for 3 minutes on each side. Pour the Italian sauce over the skewers. Reduce the heat to low. Cook for 15 minutes or until the veal is cooked through.

4. Meanwhile, bake the bread according to the package directions. Cut the bread into 2-inch diagonal slices. Serve the bread with the veal and sauce. Sprinkle with the Parmesan cheese, if desired.

Jambalaya

prep 25 minutes | **cook** 7 hours 10 minutes | **makes** 8 servings

- 3 cups Swanson® Chicken Broth **or** Swanson® Chicken Stock
- 1 tablespoon Creole seasoning
- 1 large green pepper, diced (about 1½ cups)
- 1 large onion, diced (about 1 cup)
- 2 cloves garlic, minced
- ½ teaspoon ground black pepper
- 2 large stalks celery, diced (about 1 cup)
- 1 can (14.5 ounces) diced tomatoes
- 1 pound kielbasa, diced (about 3 cups)
- ¾ pound skinless, boneless chicken thighs, cut into cubes
- 1 cup **uncooked** instant white rice
- ½ pound fresh medium shrimp, shelled and deveined

1. Stir the stock, Creole seasoning, green pepper, onion, garlic, black pepper, celery, tomatoes, kielbasa and chicken in a 6-quart slow cooker.

2. Cover and cook on LOW for 7 to 8 hours* or until the chicken is cooked through.

3. Stir the rice and shrimp in the cooker. Cover and cook for 10 minutes or until the shrimp are cooked through.

Or on HIGH for 4 to 5 hours.

Sweet Potato Dip

prep 10 minutes | **cook** 20 minutes | **makes** 18 servings (about 2 tablespoons dip **each**)

- 2 medium sweet potatoes (about 1¼ pounds)
- 2 tablespoons pure maple syrup
- 1 tablespoon butter, melted
- 1 tablespoon lemon juice
- ½ teaspoon ground ginger
- ⅛ teaspoon ground nutmeg
  Dash ground black pepper
- 4 tablespoons chopped pecans, toasted
- 2 packages (6 ounces **each**) Pepperidge Farm®
  Baked Naturals® Crackers
  Chips (any variety)

1. Place the potatoes into a 3-quart saucepan and add water to cover. Heat over medium-high heat to a boil. Reduce the heat to medium and cook for 15 minutes or until the potatoes are tender. Drain the potatoes well in a colander. Peel the potatoes. Return the potatoes to the saucepan. Mash the potatoes.

2. Stir the potatoes, syrup, butter, lemon juice, ginger, nutmeg, black pepper and **3 tablespoons** pecans in a medium bowl. Sprinkle with the remaining pecans. Serve with crackers or chips for dipping.

Tip: For a sweet, tart twist, stir in ¼ **cup** chopped dried cranberries.

Slow Cooker Veggie Beef Stew

prep 15 minutes | **cook** 10 hours | **makes** 6 servings

- 2 **tablespoons oil**
- 1½ **pounds beef for stew, cut into 1-inch pieces**
- 1 **bag (about 24 ounces) frozen vegetables for stew**
- 1 **beef bouillon cube**
- 1½ **cups V8® 100% Vegetable Juice**
- 1 **tablespoon all-purpose flour**
- ½ **teaspoon dried basil leaves, crushed**
- ½ **teaspoon dried oregano, crushed**
- ½ **teaspoon dried thyme leaves, crushed**
- ½ **teaspoon dried rosemary, crushed**
- ½ **teaspoon garlic salt**

1. Heat the oil in a 12-inch skillet over medium-high heat. Add the beef and cook until well browned, stirring often. Pour off any fat.

2. Place the beef, vegetables and bouillon cube in a 3½-quart slow cooker. Stir the vegetable juice, flour, basil, oregano, thyme, rosemary and garlic salt in a medium bowl and pour it into the slow cooker.

3. Cover and cook on LOW for 10 to 12 hours* or until the beef is fork-tender.

Or on HIGH for 5 to 6 hours.

Bloody Mary

prep 5 minutes | **makes** 4 servings

- **4 cups V8® 100% Vegetable Juice***
- **3 tablespoons lemon juice**
- **1 tablespoon Worcestershire sauce**
- **⅛ teaspoon ground black pepper**
- **⅛ teaspoon hot pepper sauce (optional)**
  Celery stalks

Also delicious with Calcium Enriched V8® or Essential Antioxidants V8®.

Stir the vegetable juice, lemon juice, Worcestershire, black pepper and hot pepper sauce in a large pitcher. Serve over ice. Garnish with celery stalks.

Tip: If you like, add ¾ **cup** vodka to vegetable juice mixture.

Penne with Creamy Vodka Sauce

prep 15 minutes | **cook** 10 minutes | **makes** 4 servings

- 5½ cups Prego® Chunky Garden Tomato, Onion & Garlic Italian Sauce
- ¼ cup vodka
- ⅓ cup chopped fresh basil leaves
- ¼ teaspoon crushed red pepper
- ½ cup heavy cream
- 9 cups medium tube-shaped pasta (penne), cooked and drained
- Grated Parmesan cheese

1. Heat the Italian sauce, vodka, basil and red pepper in a 3-quart saucepan over medium heat until the mixture comes to a boil. Remove from the heat and stir in the cream.

2. Put the pasta in a large serving bowl. Pour the sauce mixture over the pasta. Toss to coat.

3. Sprinkle with the cheese.

Mint Ice Cream & Cookie Dessert

prep 25 minutes | **freeze** 1 hour | **makes** 6 servings

- **1** bag (7 ounces) Pepperidge Farm® Chocolate Mint Milano® Cookies, crushed
- **3** tablespoons butter, melted
- **3** cups mint chocolate chip ice cream, softened
  Hot fudge topping
  Sweetened whipped cream
- **6** small candy canes

1. Stir the cookie crumbs and butter in a small bowl. Press the crumb mixture into the bottom of a greased 8-inch cake pan.

2. Spread the softened ice cream over the crumb crust. Cover and freeze for 1 hour. Serve with the hot fudge and whipped cream. Top **each** serving with **1** candy cane.

Tip: Crush the cookies by placing them into a gallon size resealable plastic bag. Close the bag and crush the cookies with a rolling pin.

Triple Chocolate Pudding Cake with Raspberry Sauce

prep 10 minutes | **cook** 6 hours | **makes** 12 servings

Vegetable cooking spray
1 package (about 18 ounces) chocolate cake mix
1 package (about 3.9 ounces) chocolate instant pudding and pie filling mix
2 cups sour cream
4 eggs
1 cup V8® 100% Vegetable Juice
¾ cup vegetable oil
1 cup semi-sweet chocolate pieces
   Raspberry dessert topping
   Whipped cream

1. Spray the inside of a 4-quart slow cooker with the cooking spray.

2. Beat the cake mix, pudding mix, sour cream, eggs, vegetable juice and oil in a large bowl with an electric mixer on medium speed for 2 minutes. Stir in the chocolate pieces. Pour the batter into the cooker.

3. Cover and cook on LOW for 6 to 7 hours or until a knife inserted in the center comes out with moist crumbs. Serve with the raspberry topping and whipped cream.

Tip: Use your favorite chocolate cake mix and pudding mix flavor in this recipe.

Spinach-Cheese Swirls

thaw 40 minutes | **prep** 20 minutes | **bake** 15 minutes | **cool** 10 minutes | **makes** 20 pieces

- ½ **of a 17.3-ounce package Pepperidge Farm® Puff Pastry Sheets (1 sheet), thawed**
- 1 **egg**
- 1 **tablespoon water**
- ½ **cup shredded Muenster cheese or Monterey Jack cheese**
- ¼ **cup grated Parmesan cheese**
- 1 **green onion, chopped (about 2 tablespoons)**
- ⅛ **teaspoon garlic powder**
- 1 **package (about 10 ounces) frozen chopped spinach, thawed and well drained**

1. Heat the oven to 400°F. Beat the egg and water in a small bowl with a fork or whisk.

2. Stir the Muenster cheese, Parmesan cheese, onion and garlic powder in a medium bowl.

3. Unfold the pastry sheet on a lightly floured surface. Brush the pastry sheet with the egg mixture. Top with the cheese mixture and spinach. Starting with a short side, roll up like a jelly roll. Cut into **20** (½-inch) slices. Place the slices cut-side down, onto baking sheets. Brush the slices with the egg mixture.

4. Bake for 15 minutes or until the pastries are golden brown. Remove the pastries from the baking sheets and let cool on wire racks for 10 minutes.

Chicken in Creamy Sun-Dried Tomato Sauce

prep 15 minutes | **cook** 7 hours | **makes** 8 servings

- 2 **cans** (10¾ ounces **each**) Campbell's® Condensed Cream of Chicken with Herbs Soup **or** Campbell's® Condensed Cream of Chicken Soup
- 1 cup Chablis **or** other dry white wine*
- ¼ cup coarsely chopped pitted kalamata **or** oil-cured olives
- 2 tablespoons drained capers
- 2 cloves garlic, minced
- 1 can (14 ounces) artichoke hearts, drained and chopped
- 1 cup drained and coarsely chopped sun-dried tomatoes
- 8 skinless, boneless chicken breast halves (about 2 pounds)
- ½ cup chopped fresh basil leaves (optional)
  Hot cooked rice, egg noodles **or** mashed potatoes

You can substitute Swanson® Chicken Broth for the wine, if desired.

1. Stir the soup, wine, olives, capers, garlic, artichokes and tomatoes in a 3½-quart slow cooker. Add the chicken and turn to coat.

2. Cover and cook on LOW for 7 to 8 hours** or until the chicken is cooked through. Sprinkle with the basil, if desired. Serve with the rice.

**Or on HIGH for 4 to 5 hours.*

Cranberry-Walnut Crostadas

prep 20 minutes | **cook** 10 minutes | **cool** 20 minutes | **makes** 6 servings

- 1 package (10 ounces) Pepperidge Farm® Puff Pastry Shells
- 1 cup heavy cream
- ¼ cup sugar
- 1½ cups toasted walnut halves, chopped
- 1 cup dried cranberries
- ¼ teaspoon ground cinnamon
  Assorted Toppings

1. Prepare the pastry shells according to the package directions.

2. Heat the heavy cream and sugar in a 1-quart heavy saucepan over medium heat to a boil. Cook for 5 minutes or until the mixture is thickened, stirring occasionally. Remove the saucepan from the heat. Let the mixture cool to room temperature. Stir in the walnuts, cranberries and cinnamon.

3. Divide the walnut mixture among the pastry shells. Top the filled shells with one of the *Assorted Toppings*, if desired.

Assorted Toppings: Almond-flavored **or** orange-flavored liqueur-sweetened whipped cream, crumbled Roquefort **or** other bleu cheese, wedges of Cheddar cheese.

Asian Tomato Beef

prep 10 minutes | **cook** 7 hours 15 minutes | **makes** 8 servings

- 2 **cans (10¾ ounces each) Campbell's® Condensed Tomato Soup**
- ⅓ **cup soy sauce**
- ⅓ **cup vinegar**
- 1½ **teaspoons garlic powder**
- ¼ **teaspoon ground black pepper**
- 1 **boneless beef round steak (3 to 3½ pounds), cut into strips**
- 6 **cups broccoli florets**
  Hot cooked rice

1. Stir the soup, soy sauce, vinegar, garlic powder, black pepper and beef in a 3½-quart slow cooker.

2. Cover and cook on LOW for 7 to 8 hours* or until the beef is fork-tender.

3. Stir in the broccoli. Increase the heat to HIGH. Cover and cook for 15 minutes or until the broccoli is tender-crisp. Serve the beef mixture with the rice.

Or on HIGH for 4 to 5 hours.

Blueberry Compote with Lemon Dumplings

prep 10 minutes | **cook** 3 hours 20 minutes | **makes** 8 servings

- 2 pounds frozen blueberries
- ¾ cup sugar
- 1 cup V8 V-Fusion® Pomegranate Blueberry Juice
- 2 cups buttermilk baking mix
- ⅔ cup milk
- 1 tablespoon grated lemon zest
  Vanilla ice cream (optional)

1. Stir the blueberries, ½ **cup** sugar and juice in a 4-quart slow cooker.

2. Cover and cook on LOW for 3 to 4 hours or until the mixture boils and thickens.

3. Stir the baking mix, remaining sugar, milk and lemon zest in a small bowl. Drop the batter by rounded tablespoonfuls over the blueberry mixture.

4. Cover and cook on HIGH for 20 minutes or until the dumplings are cooked in the center. Serve with the vanilla ice cream, if desired.

Tip: If you don't have a fresh lemon on hand for the lemon zest, try orange or lime zest instead.

February 5

Baked Pork Chops & Gravy

prep 10 minutes | **bake** 20 minutes | **makes** 6 servings

- 1 egg, beaten
- 2 tablespoons water
- 6 boneless pork chops, ¾-inch thick (about 1½ pounds)
- 2 tablespoons all-purpose flour
- 1½ cups Pepperidge Farm® Herb Seasoned Stuffing, crushed
- 1 can (10½ ounces) Campbell's® Turkey Gravy

1. Beat the egg and water in a shallow dish with a fork or whisk. Coat the pork with the flour. Dip the pork into the egg mixture. Coat with the stuffing. Place the pork onto a baking sheet.

2. Bake at 400°F. for 20 minutes or until the pork is cooked through.

3. Heat the gravy in a 1-quart saucepan over medium heat until hot and bubbling. Serve the gravy with the pork.

Easy Turkey & Biscuits

prep 20 minutes | **bake** 30 minutes | **makes** 5 servings

- 1 **can (10¾ ounces) Campbell's® Condensed Cream of Celery Soup (Regular or 98% Fat Free)**
- 1 **can (10¾ ounces) Campbell's® Condensed Cream of Potato Soup**
- 1 **cup milk**
- ¼ **teaspoon dried thyme leaves, crushed**
- ¼ **teaspoon ground black pepper**
- 4 **cups cooked cut-up vegetables (broccoli, cauliflower, carrots)**
- 2 **cups cubed cooked turkey or cooked chicken**
- 1 **package refrigerated buttermilk biscuits (10 biscuits)**

1. Stir the soups, milk, thyme, black pepper, vegetables and turkey in a 3-quart shallow baking dish.

2. Bake at 400°F. for 15 minutes. Stir the turkey mixture. Cut **each** biscuit into quarters.

3. Evenly top the turkey mixture with the cut biscuits. Bake for 15 minutes or until the turkey mixture is hot and bubbling and the biscuits are golden brown.

Tip: To microwave the vegetables, stir vegetables in a 2-quart shallow microwave-safe baking dish with ¼ **cup** water. Cover and microwave on HIGH for 10 minutes.

Balsamic Chicken with White Beans & Spinach

prep 10 minutes | **cook** 25 minutes | **makes** 4 servings

- 2 tablespoons olive oil
- 1¼ pounds skinless, boneless chicken breast halves
- 3 cloves garlic, minced
- ⅓ cup balsamic vinegar
- 1 can (10¾ ounces) Campbell's® Condensed Golden Mushroom Soup
- 1 can (about 15 ounces) white kidney beans (cannellini), rinsed and drained
- 1 bag (about 7 ounces) fresh baby spinach

1. Heat the oil in a 12-inch skillet over medium-high heat. Add the chicken and cook for 10 minutes or until well browned on both sides. Remove the chicken from the skillet.

2. Reduce the heat to medium. Add the garlic to the skillet and cook and stir for 1 minute. Stir in the vinegar and cook, scraping up the browned bits from the bottom of the pan.

3. Stir the soup and beans in the skillet and heat to a boil. Stir in the spinach. Return the chicken to the skillet. Reduce the heat to medium. Cover and cook until the chicken is cooked through and the spinach is wilted.

Holiday Banana Bread Pudding

prep 15 minutes | **bake** 25 minutes | **makes** 6 servings

- 8 slices Pepperidge Farm® Cinnamon Swirl Bread, cut into cubes (about 5 cups)
- 2 large bananas, cut into ¼-inch-thick slices
- ¾ cup semi-sweet chocolate pieces
- 1½ cups heavy cream
- 3 eggs
- ¼ cup packed brown sugar
- 2 teaspoons vanilla extract

1. Heat the oven to 350°F. Lightly grease a 1½-quart baking dish.

2. Place the bread cubes, bananas and chocolate pieces into the baking dish. Beat the heavy cream, eggs, brown sugar and vanilla extract in a medium bowl with a fork or whisk. Pour the cream mixture over the bread mixture. Stir and press the bread mixture into the cream mixture to coat.

3. Bake for 25 minutes or until a knife inserted in the center comes out clean.

Burgers Stroganoff

prep 10 minutes | **cook** 30 minutes | **makes** 6 servings

- 1½ **pounds ground beef**
- 1 **can (10¾ ounces) Campbell's® Condensed Cream of Mushroom Soup (Regular or 98% Fat Free)**
- 2 **tablespoons ketchup**
- ⅓ **cup sour cream**
- 6 **bagels, split**

1. Shape the beef into **6** (½-inch thick) burgers.

2. Cook the burgers in batches in a 10-inch skillet over medium-high heat until well browned on both sides. Remove the burgers from the skillet. Pour off any fat.

3. Stir the soup and ketchup in the skillet and heat to a boil. Return the burgers to the skillet. Reduce the heat to low. Cover and cook for 10 minutes or until the burgers are cooked through.

4. Stir in the sour cream. Serve the burgers and sauce on the bagels.

Bacon and Cheddar Puff Pastry Crisps

thaw 40 minutes | **prep** 20 minutes | **bake** 13 minutes | **cool** 10 minutes | **makes** 72 crisps

- 1 **package (17.3 ounces) Pepperidge Farm® Puff Pastry Sheets, thawed**
- 1 **cup finely shredded Cheddar cheese (about 4 ounces)**
- 1 **pound bacon, cooked and crumbled**
- ½ **cup prepared ranch salad dressing**
- 2 **tablespoons chopped fresh chives**

1. Heat the oven to 400°F.

2. Unfold **1** pastry sheet on a lightly floured surface. Roll the pastry sheet into a 12×12-inch square. Cut into **36** (2-inch) squares. Prick the pastry squares with a fork. Repeat with the remaining pastry sheet, making **72** squares in all. Place the squares onto baking sheets.

3. Bake for 8 minutes or until the pastries are golden brown. Using the back of a spoon, press down the centers of the hot pastries to make an indentation.

4. Spoon **about ½ teaspoon each** cheese and bacon onto **each** pastry. Bake for 5 minutes or until the cheese is melted. Remove the pastries from the baking sheets and let cool on wire racks for 10 minutes. Top with the dressing and chives.

Quick Bean & Rice Casserole

prep 5 minutes | **cook** 25 minutes | **makes** 6 servings

- 2½ **cups water**
- ¾ **cup uncooked regular long-grain white rice**
- 1 **envelope (about 1 ounce) dry onion soup and recipe mix**
- 1 **can (16 ounces) Campbell's® Pork and Beans**
- ¼ **cup maple-flavored syrup**

1. Heat the water in a 3-quart saucepan over medium-high heat to a boil. Stir in the rice and soup mix. Reduce the heat to low. Cover and cook for 20 minutes or until the rice is tender.

2. Stir the beans and syrup in the saucepan and cook until the mixture is hot and bubbling.

Winter Refresher

prep 5 minutes | **makes** 6 servings

- 4 **cups V8® 100% Vegetable Juice**
- 1 **can (12 ounces) ginger ale**
- ¾ **cup vodka (optional)**
- 3 **tablespoons lime juice**
  Lime slices for garnish

Stir the vegetable juice, ginger ale, vodka, if desired, and lime juice in a 2-quart pitcher. Serve over ice. Garnish with lime slices.

Sirloin, Pepper & Onion Skillet

prep 20 minutes | **cook** 20 minutes | **makes** 4 servings

- 2 **tablespoons olive oil**
- 1 **boneless beef sirloin steak, ¾-inch thick (about 1 pound), cut into 4 pieces**
- 1 **large onion, sliced (about 1 cup)**
- 2 **medium red and/or green peppers, cut into 2-inch-long strips (about 3 cups)**
- 3 **cloves garlic, minced**
- 1 **tablespoon red wine vinegar or balsamic vinegar**
- 1 **can (10¾ ounces) Campbell's® Condensed Golden Mushroom Soup**
- ½ **cup water**
- 1 **cup shredded Cheddar Jack cheese or Cheddar cheese (about 4 ounces)**

1. Heat **1 tablespoon** oil in a 10-inch skillet over medium-high heat. Add the beef and cook until well browned. Remove the beef from the skillet. Pour off any fat. Reduce the heat to medium.

2. Heat the remaining oil in the skillet. Add the onion and peppers and cook for 3 minutes, stirring occasionally. Add the garlic and cook until the vegetables are tender-crisp, stirring often.

3. Add the vinegar to the skillet and cook and stir for 1 minute. Stir in the soup and water and heat to a boil. Return the beef to the skillet. Reduce the heat to low. Cover and cook the beef for 2 minutes for medium or until desired doneness. Sprinkle with the cheese.

Brie en Croute

thaw 40 minutes | **prep** 15 minutes | **bake** 20 minutes | **stand** 45 minutes | **makes** 12 servings

- ½ **package of a 17.3-ounce Pepperidge Farm® Puff Pastry Sheets (1 sheet)**
- 1 **egg**
- 1 **tablespoon water**
- ¼ **cup toasted sliced almonds (optional)**
- ¼ **cup chopped fresh parsley**
- 1 **(about 1 pound) Brie cheese round**
- 1 **package Pepperidge Farm® Entertaining Quartet Distinctive Crackers**

1. Heat the oven to 400°F. Beat the egg and water in a small bowl with a fork or whisk.

2. Unfold the pastry sheet on a lightly floured surface. Roll the pastry sheet into a 14-inch square. Cut off the corners to make a circle. Sprinkle with the almonds and parsley in the center of the circle. Top with the cheese. Brush the edge of the circle with the egg mixture. Fold the sides of the pastry over the cheese to cover. Trim the excess pastry and press to seal. Brush the seam with the egg mixture. Place seam-side down onto a baking sheet. Decorate the top with pastry scraps, if desired. Brush with the egg mixture.

3. Bake for 20 minutes or the pastry is until golden brown. Let stand for 45 minutes. Serve with the crackers.

Shortcut Chicken Cordon Bleu

prep 10 minutes | **cook** 20 minutes | **makes** 4 servings

- 1 **tablespoon butter**
- 4 **skinless, boneless chicken breast halves (about 1 pound)**
- 1 **can (10¾ ounces) Campbell's® Condensed Cream of Chicken Soup (Regular or 98% Fat Free)**
- 2 **tablespoons water**
- 2 **tablespoons Chablis or other dry white wine**
- ½ **cup shredded Swiss cheese**
- ½ **cup chopped cooked ham**
- 4 **cups medium egg noodles, cooked and drained**

1. Heat the butter in a 10-inch skillet over medium-high heat. Add the chicken and cook for 10 minutes or until well browned on both sides.

2. Stir the soup, water, wine, cheese and ham in the skillet and heat to a boil. Reduce the heat to low. Cover and cook for 5 minutes or until the chicken is cooked through. Serve the chicken and sauce with the noodles.

December 4

Cranberry & Pecan Stuffing

prep 20 minutes | **bake** 30 minutes | **makes** 11 servings

- 2 **tablespoons butter**
- 1 **large onion, chopped (about 1 cup)**
- 2 **stalks celery, chopped (about 1 cup)**
- 2½ **cups Swanson® Chicken Broth (Regular, Natural Goodness® or Certified Organic)**
- 1 **cup dried cranberries**
- ½ **cup chopped pecans**
- 1 **package (16 ounces) Pepperidge Farm® Herb Seasoned Stuffing**

1. Heat the butter in a 3-quart saucepan over medium-high heat. Add the onion and celery and cook until tender, stirring occasionally. Remove the saucepan from the heat.

2. Stir the broth, cranberries and pecans in the saucepan. Add the stuffing and mix lightly. Spoon the stuffing mixture into a greased 3-quart casserole. Cover the casserole.

3. Bake at 350°F. for 30 minutes or until the stuffing mixture is hot.

Creamy Beef Stroganoff

prep 15 minutes | **cook** 8 hours | **makes** 9 servings

- 2 cans (10¾ ounces **each**) Campbell's® Condensed Cream of Mushroom Soup
- ¼ cup water
- 2 tablespoons Worcestershire sauce
- 1 package (8 ounces) sliced white mushrooms
- 3 medium onions, coarsely chopped (about 1½ cups)
- 3 cloves garlic, minced
- ½ teaspoon ground black pepper
- 2 pounds boneless beef bottom round steaks, sliced diagonally into strips
- 1 cup sour cream
  Hot cooked egg noodles
  Chopped fresh parsley (optional)

1. Stir the soup, water, Worcestershire sauce, mushrooms, onions, garlic and black pepper in a 6-quart slow cooker. Add the beef and stir to coat.

2. Cover and cook on LOW for 8 to 9 hours* or until the beef is cooked through.

3. Stir the sour cream into the cooker. Serve with the egg noodles. Top with the parsley, if desired.

Or on HIGH for 4 to 5 hours.

Tip: For more overall flavor and color, brown the beef before adding it to the slow cooker.

Heavenly Sweet Potatoes

prep 10 minutes | **bake** 20 minutes | **makes** 8 servings

Vegetable cooking spray
1   can (40 ounces) cut sweet potatoes in heavy syrup, drained
¼   teaspoon ground cinnamon
⅛   teaspoon ground ginger
¾   cup Swanson® Chicken Broth (Regular, Natural Goodness® **or** Certified Organic)
2   cups miniature marshmallows

1. Heat the oven to 350°F.

2. Spray a 1½-quart casserole with cooking spray.

3. Put the potatoes, cinnamon and ginger in an electric mixer bowl. Beat at medium speed until almost smooth. Add the broth and beat until potatoes are fluffy. Spoon the potato mixture in the prepared dish. Top with the marshmallows.

4. Bake for 20 minutes or until heated through and marshmallows are golden brown.

Easy Taco Tamale Pie

prep 15 minutes | **bake** 25 minutes | **makes** 4 servings

- 1 **pound ground beef**
- 1 **can (16 ounces) whole kernel corn, undrained**
- 1 **jar (16 ounces) Pace® Picante Sauce**
- ½ **cup shredded Cheddar cheese**
- 1 **box (about 8 ounces) corn muffin mix**

1. Heat the oven to 375°F. Cook the beef in a 10-inch skillet over medium-high heat until well browned, stirring often to separate the meat. Pour off any fat.

2. Stir the corn with liquid, picante sauce and cheese in the skillet. Spoon the beef mixture into a 2-quart shallow baking dish. Mix the corn muffin mix according to the package directions. Drop the batter by spoonfuls on top of the beef mixture.

3. Bake for 25 minutes or until the topping is golden brown.

Baked Apple Cranberry Stuffing

prep 20 minutes | **bake** 35 minutes | **makes** 11 servings

Non-stick aluminum foil
3 tablespoons butter
4 stalks celery, sliced (about 2 cups)
1 large onion, chopped (about 1 cup)
2¼ cups Swanson® Chicken Broth (Regular, Natural Goodness® **or** Certified Organic)
1 medium Granny Smith apple, chopped
1 cup dried cranberries
1 package (12 ounces) Pepperidge Farm® Herb Seasoned Cubed Stuffing

1. Heat the oven to 350°F. Line a 3-quart shallow baking pan with the foil, dull-side down.

2. Heat the butter in a 3-quart saucepan over medium heat. Add the celery and onion and cook until tender, stirring occasionally. Stir in the broth, apple and cranberries. Remove the saucepan from the heat. Add the stuffing and mix lightly. Spoon the stuffing mixture into the baking pan.

3. Bake for 35 minutes or until the stuffing mixture is hot.

Hearty Mixed Bean Stew with Sausage

prep 15 minutes | **cook** 8 hours | **makes** 8 servings

- ¾ **pound sweet Italian pork sausage, casing removed**
- 10 **cups Swanson® Chicken Stock**
- ¼ **teaspoon ground black pepper**
- 2 **medium carrots, chopped (about ⅔ cup)**
- 1 **stalk celery, chopped (about ½ cup)**
- 4 **ounces dried pinto beans (about ¾ cup)**
- 4 **ounces dried navy beans (about ¾ cup)**
- 4 **ounces dried kidney beans (about ¾ cup)**
- 6 **sun-dried tomatoes in oil, drained and thinly sliced (about ¼ cup)**
   Grated Parmesan cheese

1. Cook the sausage in a 10-inch skillet over medium-high heat until well browned, stirring often to separate the meat. Pour off any fat.

2. Stir the sausage, stock, black pepper, carrots, celery and beans in a 5-quart slow cooker.

3. Cover and cook on LOW for 7 to 8 hours.*

4. Stir in the tomatoes. Cover and cook for 1 hour or until the beans are tender. Sprinkle with the cheese.

Or on HIGH for 4 to 5 hours.

Chocolate Pirouette-Crusted Cake

thaw 1 hour 30 minutes | **prep** 10 minutes | **makes** 8 servings

1	**box (19.6 ounces) Pepperidge Farm® Chocolate Fudge 3 Layer Cake**
½	**of a 13.5-ounce canister Pepperidge Farm® Chocolate Hazelnut Pirouette® (about 18)**

1. Thaw the cake according to the package directions. Place the cake onto a serving dish.

2. Cut the wafers into 2½-inch-long pieces. Place the wafers upright, side-by-side, all around the edge of the cake, pressing them gently into the frosting. Place any remaining wafers on top of the cake.

Tip: This cake can be prepared up to 2 days ahead and stored in the refrigerator.

Chocolate Velvet Torte

thaw 40 minutes | **prep** 15 minutes | **bake** 20 minutes | **cool** 10 minutes | **chill** 2 hours |
makes 8 servings

- ½ of a 17.3-ounce package Pepperidge Farm® Puff Pastry Sheets (1 sheet), thawed
- 16 ounces semi-sweet chocolate, chopped
- 1 cup heavy cream
- 1 egg yolk
- 2 cups fresh raspberries **or** strawberries

1. Heat the oven to 425°F. Unfold the pastry sheet on a lightly floured surface. Roll the pastry sheet into a 12-inch square. Cut off the corners to make a circle. Press the pastry into the bottom and up the sides of a 9-inch springform pan. Prick the pastry with a fork.

2. Bake for 20 minutes or until the pastry is golden brown. Let the pastry cool in the pan on a wire rack for 10 minutes.

3. Heat and stir the chocolate and cream in a 1-quart heavy saucepan over low heat until the mixture is melted and smooth. Remove the saucepan from the heat. Stir some chocolate mixture into the egg yolk. Return the egg mixture to the remaining chocolate mixture. Cook and stir for 1 minute. Pour the chocolate mixture into the pastry crust. Cover and refrigerate for 2 hours or until firm. Top the torte with the raspberries.

Easy Turkey Pot Pie

prep 10 minutes | **bake** 30 minutes | **makes** 4 servings

- **1** **can (10¾ ounces) Campbell's® Condensed Cream of Chicken Soup (Regular or 98% Fat Free)**
- **1** **package (about 9 ounces) frozen mixed vegetables, thawed**
- **1** **cup cubed cooked turkey or chicken**
- **½** **cup milk**
- **1** **egg**
- **1** **cup all-purpose baking mix**

1. Heat the oven to 400°F.
2. Stir the soup, vegetables and turkey in a 9-inch pie plate.
3. Stir the milk, egg and baking mix in a small bowl. Spread the batter over the turkey mixture.
4. Bake for 30 minutes or until the topping is golden brown.

Tip: Substitute Campbell's® Condensed Cream of Chicken with Herbs Soup for the Cream of Chicken.

Garlic Potato Soup

prep 15 minutes | **cook** 25 minutes | **makes** 4 servings

- 3½ **cups Swanson® Chicken Broth (Regular, Natural Goodness® or Certified Organic)**
- 4 **cloves garlic, minced**
- 4 **medium red potatoes, cut into cubes (about 4 cups)**
- 2 **medium carrots, diced (about 1 cup)**
- 1 **medium onion, chopped (about ½ cup)**
- 1 **stalk celery, chopped (about ½ cup)**
- 2 **slices bacon, cooked and crumbled**
- 1 **cup milk**
- 1 **cup instant mashed potato flakes or buds**
- 1 **tablespoon chopped fresh parsley**

1. Heat the broth, garlic, potatoes, carrots, onion, celery and bacon in a 4-quart saucepan over medium-high heat to a boil. Reduce the heat to low. Cover and cook for 15 minutes or until the vegetables are tender.

2. Reduce the heat to medium. Stir the milk, potato flakes and parsley in the saucepan. Cook until the mixture is hot and bubbling, stirring occasionally.

Hot Turkey Sandwiches

prep 5 minutes | **cook** 10 minutes | **makes** 4 servings

- **1**   **can (10½ ounces) Campbell's® Turkey Gravy**
- **12** **ounces sliced roasted or deli turkey breast**
- **8**   **slices Pepperidge Farm® Farmhouse™ Hearty White Bread**

1. Heat the gravy in a 10-inch skillet over medium-high heat to a boil. Add the turkey to the skillet. Reduce the heat to low. Cook until the mixture is hot and bubbling.

2. Place **2** bread slices onto each of **4** plates. Spoon **about ¾ cup** turkey mixture onto **each** plate.

Roasted Tomato & Barley Soup

prep 10 minutes | **roast** 25 minutes | **cook** 40 minutes | **makes** 8 servings

- **1** can (about 28 ounces) diced tomatoes, undrained
- **2** large onions, diced (about 2 cups)
- **2** cloves garlic, minced
- **2** tablespoons olive oil
- **4** cups Swanson® Chicken Broth (Regular, Natural Goodness® **or** Certified Organic)
- **2** stalks celery, diced (about 1 cup)
- **½** cup **uncooked** pearl barley
- **2** tablespoons chopped fresh parsley

1. Heat the oven to 425°F. Drain the tomatoes, reserving the juice. Place the tomatoes, onions and garlic into a 17×11-inch roasting pan. Pour the oil over the vegetables and toss to coat. Roast for 25 minutes.

2. Place the roasted vegetables into a 3-quart saucepan. Stir in the reserved tomato juice, broth, celery and barley and heat to a boil. Reduce the heat to low. Cover and cook for 35 minutes or until the barley is tender. Stir in the parsley.

Green Bean Casserole

prep 10 minutes | **bake** 30 minutes | **makes** 5 servings

- 1 **can (10¾ ounces) Campbell's® Condensed Cream of Mushroom Soup (Regular or 98% Fat Free)**
- ½ **cup milk**
- 1 **teaspoon soy sauce**
  Dash ground black pepper
- 2 **packages (10 ounces each) frozen cut green beans, cooked and drained**
- 1 **can (2.8 ounces) French fried onions (1⅓ cups)**

1. Stir the soup, milk, soy sauce, black pepper, green beans and ⅔ **cup** onions in a 1½-quart casserole.

2. Bake at 350°F. for 25 minutes or until hot. Stir the green bean mixture.

3. Sprinkle the remaining onions over the green bean mixture. Bake for 5 minutes more or until onions are golden brown.

Tip: You can also make this classic side dish with fresh **or** canned green beans. You will need either 1½ **pounds** fresh green beans, cut into 1-inch pieces, cooked and drained, **or 2 cans** (about 16 ounces **each**) cut green beans, drained, for the frozen green beans.

February 17

Savory Orange Chicken with Sage

prep 10 minutes | **cook** 20 minutes | **makes** 4 servings

- **4** skinless, boneless chicken breasts halves (about 1 pound)
- **½** cup all-purpose flour
- **1** tablespoon vegetable oil
- **1** tablespoon butter
- **1¾** cups Swanson® Chicken Stock
- **⅓** cup orange juice
- **¼** cup Chablis **or** other dry white wine
- **1** tablespoon grated orange zest
- **1** tablespoon chopped fresh sage leaves **or** 1 teaspoon ground sage
- **¼** teaspoon ground black pepper
- **2** cups chopped shiitake mushrooms (about 3½ ounces)
  Hot cooked rice

1. Coat the chicken with the flour.

2. Heat the oil and butter in a 12-inch skillet over medium-high heat. Add the chicken and cook for 10 minutes or until well browned on both sides. Remove the chicken from the skillet.

3. Stir the stock, juice, wine, orange zest, sage and black pepper in the skillet and heat to a boil. Stir in the mushrooms. Return the chicken to the skillet. Reduce the heat to low. Cook for 5 minutes or until the chicken is cooked through and liquid is reduced by one-fourth. Serve with the rice.

Holiday Potato Pancakes

prep 25 minutes | **cook** 30 minutes | **makes** 36 pancakes

- **8** medium all-purpose potatoes (about 3 pounds), peeled and grated (about 7 cups)
- **2** cans (10¾ ounces **each**) Campbell's® Condensed Broccoli Cheese Soup (Regular **or** 98% Fat Free)
- **3** eggs, beaten
- **2** tablespoons all-purpose flour
- ¼ teaspoon freshly ground black pepper
- ½ cup vegetable oil
  Sour cream
  Chopped chives

1. Wrap the grated potatoes in a clean dish or paper towel. Twist the towel and squeeze to wring out as much of the liquid as possible.

2. Mix the soup, eggs, flour, black pepper and potatoes in a 3-quart bowl.

3. Heat ¼ **cup** oil in a deep nonstick 12-inch skillet over medium-high heat. Drop a scant ¼ **cup** potato mixture into the pan, making **4** pancakes at a time. Press on **each** pancake to flatten to 3 or 4 inches. Cook 4 minutes, turning once or until pancakes are dark golden brown. Remove the pancakes and keep warm. Repeat with the remaining potato mixture, adding more of the remaining oil as needed. Serve with the sour cream and chives.

Quick Barbecued Beef Sandwiches

prep 10 minutes | **cook** 20 minutes | **makes** 12 servings

1	tablespoon vegetable oil
1	medium onion, chopped (about ½ cup)
1	can (26 ounces) Campbell's® Condensed Tomato Soup
¼	cup water
2	tablespoons packed brown sugar
2	tablespoons vinegar
1	tablespoon Worcestershire sauce
1½	pounds thinly sliced deli roast beef
12	Pepperidge Farm® Classic Sandwich Buns with Sesame Seeds, split and toasted

1. Heat the oil in a 4-quart saucepot over medium heat. Add the onion and cook until tender, stirring occasionally.

2. Stir the soup, water, brown sugar, vinegar and Worcestershire in the saucepot and heat to a boil. Reduce the heat to low. Cook for 5 minutes. Add the beef to the saucepot and cook until the mixture is hot and bubbling. Divide the beef and sauce among the buns.

Swiss Vegetable Casserole

prep 5 minutes | **bake** 45 minutes | **makes** 4 servings

- 1 can (10¾ ounces) Campbell's® Condensed Cream of Mushroom Soup (Regular **or** 98% Fat Free)
- ⅓ cup sour cream
- ¼ teaspoon ground black pepper
- 1 bag (16 ounces) frozen vegetable combination (broccoli, cauliflower, carrots), thawed
- 1 can (2.8 ounces) French fried onions (1⅓ cups)
- ½ cup shredded Swiss cheese

1. Stir soup, sour cream, black pepper, vegetables, ⅔ **cup** onions and ¼ **cup** cheese in 2-quart casserole. Cover the casserole.

2. Bake at 350°F. for 40 minutes or until the vegetables are tender. Stir the vegetable mixture. Top with the remaining onions and cheese.

3. Bake for 5 minutes or until the cheese is melted.

For Cheddar Cheese Lovers: Use Cheddar cheese instead of Swiss cheese.

Tip: If you like, stir **1 jar** (4 ounces) chopped pimientos, drained, into the vegetable mixture before baking.

Ranchero Enchilada Casserole

prep 10 minutes | **bake** 25 minutes | **makes** 4 servings

- 1 **can (10¾ ounces) Campbell's® Condensed Cream of Chicken Soup (Regular or 98% Fat Free)**
- ½ **cup water**
- 1 **teaspoon chili powder**
- ½ **teaspoon garlic powder**
- 1 **can (about 4 ounces) chopped green chiles**
- ¼ **cup rinsed, drained canned black beans**
- 3 **tablespoons tomato paste**
- 2 **tablespoons chopped red peppers**
- 2 **cups cubed cooked chicken**
- 4 **flour tortillas (8-inch) or 6 corn tortillas (6-inch), cut into strips**
- ½ **cup shredded Cheddar cheese**

1. Stir the soup, water, chili powder, garlic powder, chiles, beans, tomato paste, red pepper, chicken and tortillas in a large bowl.

2. Spoon the chicken mixture into a 2-quart shallow baking dish. Top with the cheese. Cover the baking dish.

3. Bake at 350°F. for 25 minutes or until the mixture is hot and bubbling.

Herb Roasted Turkey

prep 15 minutes | **roast** 4 hours | **stand** 10 minutes | **makes** 12 servings

- 1¾ **cups Swanson® Chicken Stock**
- 3 **tablespoons lemon juice**
- 1 **teaspoon dried basil leaves, crushed**
- 1 **teaspoon dried thyme leaves, crushed**
- ⅛ **teaspoon ground black pepper**
- **12- to 14-pound turkey**
- 2 **cans (14½ ounces each) Campbell's® Turkey Gravy**

1. Stir the stock, lemon juice, basil, thyme and black pepper in a small bowl.

2. Roast the turkey according to the package directions, basting occasionally with the stock mixture during cooking. Let the turkey stand for 10 minutes before slicing. Discard any remaining stock mixture.

3. Heat the gravy in a 1-quart saucepan over medium heat until hot and bubbling. Serve with the turkey.

Tip: The turkey may be roasted in an oven bag, following the package directions, pouring the stock mixture over the turkey before closing the bag.

Italian-Style Pot Roast

prep 5 minutes | **cook** 2 hours | **makes** 8 servings

- 2 tablespoons oil
- 1 boneless beef bottom round roast **or** beef chuck pot roast (about 4 pounds)
- 1 jar (24 ounces) Prego® Traditional Italian Sauce
- 6 medium potatoes, cut into quarters
- 6 medium carrots, cut into 2-inch pieces

1. Heat the oil in a 6-quart saucepot over medium-high heat. Add the roast and cook until browned on all sides. Pour off any fat.

2. Stir the Italian sauce in the saucepot. Heat to a boil. Reduce the heat to low. Cover and cook for 45 minutes.

3. Add the potatoes and carrots. Cover and cook for 1 hour or until the beef and vegetables are fork-tender.

Quick Creamy Chicken & Corn

prep 15 minutes | **cook** 25 minutes | **makes** 4 servings

- 1 tablespoon vegetable oil
- 4 skinless, boneless chicken breasts halves (about 1 pound)
- 1 can (10¾ ounces) Campbell's® Condensed Cream of Chicken Soup (Regular **or** 98% Fat Free)
- ¾ cup water
- ½ teaspoon poultry seasoning
- 1 package (10 ounces) frozen whole kernel corn
- 2 cups refrigerated cubed potatoes
- 2 tablespoons chopped fresh parsley
- 1 cup shredded Cheddar cheese (about 4 ounces)

1. Heat the oil in a 10-inch skillet over medium-high heat. Add the chicken and cook for 10 minutes or until well browned on both sides.

2. Stir the soup, water, poultry seasoning, corn and potatoes into the skillet. Heat to a boil. Reduce the heat to low. Cover and cook for 10 minutes or until the chicken is cooked through. Stir in the parsley and sprinkle with the cheese.

February 21

Savory Meatloaf

prep 15 minutes | **bake** 1 hour | **stand** 10 minutes | **cook** 5 minutes | **makes** 6 servings

- 1½ **pounds ground beef**
- 1 **can (10¾ ounces) Campbell's® Condensed Tomato Soup**
- ½ **cup dry bread crumbs**
- 1 **egg, beaten**
- 1 **small onion, finely chopped (about ¼ cup)**
- 1 **tablespoon Worcestershire sauce**
- ⅛ **teaspoon ground black pepper**
- ¼ **cup water**

1. Thoroughly mix the beef, ½ **cup** soup, bread crumbs, egg, onion, Worcestershire sauce and black pepper. Place the beef mixture into a shallow 3-quart baking pan and firmly shape into an 8×4-inch loaf.

2. Bake at 350°F. for 1 hour or until the meatloaf is cooked through. Let the meatloaf stand for 10 minutes before slicing.

3. Heat **2 tablespoons** pan drippings, remaining soup and water in a 1-quart saucepan over medium-high heat until the mixture is hot and bubbling. Serve the gravy with the meatloaf.

Legendary Twice-Baked Potatoes

prep 20 minutes | **broil** 5 minutes | **makes** 4 servings

- 4 hot baked potatoes
- 1 cup shredded smoked Gouda cheese **or** shredded Monterey Jack cheese
- ½ cup sour cream
- ⅓ cup Pace® Picante Sauce
- ¼ cup diced cooked bacon
- 2 green onions, chopped (about ¼ cup)
- 1 jar (16 ounces) Pace® Chunky Salsa

1. Cut the potatoes into lengthwise halves. Scoop out the inside of the potatoes and place in a medium bowl. Set the potato skins aside.

2. Stir ¾ **cup** cheese, sour cream, picante sauce, bacon and onions into the bowl. Mix well. Spoon the mixture into the potato skins and place on a baking sheet.

3. Broil until they're browned. Sprinkle with the remaining cheese. Broil until the cheese is bubbly. Top with the salsa.

Broccoli Fish Bake

prep 15 minutes | **bake** 20 minutes | **makes** 4 servings

1	package (about 10 ounces) frozen broccoli spears, cooked and drained
4	fresh **or** thawed frozen firm white fish fillets (cod, haddock **or** halibut) (about 1 pound)
1	can (10¾ ounces) Campbell's® Condensed Cream of Broccoli Soup
⅓	cup milk
¼	cup shredded Cheddar cheese
2	tablespoons dry bread crumbs
1	teaspoon butter, melted
⅛	teaspoon paprika

1. Place the broccoli into a 2-quart shallow baking dish. Top with the fish. Stir the soup and milk in a small bowl. Pour the soup mixture over the fish. Sprinkle with the cheese.

2. Stir the bread crumbs, butter and paprika in a small bowl. Sprinkle the crumb mixture over all.

3. Bake at 450°F. for 20 minutes or until the fish flakes easily when tested with a fork.

Tip: You can substitute **1 pound** fresh broccoli spears, cooked and drained, for the frozen.

Italian Sausage Sandwiches

prep 5 minutes | **cook** 15 minutes | **makes** 4 servings

- 1 pound Italian pork sausage, casing removed
- 1½ cups Prego® Chunky Garden Mushroom & Green Pepper Italian Sauce
- 4 long hard rolls, split

1. Cook the sausage in a 10-inch skillet over medium-high heat until well browned, stirring often to separate the meat. Pour off any fat.

2. Stir in the Italian sauce and cook until the mixture is hot and bubbling. Serve the sausage mixture on the rolls.

Tip: You can use any favorite Prego® Italian Sauce in this recipe.

Swiss Cheese Fondue

prep 10 minutes | **cook** 1 hour | **makes** 6 servings

- 1 clove garlic, cut in half
- 1 can (10½ ounces) Campbell's® Condensed Chicken Broth
- 2 cans (10¾ ounces **each**) Campbell's® Condensed Cheddar Cheese Soup
- 1 cup water
- ½ cup Chablis **or** other dry white wine
- 1 tablespoon Dijon-style mustard
- 1 tablespoon cornstarch
- 4 cups shredded Emmentaler **or** Gruyère cheese (about 1 pound), at room temperature
- ¼ teaspoon ground nutmeg
  Dash ground black pepper
  Pepperidge Farm® Garlic Bread, prepared and cut into cubes
  Fresh vegetables

1. Rub the inside of a 5½-quart slow cooker with the cut sides of the garlic. Discard the garlic. Stir the broth, soup, water, wine, mustard, cornstarch, cheese, nutmeg and black pepper in the cooker.
2. Cover and cook on LOW for 1 hour or until the cheese is melted, stirring occasionally.
3. Serve with the bread and vegetables on skewers for dipping.

Spinach Ricotta Gnocchi

prep 5 minutes | **cook** 25 minutes | **makes** 6 servings

- 1 package (16 ounces) frozen dumpling-shaped pasta (gnocchi)
- 2 cups frozen cut leaf spinach, thawed and well drained
- 1½ cups Prego® Heart Smart Onion and Garlic Italian Sauce **or** Heart Smart Traditional Italian Sauce
- ¼ cup grated Romano cheese
- ½ cup ricotta cheese
- 1 cup shredded mozzarella cheese (about 4 ounces)

1. Prepare the gnocchi according to the package directions in a 6-quart saucepot. Add the spinach during the last 3 minutes of cooking time. Drain the gnocchi mixture well in a colander. Return the gnocchi mixture to the saucepot.

2. Stir the Italian sauce, Romano cheese and ricotta cheese in the saucepot. Cook over medium heat until the mixture is hot and bubbling, stirring occasionally. Top with the mozzarella cheese.

Slow Cooker Savory Pot Roast

prep 10 minutes | **cook** 8 hours | **makes** 6 servings

- 1 can (10¾ ounces) Campbell's® Condensed Cream of Mushroom Soup (Regular **or** 98% Fat Free)
- 1 envelope (about 1 ounce) dry onion soup and recipe mix
- 6 small red potatoes, cut in half
- 6 medium carrots, cut into 2-inch pieces (about 3 cups)
- 1 boneless beef bottom round roast **or** chuck pot roast (3 to 3½ pounds)

1. Stir the mushroom soup, soup mix, potatoes and carrots in a 4½-quart slow cooker. Add the beef and turn to coat.

2. Cover and cook on LOW for 8 to 9 hours* or until the beef is fork-tender.

Or on HIGH for 4 to 5 hours.

Greek Rice Bake

prep 15 minutes | **bake** 40 minutes | **stand** 5 minutes |
makes 6 servings

- 1 **can (10¾ ounces) Campbell's® Condensed Cream of Mushroom Soup (Regular or 98% Fat Free)**
- ½ **cup water**
- 1 **can (about 14.5 ounces) diced tomatoes, undrained**
- 1 **jar (6 ounces) marinated artichoke hearts, drained and cut in half**
- 2 **portobello mushrooms, coarsely chopped (about 2 cups)**
- ¾ **cup uncooked quick-cooking brown rice**
- 1 **can (about 15 ounces) small white beans, rinsed and drained**
- 3 **to 4 tablespoons crumbled feta cheese**

1. Heat the oven to 400°F. Stir the soup, water, tomatoes, artichokes, mushrooms, rice and beans in a 2-quart casserole. Cover the casserole.

2. Bake for 40 minutes or until the rice is tender. Stir the rice mixture. Let stand for 5 minutes. Sprinkle with the cheese before serving.

Tip: Different brands of quick-cooking brown rice cook differently, so the bake time for this recipe may be slightly longer or shorter than indicated.

February 25

Easy Skillet Chicken Parmesan

prep 5 minutes | **cook** 20 minutes | **stand** 5 minutes |
makes 6 servings

- 1 tablespoon olive oil
- 6 skinless, boneless chicken breast halves (about 1½ pounds)
- 1½ cups Prego® Traditional **or** Organic Tomato & Basil Italian Sauce
- ¼ cup grated Parmesan cheese
- 1½ cups shredded part-skim mozzarella cheese (about 6 ounces)

1. Heat the oil in a 12-inch skillet over medium-high heat. Add the chicken and cook for 10 minutes or until well browned on both sides.

2. Stir the Italian sauce and **3 tablespoons** Parmesan cheese in the skillet. Reduce the heat to low. Cover and cook for 10 minutes or until the chicken is cooked through. Sprinkle with the mozzarella and remaining Parmesan cheese. Let stand for 5 minutes or until the cheese is melted.

Baked Corn Casserole

prep 10 minutes | **bake** 35 minutes | **makes** 6 servings

- 1 **can (10¾ ounces) Campbell's® Condensed Cream of Chicken Soup (Regular or 98% Fat Free)**
- ½ **cup milk**
- 2 **eggs**
- 1 **can (about 16 ounces) whole kernel corn, drained**
- 1 **package (about 8 ounces) corn muffin mix**
- ¼ **cup grated Parmesan cheese**
- 1 **can (2.8 ounces) French fried onions (about 1⅓ cups)**

1. Beat the soup, milk and eggs in a medium bowl with a fork or whisk. Stir in the corn, corn muffin mix, cheese and ⅔ **cup** onions. Pour the soup mixture into a 1½-quart casserole.

2. Bake at 350°F. for 30 minutes or until the mixture is hot.

3. Top with the remaining onions. Bake for 5 minutes or until the onions are golden brown.

Slow-Cooked Pulled Pork Sliders

prep 10 minutes | **cook** 8 hours | **stand** 10 minutes |
makes 12 mini sandwiches

- 1 **can** (10¾ ounces) Campbell's® Condensed Tomato Soup
- ½ cup packed brown sugar
- ¼ cup cider vinegar
- 1 teaspoon garlic powder
- 1 boneless pork shoulder roast (3½ to 4½ pounds)
- 2 packages (15 ounces **each**) Pepperidge Farm® Slider Mini Sandwich Rolls
  Hot pepper sauce (optional)

1. Stir the soup, brown sugar, vinegar and garlic powder in a 6-quart slow cooker. Add the pork and turn to coat.

2. Cover and cook on LOW for 8 to 9 hours* or until the pork is fork-tender. Spoon off any fat.

3. Remove the pork from the cooker to a cutting board and let stand for 10 minutes. Using 2 forks, shred the pork. Return the pork to the cooker.

4. Divide the pork mixture among the rolls. Serve with the hot pepper sauce, if desired.

Or on HIGH for 5 to 6 hours.

Apple-Raisin Stuffing

prep 25 minutes | **bake** 25 minutes | **makes** 4 servings

- ¼ **cup (½ stick) butter**
- 1 **stalk celery, chopped (about ½ cup)**
- 1 **small onion, chopped (about ¼ cup)**
- 1 **can (10½ ounces) Campbell's® Condensed Chicken Broth**
- 4 **cups Pepperidge Farm® Herb Seasoned Stuffing**
- 1 **medium apple, cored and chopped (about 1 cup)**
- ¼ **cup raisins**
- ¼ **teaspoon ground cinnamon**

1. Heat the butter in a 10-inch skillet over medium heat. Add the celery and onion and cook until tender, stirring occasionally. Add the broth and heat to a boil. Remove the skillet from the heat. Add the stuffing, apple, raisins and cinnamon and mix lightly. Spoon the stuffing mixture into a 1½-quart casserole.

2. Bake at 350°F. for 25 minutes or until the stuffing is hot.

Tomato-Basil Chicken

prep 15 minutes | **cook** 15 minutes | **makes** 4 servings

- 1 tablespoon vegetable oil
- 1 pound skinless, boneless breast halves
- 1 can (10¾ ounces) Campbell's® Condensed Tomato Soup
- ½ cup milk
- 2 tablespoons grated Parmesan cheese
- ½ teaspoon dried basil leaves, crushed
- ¼ teaspoon garlic powder **or** 1 clove garlic, minced
- ½ package medium tube-shaped pasta (ziti), cooked according to package directions (about 4 cups)

1. Heat the oil in a 10-inch skillet over medium-high heat. Add the chicken and cook for 10 minutes or until well browned on both sides.

2. Stir in the soup, milk, cheese, basil and garlic powder. Heat to a boil. Return the chicken to the skillet and reduce the heat to low. Cover and cook for 5 minutes or until chicken is cooked through. Serve with the pasta.

Orange Cranberry Sauce

prep 5 minutes | **cook** 15 minutes | **makes** 12 servings

- 1 cup Swanson® Chicken Broth (Regular, Natural Goodness® **or** Certified Organic)
- 1 cup packed brown sugar
- 1 teaspoon ground cinnamon
- 1 package (about 12 ounces) fresh **or** frozen cranberries
- 1 cup coarsely chopped orange

Heat the broth, brown sugar, cinnamon, cranberries and orange in a 2-quart saucepan over high heat to a boil. Reduce the heat to low. Cook for 10 minutes or until the mixture thickens. Refrigerate until serving time.

Tip: Make the sauce a day in advance and chill overnight.

Roasted Orange Cranberry Sauce: Use **1¾ cups** Swanson® Chicken Broth. Mix all the ingredients in a 17×15-inch roasting pan. Roast at 450°F. for 25 minutes or until the mixture thickens. Refrigerate until serving time.

Chicken Tetrazzini

prep 20 minutes | cook 5 minutes | makes 4 servings

- 1 can (10¾ ounces) Campbell's® Condensed Cream of Mushroom Soup (Regular **or** 98% Fat Free)
- ¾ cup water
- ½ cup grated Parmesan cheese
- 2 tablespoons chopped fresh parsley **or** 2 teaspoons dried parsley flakes
- ¼ cup chopped red pepper **or** pimiento (optional)
- ½ package (8 ounces) spaghetti, cooked and drained
- 2 cans (4.5 ounces **each**) Swanson® Premium White Chunk Chicken Breast in Water, drained

Heat the soup, water, cheese, parsley, pepper, if desired, spaghetti and chicken in a 2-quart saucepan over medium heat until the mixture is hot and bubbling.

Smokey Sausage Cups

thaw 40 minutes | **prep** 15 minutes | **bake** 15 minutes | **makes** 12 servings

All-purpose flour
½ **of a 17.3-ounce package Pepperidge Farm® Puff Pastry Sheets (1 sheet) thawed**
6 **ounces kielbasa, diced (about 1½ cups)**
2 **tablespoons orange marmalade or your favorite jam**
1 **tablespoon Dijon-style mustard**
Chopped fresh parsley

1. Heat the oven to 400°F. Sprinkle flour on the work surface. Unfold the pastry sheet on the work surface. Roll the pastry sheet into a 10×15-inch rectangle. Cut the pastry sheet into 24 (2½-inch) squares. Press the pastry squares into 24 (1¾-inch) mini muffin-pan cups.

2. Stir the kielbasa, marmalade and mustard in a medium bowl. Spoon about **1 tablespoon** kielbasa mixture into **each** pastry cup.

3. Bake for 15 minutes or until the pastries are golden brown. Sprinkle the pastries with the parsley before serving.

Baked Macaroni and Cheese

prep 20 minutes | **bake** 20 minutes | **makes** 4 servings

- 1 can (10¾ ounces) Campbell's® Condensed Cheddar Cheese Soup
- ½ soup can milk
- ⅛ teaspoon ground black pepper
- 2 cups corkscrew–shaped pasta (rotini) **or** shell–shaped pasta, cooked and drained
- 1 tablespoon dry bread crumbs
- 2 teaspoons butter, melted

1. Stir the soup, milk, black pepper and pasta in a 1-quart baking dish.

2. Stir the bread crumbs and butter in a small bowl. Sprinkle the bread crumb mixture over the pasta mixture.

3. Bake at 400°F. for 20 minutes or until the pasta mixture is hot and bubbling.

Texas Cowboy Chili

prep 20 minutes | **cook** 40 minutes | **makes** 4 servings

- 1 **tablespoon olive oil**
- 1 **beef sirloin steak or boneless beef top round steak,** cut into cubes (about 1 pound)
- 1 **medium onion, chopped** (about ½ cup)
- 1 **small green pepper, chopped** (about ½ cup)
- 1 **teaspoon ground cumin**
- 1 **tablespoon all-purpose flour**
- 1 **cup Pace® Picante Sauce**
- 1¾ **cups Swanson® Beef Broth or Swanson® Beef Stock**
  Assorted Toppers

1. Heat the oil in a 4-quart nonstick saucepan over medium-high heat. Add the beef and cook until well browned, stirring often. Pour off any fat.

2. Reduce the heat to medium. Stir the onion, pepper and cumin in the saucepan and cook until the vegetables are tender-crisp, stirring occasionally. Add the flour and cook and stir for 1 minute.

3. Add the picante sauce and broth and heat to a boil. Reduce the heat to low. Cook for 20 minutes or until the beef is cooked through and the mixture is thickened. Serve with the *Assorted Toppers*.

Assorted Toppers: Shredded Cheddar cheese, chopped green onions and Pace® Chunky Salsa.

Classic Lasagna

prep 30 minutes | **bake** 30 minutes | **stand** 10 minutes | **makes** 12 servings

- 3 **cups ricotta cheese**
- 12 **ounces shredded mozzarella cheese (about 3 cups)**
- ¾ **cup grated Parmesan cheese**
- 2 **eggs**
- 1 **pound ground beef**
- 1 **jar (45 ounces) Prego® Three Cheese Italian Sauce**
- 12 **lasagna noodles, cooked and drained**

1. Stir the ricotta cheese, mozzarella cheese, ½ **cup** Parmesan cheese and eggs in a medium bowl and set it aside.

2. In a 3-quart saucepan over medium-high heat, cook the beef until well browned, stirring often to separate the meat. Pour off any fat. Stir the Italian sauce in the saucepan.

3. Spoon **1 cup** meat mixture in **each** of two 2-quart shallow baking dishes. Top **each** with **2** lasagna noodles and **about 1¼ cups** cheese mixture. Repeat the layers. Top with the remaining **2** lasagna noodles, remaining meat mixture and the Parmesan cheese.

4. Bake at 400°F. for 30 minutes or until hot and bubbling. Let stand for 10 minutes.

Tip: To freeze, prepare lasagna but do not bake. Cover tightly with foil and freeze. Bake frozen lasagna, uncovered, at 350°F. for 1 hour 15 minutes or until hot. Or, refrigerate 24 hours to thaw. Bake thawed lasagna, uncovered, at 350°F. for 50 minutes or until hot. Let stand for 10 minutes.

Cornbread Chicken Pot Pie

prep 15 minutes | **bake** 30 minutes | **makes** 4 servings

1 can (10¾ ounces) Campbell's® Condensed Cream of Chicken Soup (Regular **or** 98% Fat Free)
1 can (about 8 ounces) whole kernel corn, drained
2 cups cubed cooked chicken **or** turkey
1 package (about 8 ounces) corn muffin mix
¾ cup milk
1 egg
½ cup shredded Cheddar cheese

1. Heat the oven to 400°F. Stir the soup, corn and chicken in a 9-inch pie plate.

2. Stir the muffin mix, milk and egg in a small bowl just until blended. Spread the batter over the chicken mixture.

3. Bake for 30 minutes or until the topping is golden brown. Sprinkle with the cheese. Let stand until the cheese is melted.

Tip: Don't overmix the cornbread batter. Stir just enough to combine the wet ingredients with the dry. Most lumps will disappear during baking.

Chicken with Wild Mushroom Cream Sauce

prep 15 minutes | **cook** 25 minutes | **makes** 4 servings

- 4 **skinless, boneless chicken breast halves (about 1 pound)**
   Ground black pepper
- 2 **tablespoons all-purpose flour**
- 2 **tablespoons butter**
- 4 **ounces sliced mixed wild mushrooms (cremini, shiitake, oyster) (about 2 cups)**
- 4 **green onions, sliced (about ½ cup)**
- 1 **cup Swanson® Chicken Stock**
- ½ **cup chopped roasted red pepper**
- ½ **cup sour cream**
- 2 **tablespoons chopped fresh parsley**

1. Season the chicken with the black pepper and coat with the flour.

2. Heat the butter in a 10-inch skillet over medium-high heat. Add the chicken and cook for 10 minutes or until well browned on both sides. Add the mushrooms and onions and cook until tender.

3. Stir the stock in the skillet and heat to a boil. Reduce the heat to low. Cover and cook for 5 minutes or until the chicken is cooked through. Stir in the pepper and sour cream and heat through. Sprinkle with the parsley.

Chicken & Vegetable Bake

prep 20 minutes | **bake** 30 minutes | **makes** 4 servings

- 1 **can (10¾ ounces) Campbell's® Condensed Cream of Celery Soup (Regular or 98% Fat Free)**
- ½ **cup milk**
  Dash ground black pepper
- 1 **cup cooked broccoli or cauliflower florets**
- 1 **cup cooked sliced carrots**
- 1 **cup cooked cut green beans**
- ¼ **cup cooked red pepper strips**
- 1 **can (12.5 ounces) Swanson® Premium White Chunk Chicken Breast in Water, drained**
- 1 **can (2.8 ounces) French fried onions (1⅓ cups)**

1. Stir the soup, milk, black pepper, broccoli, carrots, green beans, red pepper, chicken and ½ **can** onions in a 1½-quart casserole.

2. Bake at 350°F. for 20 minutes or until the chicken mixture is hot and bubbling. Stir the chicken mixture. Sprinkle with the remaining onions.

3. Bake for 10 minutes or until the onions are golden brown.

Beefy Pasta Skillet

prep 10 minutes | **cook** 15 minutes | **makes** 4 servings

- 1 **pound ground beef**
- 1 **medium onion, chopped (about ½ cup)**
- 1 **can (10¾ ounces) Campbell's® Condensed Tomato Soup (Regular or Healthy Request®)**
- ¼ **cup water**
- 1 **tablespoon Worcestershire sauce**
- ½ **cup shredded Cheddar cheese**
- 1½ **cups corkscrew-shaped pasta (rotini), cooked and drained**

1. Cook the beef and onion in a 10-inch skillet over medium-high heat until the beef is well browned, stirring often to separate the meat. Pour off any fat.

2. Stir the soup, water, Worcestershire, cheese and pasta in the skillet and cook until the mixture is hot and bubbling.

Tip: You can substitute **1 cup uncooked** elbow pasta, cooked and drained, for the corkscrew pasta, if you like.

Terrific Tacos

prep 15 minutes | **cook** 15 minutes | **makes** 24 tacos

- **2 pounds ground beef**
- **1 jar (16 ounces) Pace® Picante Sauce**
- **24 taco shells**
- **Shredded Cheddar cheese**
- **Shredded lettuce**
- **Chopped tomato**
- **Sour cream**

1. In a 12-inch skillet over medium-high heat, cook ground beef until browned, stirring to separate the meat. Pour off any fat. Add picante sauce. Heat to a boil. Simmer 5 minutes.

2. Spoon taco mixture into taco shells. Top with cheese, lettuce, tomatoes and sour cream.

Broccoli Chicken Potato Parmesan

prep 10 minutes | **cook** 20 minutes | **makes** 4 servings

- 2 tablespoons vegetable oil
- 1 pound small red potatoes, sliced ¼-inch thick
- 1 can (10¾ ounces) Campbell's® Condensed Broccoli Cheese Soup (Regular **or** 98% Fat Free)
- ½ cup milk
- ¼ teaspoon garlic powder
- 2 cups fresh **or** frozen broccoli florets
- 1 package (about 10 ounces) refrigerated cooked chicken breast strips
- ¼ cup grated Parmesan cheese

1. Heat the oil in a 10-inch skillet over medium heat. Add the potatoes. Cover and cook for 10 minutes, stirring occasionally.

2. Stir the soup, milk, garlic powder, broccoli and chicken in the skillet. Add the cheese and heat to a boil. Reduce the heat to low. Cover and cook for 5 minutes or until the potatoes are fork-tender.

Chicken Mushroom Risotto

prep 15 minutes | **cook** 35 minutes | **makes** 4 servings

- 3 skinless, boneless chicken breast halves (about ¾ pound), cut into cubes
- 1 small onion, finely chopped (about ¼ cup)
- 1 small carrot, chopped (about ¼ cup)
- 1 cup **uncooked** regular long-grain white rice
- 1 can (10¾ ounces) Campbell's® Healthy Request® Condensed Cream of Mushroom Soup
- 1¾ cups Swanson® Chicken Stock
- ⅛ teaspoon ground black pepper
- ½ cup frozen peas

1. Cook the chicken in a 10-inch nonstick skillet over medium-high heat until well browned, stirring often. Remove the chicken from the skillet.

2. Stir the onion, carrot and rice in the skillet and cook and stir until the rice is browned.

3. Stir in the soup, stock and black pepper and heat to a boil. Reduce the heat to low. Cover and cook for 15 minutes.

4. Stir in the peas. Return the chicken to the skillet. Cover and cook for 5 minutes or until the chicken is cooked through and the rice is tender.

March 6

Beefy Enchilada Skillet

prep 5 minutes | **cook** 15 minutes | **makes** 4 servings

- 1 **pound ground beef**
- 1 **jar (17.5 ounces) Pace® Picante Sauce**
- 8 **corn tortillas (6-inch), cut into 1-inch squares**
- 1 **cup shredded Cheddar cheese (about 4 ounces)**
  Sour cream
  Chopped green onions

1. Cook the beef in a 10-inch skillet over medium-high heat until well browned, stirring often to separate the meat. Pour off any fat.

2. Stir the picante sauce, tortillas and **half** of the cheese in the skillet and heat to a boil. Reduce the heat to low. Cover and cook for 5 minutes or until hot and bubbling.

3. Top with the remaining cheese. Serve with sour cream and green onions.

Now & Later Baked Ziti

prep 15 minutes | **bake** 30 minutes | **makes** 12 servings

- 2 **pounds ground beef**
- 1 **large onion, chopped (about 1 cup)**
- 7½ **cups Prego® Fresh Mushroom Italian Sauce**
- 9 **cups tube-shaped pasta (ziti), cooked and drained**
- 12 **ounces shredded mozzarella cheese (about 3 cups)**
- ½ **cup grated Parmesan cheese**

1. Cook the beef and onion in an 8-quart saucepot over medium-high heat until the beef is well browned, stirring often to separate the meat. Pour off any fat.

2. Stir the Italian sauce, ziti and **2 cups** mozzarella cheese in the saucepot. Spoon the beef mixture into **2** (12½×8½×2-inch) disposable foil pans. Top with the remaining mozzarella and Parmesan cheeses.

3. Bake at 350°F. for 30 minutes or until the beef mixture is hot and the cheese is melted.

Tip: To make ahead and freeze, prepare the ziti as directed above but do not bake. Cover the pans with foil and freeze. Bake the frozen ziti, uncovered, at 350°F. for 1 hour or until it's hot. Or, thaw the ziti in the refrigerator for 24 hours, then bake, uncovered, at 350°F. for 45 minutes or until it's hot.

Best Ever Meatloaf

prep 10 minutes | **bake** 1 hour 15 minutes | **stand** 10 minutes | **cook** 5 minutes | **makes** 8 servings

- **2** pounds ground beef
- **1** can (10¾ ounces) Campbell's® Condensed Tomato Soup (Regular **or** Healthy Request®)
- **1** envelope (about 1 ounce) dry onion soup and recipe mix
- **½** cup dry bread crumbs
- **1** egg, beaten
- **¼** cup water

1. Thoroughly mix the beef, ½ **cup** tomato soup, onion soup mix, bread crumbs and egg in a large bowl. Place the mixture into a 13×9×2-inch baking pan and firmly shape into an 8×4-inch loaf.

2. Bake at 350°F. for 1 hour 15 minutes or until the meatloaf is cooked through. Let the meatloaf stand for 10 minutes before slicing.

3. Heat **2 tablespoons** pan drippings, remaining tomato soup and water in a 1-quart saucepan over medium heat until the mixture is hot and bubbling. Serve the sauce with the meatloaf.

Tip: You can substitute Campbell's® Condensed Cream of Mushroom Soup (Regular **or** 98% Fat Free) for the Tomato Soup.

Mediterranean Chicken & Rice Bake

prep 10 minutes | **bake** 50 minutes | **makes** 6 servings

- 2 cups Swanson® Chicken Stock
- ¼ cup chopped fresh parsley
- 1 can (2.25 ounces) sliced pitted ripe olives
- 1 tablespoon fresh lemon juice
- ¼ teaspoon ground black pepper
- 1 can (about 14.5 ounces) stewed tomatoes
- 1¼ cups **uncooked** regular long-grain white rice
- 6 skinless, boneless chicken breast halves (about 1½ pounds)
- 1 teaspoon garlic powder
  Paprika

1. Stir the stock, parsley, olives, lemon juice, black pepper, tomatoes and rice in a 13×9×2-inch baking dish. Cover the dish.

2. Bake at 375°F. for 20 minutes.

3. Place the chicken onto the rice mixture. Sprinkle the chicken with the garlic powder and paprika. Cover the dish.

4. Bake for 30 minutes or until the chicken is cooked through and the rice is tender.

Fish Stuffing Bake

prep 30 minutes | **bake** 15 minutes | **makes** 6 servings

- 1 **cup water***
- ¼ **cup (½ stick) butter**
- 2 **medium carrots, sliced (about 1 cup)**
- 1 **small green pepper, chopped (about ½ cup)**
- 4 **cups Pepperidge Farm® Herb Seasoned Stuffing**
- 6 **fresh or thawed frozen firm white fish fillets (cod,**
  haddock or halibut) (about 1½ pounds)
- 1 **tablespoon lemon juice**
- 1 **tablespoon chopped fresh parsley or 1 teaspoon dried parsley flakes**

*For moister stuffing increase the water to 1½ cups.

1. Heat the water, **2 tablespoons** butter, carrots and pepper in a 3-quart saucepan over medium-high heat to a boil. Remove the saucepan from the heat. Add the stuffing and mix lightly.

2. Spoon the stuffing across the center of a 3-quart shallow baking dish. Arrange the fish on each side of the stuffing.

3. Heat the remaining butter in an 8-inch skillet over medium heat until melted. Stir in the lemon juice and parsley. Spoon the butter mixture over the fish.

4. Bake at 400°F. for 15 minutes or until the fish flakes easily when tested with a fork.

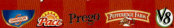
Apricot Glazed Pork Roast

prep 5 minutes | **cook** 8 hours | **makes** 8 servings

- **1** **can (10½ ounces) Campbell's®
  Condensed Chicken Broth**
- **1** **jar (18 ounces) apricot preserves**
- **1** **large onion, chopped (about 1 cup)**
- **2** **tablespoons Dijon-style mustard**
- **1** **boneless pork loin roast (about 4 pounds)**

1. Stir the broth, preserves, onion and mustard in a 3½-quart slow cooker. Add the pork to the cooker, cutting to fit, if needed, and turn to coat.

2. Cover and cook on LOW for 8 to 9 hours* or until the pork is fork-tender.

Or on HIGH for 4 to 5 hours.

Tip: For thicker sauce, mix **2 tablespoons** cornstarch and **2 tablespoons** water in a small bowl until smooth. Remove the pork from the cooker. Stir the cornstarch mixture in the cooker. Cover and cook on HIGH for 10 minutes or until the mixture boils and thickens.

Slow-Cooked Taco Shredded Beef

prep 10 minutes | **cook** 6 hours | **stand** 10 minutes | **makes** 16 servings

- 1 **can (10¾ ounces) Campbell's® Condensed French Onion Soup**
- 1 **tablespoon chili powder**
- ½ **teaspoon ground cumin**
  2-pound boneless beef chuck roast
- 2 **tablespoons finely chopped fresh cilantro leaves**
- 16 **taco shells**
- 1 **cup shredded Cheddar cheese (about 4 ounces)**
  Shredded lettuce
  Sour cream

1. Stir the soup, chili powder and cumin in a 4-quart slow cooker. Add the beef and turn to coat.

2. Cover and cook on LOW for 6 to 7 hours* or until the beef is fork-tender.

3. Remove the beef from the cooker to a cutting board and let stand for 10 minutes. Using 2 forks, shred the beef. Return the beef to the cooker. Stir the cilantro in the cooker.

4. Spoon **about ¼ cup** beef mixture into **each** taco shell. Top **each** with **about 1 tablespoon** cheese. Top with the lettuce and the sour cream.

Or on HIGH for 4 to 5 hours.

Chipotle Chili

prep 15 minutes | **cook** 8 hours | **makes** 8 servings

- 1 jar (16 ounces) Pace® Picante Sauce
- 1 cup water
- 2 tablespoons chili powder
- 1 teaspoon ground chipotle chile pepper
- 1 large onion, chopped (about 1 cup)
- 2 pounds beef for stew, cut into ½-inch pieces
- 1 can (about 19 ounces) red kidney beans, rinsed and drained
  Shredded Cheddar cheese (optional)
  Sour cream (optional)

1. Stir the picante sauce, water, chili powder, chipotle pepper, onion, beef and beans in a 3½-quart slow cooker.

2. Cover and cook on LOW for 8 to 9 hours* or until the beef is fork-tender. Serve with the cheese and sour cream, if desired.

Or on HIGH for 4 to 5 hours.

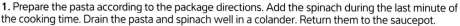

March 10

Three Cheese Baked Ziti with Spinach

prep 15 minutes | **bake** 30 minutes | **makes** 6 servings

- 1 package (16 ounces) **uncooked** medium tube-shaped pasta (ziti)
- 1 bag (6 ounces) baby spinach, washed (about 4 cups)
- 1 jar (1 pound 9 ounces) Prego® Marinara Italian Sauce
- 1 cup ricotta cheese
- 4 ounces shredded mozzarella cheese (about 1 cup)
- ¾ cup grated Parmesan cheese
- ½ teaspoon garlic powder
- ¼ teaspoon ground black pepper

1. Prepare the pasta according to the package directions. Add the spinach during the last minute of the cooking time. Drain the pasta and spinach well in a colander. Return them to the saucepot.

2. Stir the Italian sauce, ricotta, ½ **cup** of the mozzarella cheese, ½ **cup** of the Parmesan cheese, garlic powder and black pepper into the pasta mixture. Spoon the pasta mixture into a 13×9×2-inch shallow baking dish. Sprinkle with the remaining mozzarella and Parmesan cheeses.

3. Bake at 350°F. for 30 minutes or until hot and bubbling.

Tip: Save valuable time by putting together the casserole a day or less in advance, covering and refrigerating it to bake later to everyone's delight.

Chicken Nachos

prep 10 minutes | **cook** 5 minutes | **makes** 6 servings

- ½ cup Pace® Picante Sauce
- 1 can (10¾ ounces) Campbell's® Condensed Cheddar Cheese Soup
- 2 cans (4.5 ounces **each**) Swanson® Premium White Chunk Chicken Breast in Water, drained
- 1 bag (about 10 ounces) tortilla chips
  Chopped tomato
  Sliced green onions
  Sliced pitted ripe olives

1. Heat the picante sauce, soup and chicken in a 1-quart saucepan over medium heat until the mixture is hot and bubbling, stirring often.

2. Place the chips on a platter. Spoon the chicken mixture over the chips. Top with the tomato, onions and olives.

Sensational Chicken Noodle Soup

prep 5 minutes | **cook** 25 minutes | **makes** 4 servings

- 4 cups Swanson® Chicken Broth (Regular, Natural Goodness® **or** Certified Organic)
  Generous dash ground black pepper
- 1 medium carrot, sliced (about ½ cup)
- 1 stalk celery, sliced (about ½ cup)
- ½ cup **uncooked** extra-wide egg noodles
- 1 cup shredded cooked chicken **or** turkey

1. Heat the broth, black pepper, carrot and celery in a 2-quart saucepan over medium-high heat to a boil.

2. Stir the noodles and chicken into the saucepan. Reduce the heat to medium. Cook for 10 minutes or until the noodles are tender.

Asian Soup: Add **2** green onions cut into ½-inch pieces, **1 clove** garlic, minced, **1 teaspoon** ground ginger and **2 teaspoons** soy sauce. Substitute **uncooked** curly Asian noodles for egg noodles.

Mexican Soup: Add ½ **cup** Pace® Chunky Salsa, **1 clove** garlic, minced, **1 cup** rinsed and drained black beans and ½ **teaspoon** chili powder. Substitute **2** corn tortillas (4- or 6-inch) cut into thin strips for the noodles, adding them just before serving.

Black Bean, Corn and Turkey Chili

prep 15 minutes | **cook** 40 minutes | **makes** 6 servings

1 tablespoon vegetable oil
1 pound ground turkey
1 large onion, chopped (about 1 cup)
2 tablespoons chili powder
1 teaspoon ground cumin
1 teaspoon dried oregano leaves, crushed
½ teaspoon ground black pepper
¼ teaspoon garlic powder **or** 2 cloves garlic, minced
1¾ cups Swanson® Chicken Stock
1 cup Pace® Picante Sauce
1 tablespoon sugar
1 can (about 15 ounces) black beans, rinsed and drained
1 can (about 16 ounces) whole kernel corn, drained

1. Heat the oil in a 4-quart saucepan over medium-high heat. Add the turkey, onion, chili powder, cumin, oregano, black pepper and garlic powder. Cook until the turkey is well browned, stirring often to separate the meat.

2. Stir the stock, picante sauce, sugar, beans and corn in the saucepan and heat to a boil. Reduce the heat to low. Cover and cook for 30 minutes or until the mixture is hot and bubbling.

March 12

Chicken & Broccoli Alfredo

prep 10 minutes | **cook** 20 minutes | **makes** 4 servings

- ½ of a 16-ounce package linguine
- 1 cup fresh **or** frozen broccoli florets
- 2 tablespoons butter
- 4 skinless, boneless chicken breast halves (about 1 pound), cut into 1½-inch pieces
- 1 can (10¾ ounces) Campbell's® Condensed Cream of Mushroom Soup (Regular, 98% Fat Free **or** Healthy Request®)
- ½ cup milk
- ½ cup grated Parmesan cheese
- ¼ teaspoon ground black pepper

1. Prepare the linguine according to the package directions in a 3-quart saucepan. Add the broccoli during the last 4 minutes of the cooking time. Drain the linguine mixture well in a colander.

2. Heat the butter in a 10-inch skillet over medium-high heat. Add the chicken and cook until well browned, stirring often.

3. Stir the soup, milk, cheese, black pepper and linguine mixture in the skillet and cook until the chicken is cooked through, stirring occasionally. Serve with additional Parmesan cheese.

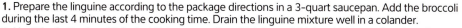

Walnut-Cheddar Ball

prep 20 minutes | **chill** 2 hours | **makes** 2 cups

- 2 cups shredded Cheddar cheese (8 ounces)
- ½ cup finely chopped walnuts
- ¼ cup mayonnaise
- 1 medium green onion, chopped (about 2 tablespoons)
- 1 tablespoon Dijon-style mustard
- 1 teaspoon Worcestershire sauce
- ¼ cup chopped fresh parsley
- 1 tablespoon paprika
  Pepperidge Farm® Cracker Quartet **or** Cracker Trio Entertaining Collection Cracker Assortment

Stir the cheese, walnuts, mayonnaise, green onion, mustard and Worcestershire in a medium bowl. Shape the mixture into a ball. Roll the ball in parsley and paprika to coat. Refrigerate for at least 2 hours. Serve with the crackers.

One-Dish Chicken & Rice Bake

prep 5 minutes | **bake** 45 minutes | **makes** 4 servings

- 1 **can (10¾ ounces) Campbell's® Condensed Cream of Mushroom Soup (Regular or 98% Fat Free)**
- 1 **cup water***
- ¾ **cup uncooked regular long-grain white rice**
- ¼ **teaspoon paprika**
- ¼ **teaspoon ground black pepper**
- 4 **skinless, boneless chicken breast halves (about 1 pound)**

For creamier rice, increase the water to 1⅓ cups.

1. Stir the soup, water, rice, paprika and black pepper in a 2-quart shallow baking dish. Top with the chicken. Season with additional paprika and black pepper. Cover the baking dish.
2. Bake at 375°F. for 45 minutes or until the chicken is cooked through and the rice is tender.

Chocolate-Cinnamon Bread Pudding

prep 15 minutes | **bake** 40 minutes | **makes** 6 servings

12	slices Pepperidge Farm® Cinnamon Swirl Bread, any variety, cut into cubes (about 6 cups)
½	cup semi-sweet chocolate pieces
2½	cups milk
4	eggs
½	cup packed brown sugar
1	teaspoon vanilla extract
	Sweetened whipped cream (optional)

1. Heat the oven to 350°F.

2. Place the bread cubes into a lightly greased 2-quart shallow baking dish. Sprinkle the chocolate pieces over the bread cubes. Beat the milk, eggs, brown sugar and vanilla extract in a small bowl with a fork or whisk. Pour the milk mixture over the bread cubes. Stir and press the bread cubes into the milk mixture to coat.

3. Bake for 40 minutes or until a knife inserted in the center comes out clean. Serve with the whipped cream, if desired.

Tip: This bread pudding can be served with the whipped cream as a dessert, or with a sprinkle of confectioners' sugar as a decadent brunch dish.

Southwestern Chicken & White Bean Soup

prep 15 minutes | **cook** 8 minutes | **makes** 6 servings

- 1 tablespoon vegetable oil
- 1 pound skinless, boneless chicken breasts, cut into 1-inch pieces
- 1¾ cups Swanson® Chicken Broth (Regular, Natural Goodness® **or** Certified Organic)
- 1 cup Pace® Picante Sauce
- 3 cloves garlic, minced
- 2 teaspoons ground cumin
- 1 can (about 16 ounces) small white beans, rinsed and drained
- 1 cup frozen whole kernel corn
- 1 large onion, chopped (about 1 cup)

1. Heat the oil in a 10-inch skillet over medium-high heat. Add the chicken and cook until well browned, stirring often.

2. Stir the chicken, broth, picante sauce, garlic, cumin, beans, corn and onion in a 3½-quart slow cooker.

3. Cover and cook on LOW for 8 to 9 hours* or until the chicken is cooked through.

Or on HIGH for 4 to 5 hours.

Moist & Savory Stuffing

prep 10 minutes | **cook** 10 minutes | **bake** 30 minutes |
makes 10 servings

2½ **cups** Swanson® Chicken Broth (Regular, Natural
  Goodness® **or** Certified Organic)
  Generous dash ground black pepper
2 **stalks celery, coarsely chopped (about 1 cup)**
1 **large onion, coarsely chopped (about 1 cup)**
1 **package (16 ounces) Pepperidge Farm® Herb Seasoned
  Stuffing**

1. Heat the broth, pepper, celery and onion in a 3-quart saucepan over medium-high heat to a boil.
Reduce the heat to low. Cover and cook for 5 minutes or until the vegetables are tender, stirring
often. Remove the saucepan from the heat. Add the stuffing and mix lightly.

2. Spoon the stuffing mixture into a greased 3-quart shallow baking dish. Cover the baking dish.

3. Bake at 350°F. for 30 minutes or until the stuffing is hot.

Tip: For crunchier stuffing, bake the casserole uncovered.

Cranberry & Pecan Stuffing: Stir ½ **cup each** dried cranberries and chopped pecans into the stuffing
mixture.

Sausage & Mushroom Stuffing: Add **1 cup** sliced mushrooms to the vegetables during cooking.
Stir ½ **pound** pork sausage, cooked and crumbled, into the stuffing mixture before baking.

Picante Macaroni and Cheese

prep 20 minutes | **bake** 30 minutes | **makes** 4 servings

- 1 **can** (10¾ ounces) Campbell's® Condensed Cream of Mushroom Soup (Regular **or** 98% Fat Free)
- ½ **cup** Pace® Picante Sauce
- 2 **cups** shredded Cheddar cheese (about 8 ounces)
- 3 **cups** hot cooked elbow macaroni (about 1½ cups dry)
- ½ **cup** crumbled tortilla chips

1. Stir the soup, picante sauce, 1½ **cups** cheese and macaroni in a 1½-quart casserole.

2. Bake at 400°F. for 25 minutes or until hot and bubbling. Stir the macaroni mixture.

3. Sprinkle with the chips and remaining cheese. Bake for 5 minutes or until the cheese is melted.

Ultra Creamy Mashed Potatoes

prep 15 minutes | **cook** 20 minutes | **makes** 6 servings

- 3½ cups Swanson® Chicken Broth (Regular, Natural Goodness® **or** Certified Organic)
- 5 large potatoes, cut into 1-inch pieces (about 7½ cups)
- ½ cup light cream
- 2 tablespoons butter
  Generous dash ground black pepper
- 1 can (14½ ounces) Campbell's® Turkey Gravy

1. Heat the broth and potatoes in a 3-quart saucepan over medium-high heat to a boil.

2. Reduce the heat to medium. Cover and cook for 10 minutes or until the potatoes are tender. Drain, reserving the broth.

3. Mash the potatoes with ¼ **cup** broth, cream, butter and black pepper. Add additional broth, if needed, until desired consistency. Serve with the gravy.

Ultimate Mashed Potatoes: Stir ½ **cup** sour cream, **3** slices bacon, cooked and crumbled (reserve some for garnish), and ¼ **cup** chopped fresh chives into the hot mashed potatoes. Sprinkle with the reserved bacon.

Glorified Onion Pork Chops

prep 10 minutes | **cook** 25 minutes | **makes** 6 servings

- 1 tablespoon vegetable oil
- 6 bone-in pork chops, ½-inch thick (about 3 pounds)
- 1 medium onion, sliced (about ½ cup)
- 1 can (10¾ ounces) Campbell's® Condensed Cream of Celery Soup (Regular **or** 98% Fat Free)
- ½ cup water

1. Heat the oil in a 12-inch skillet over medium-high heat. Add the pork and cook until well browned on both sides.

2. Add the onion and cook until the onion is tender, stirring occasionally. Stir in the soup and water and heat to a boil. Reduce the heat to low. Cook for 5 minutes or until the pork is cooked through.

Graveyard Cupcakes

prep 20 minutes | **makes** 24 servings

24 Pepperidge Farm® Milano® Cookies **and/or** Brussels® Distinctive Cookies **and/or** Old Fashioned Homestyle Sugar Cookies

 4 tubes (4.25 ounces **each**) decorating icing (black, white, orange **and** green) **or** 4 tubes (.68 ounces **each**) decorating gel (black, white, orange **and** green) Orange-colored sugar crystals

24 store-purchased frosted cupcakes

1. Decorate the Milano® cookies using the black and white icing to resemble tombstones and ghosts.

2. Decorate the Brussels® or Sugar cookies using the orange and green icing and sugar crystals to resemble pumpkins and spider webs.

3. Press the decorated cookies into the tops of the cupcakes.

Creamy Irish Potato Soup

prep 15 minutes | **cook** 25 minutes | **makes** 5 servings

- 2 **tablespoons butter**
- 4 **medium green onions, sliced (about ½ cup)**
- 1 **stalk celery, sliced (about ½ cup)**
- 1¾ **cups Swanson® Chicken Broth (Regular, Natural Goodness® or Certified Organic)**
- ⅛ **teaspoon ground black pepper**
- 3 **medium potatoes, sliced ¼-inch thick (about 3 cups)**
- 1½ **cups milk**

1. Heat the butter in a 3-quart saucepan over medium heat. Add the onions and celery and cook until tender.

2. Stir the broth, black pepper and potatoes in the saucepan and heat to a boil. Reduce the heat to low. Cover and cook for 15 minutes or until the potatoes are tender.

3. Place **half** of the broth mixture and **half** of the milk in a blender or food processor. Cover and blend until smooth. Repeat with the remaining broth mixture and remaining milk. Return to the saucepan and heat through.

Baked Eyeballs Casserole

prep 15 minutes | **bake** 25 minutes | **stand** 10 minutes | **makes** 8 servings

Vegetable cooking spray
- 1 **jar (24 ounces) Prego® Italian Sausage & Garlic Italian Sauce**
- 1 **container (15 ounces) part-skim ricotta cheese**
- ¾ **cup grated Parmesan cheese**
- 7 **cups bow tie-shaped pasta, cooked and drained**
- 1 **container (8 ounces) small fresh mozzarella cheese balls (about 1 inch)**
- 2 **tablespoons sliced pitted ripe olives**

1. Spray a 13×9×2-inch shallow baking dish with the cooking spray.

2. Mix **1½ cups** of the Italian sauce, ricotta cheese, ½ **cup** Parmesan cheese and pasta in the prepared dish. Spread the remaining sauce over the pasta mixture. Sprinkle with the remaining Parmesan cheese and cover the dish with foil.

3. Bake at 400°F. for 25 minutes or until hot and bubbling. Arrange the cheese balls randomly over the pasta mixture. Place a sliced olive on **each** cheese ball. Let stand for 10 minutes before serving.

Tip: If fresh mozzarella cheese balls are not available, substitute **1 package** (8 ounces) fresh mozzarella cheese. Cut crosswise into thirds. Cut **each** third into **6** wedges, for triangle-shaped eyes.

Tomato Walnut Pesto Penne

prep 15 minutes | **cook** 5 minutes | **makes** 8 servings

- ¼ **cup walnuts, toasted**
- 2 **cloves garlic**
- ½ **cup loosely-packed fresh basil leaves**
- 4 **cups loosely-packed fresh baby spinach**
- 3 **cups Prego® Heart Smart Ricotta Parmesan Italian Sauce**
- 1 **package (16 ounces) penne pasta, cooked and drained (about 9 cups)**
- 2 **tablespoons grated Parmesan cheese (optional)**

1. Place the walnuts and garlic into a food processor or blender. Cover and process until the mixture is finely chopped. Add the basil and spinach and process until the mixture forms a smooth paste.

2. Heat the Italian sauce and the walnut mixture in a 2-quart saucepan over medium heat for 5 minutes or until the mixture is hot and bubbling.

3. Toss the sauce mixture with the pasta. Sprinkle with the cheese.

Tip: If you're using a blender, reserve ¼ **cup** pasta water and add it to the walnut mixture to help the blending.

Chicken Scampi

prep 10 minutes | **cook** 20 minutes | **makes** 6 servings

- **2 tablespoons butter**
- **6 skinless, boneless chicken breast halves (about 1½ pounds)**
- **1 can (10¾ ounces) Campbell's® Condensed Cream of Chicken Soup (Regular or 98% Fat Free)**
- **¼ cup water**
- **2 teaspoons lemon juice**
- **2 cloves garlic, minced**
- **Hot cooked pasta**

1. Heat the butter in a 10-inch skillet over medium-high heat. Add the chicken and cook for 10 minutes or until well browned on both sides. Remove the chicken from the skillet.

2. Stir the soup, water, lemon juice and garlic in the skillet and heat to a boil. Return the chicken to the skillet. Reduce the heat to low. Cover and cook for 5 minutes or until the chicken is cooked through. Serve the chicken and sauce with the pasta.

Cheesy Chicken & Rice Casserole

prep 15 minutes | **bake** 50 minutes | **stand** 10 minutes |
makes 4 servings

- 1 can (10¾ ounces) Campbell's® Condensed Cream of Chicken Soup (Regular, 98% Fat Free **or** Healthy Request®)
- 1⅓ cups water
- ¾ cup **uncooked** regular long-grain white rice
- ½ teaspoon onion powder
- ¼ teaspoon ground black pepper
- 2 cups frozen mixed vegetables
- 4 skinless, boneless chicken breast halves (about 1 pound)
- ½ cup shredded Cheddar cheese

1. Heat the oven to 375°F. Stir the soup, water, rice, onion powder, black pepper and vegetables in a 2-quart shallow baking dish.

2. Top with the chicken. Cover the baking dish.

3. Bake for 50 minutes or until the chicken is cooked through and the rice is tender. Top with the cheese. Let the casserole stand for 10 minutes. Stir the rice before serving.

To Make Alfredo: Substitute broccoli florets for the vegetables and substitute ¼ **cup** grated Parmesan for the Cheddar cheese. Add **2 tablespoons** Parmesan cheese with the soup. Sprinkle the chicken with the remaining Parmesan cheese.

Onion-Crusted Meatloaf with Roasted Potatoes

prep 10 minutes | **bake** 1 hour 3 minutes | **makes** 6 servings

1	can (10¾ ounces) Campbell's® Condensed Tomato Soup
1½	pounds ground beef
1	can (2.8 ounces) French fried onions
1	egg, beaten
1	tablespoon Worcestershire sauce
6	small potatoes, cut into quarters

1. Thoroughly mix ½ **cup** soup, beef, ½ **can** onions, egg and Worcestershire in a large bowl. Place the mixture in a 13×9×2-inch baking pan and firmly shape into an 8×4-inch loaf. Spoon the remaining soup over the meatloaf. Arrange the potatoes around the meatloaf.

2. Bake at 400°F. for 1 hour or until the meatloaf is cooked through. Stir the potatoes. Sprinkle the remaining onions over the meatloaf and bake for 3 minutes or until the onions are golden.

Quick Chicken Parmesan

prep 5 minutes | **bake** 25 minutes | **makes** 4 servings

- **4**   skinless, boneless chicken breast halves (about 1 pound)
- **2**   cups Prego® Traditional Italian Sauce **or** Fresh Mushroom Italian Sauce
- **2**   ounces shredded mozzarella cheese (about ½ cup)
- **2**   tablespoons grated Parmesan cheese
- **½**   of a 16-ounce package spaghetti, cooked and drained (about 4 cups)

1. Place the chicken in a 2-quart shallow baking dish. Top the chicken with the Italian sauce. Sprinkle with the mozzarella cheese and Parmesan cheese.

2. Bake at 400°F. for 25 minutes or until cooked through. Serve with the spaghetti.

Chicken Seasoned Rice and Vegetable Casserole

prep 5 minutes | **bake** 1 hour | **makes** 6 servings

- 1 can (10¾ ounces) Campbell's® Condensed Cream of Mushroom Soup (Regular **or** 98% Fat Free)
- 1 cup water
- 1 package (6 ounces) seasoned long-grain and wild rice mix
- 1 bag (16 ounces) frozen vegetable combination (broccoli, carrots, water chestnuts)
- 1 cup shredded Cheddar cheese (about 4 ounces)
- 6 skinless, boneless chicken breast halves (about 1½ pounds) Paprika

1. Stir the soup, water, rice and seasoning packet, vegetables and **half** of the cheese in a 3-quart shallow baking dish. Top with the chicken. Sprinkle the chicken with the paprika. Cover the baking dish.

2. Bake at 375°F. for 1 hour or until the chicken is cooked through and the rice is tender. Uncover the dish and sprinkle with the remaining cheese.

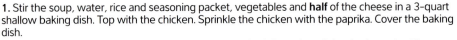

Salsa Chicken Soup

prep 5 minutes | **cook** 25 minutes | **makes** 4 servings

- 3½ **cups** Swanson® Chicken Broth (Regular, Natural Goodness® **or** Certified Organic)
- ½ cup **uncooked** regular long-grain white rice
- 1 can (16 ounces) Campbell's® Pork and Beans
- ½ cup Pace® Chunky Salsa
- 1 cup cubed cooked chicken

1. Heat the broth in a 2-quart saucepan over medium-high heat to a boil. Stir the rice in the saucepan. Reduce the heat to low. Cover and cook for 20 minutes or until rice is done.

2. Stir the beans, salsa and chicken in the saucepan and heat through.

Bloody Fingers

prep 15 minutes | **bake** 5 minutes | **makes** 8 servings

24	sliced blanched almonds
	Red liquid **or** paste food coloring
2	packages (about 9 ounces **each**) refrigerated fully cooked breaded chicken strips (about 24)
1	egg, slightly beaten
1	jar (24 ounces) Prego® Traditional Italian Sauce

1. Heat the oven to 400°F. Brush the almonds with the food coloring to coat. Set them aside to dry for about 10 minutes.

2. Place the chicken strips on a baking sheet. Brush the narrow end of the chicken strips with egg and press almonds on the egg wash to attach. Bake for 5 minutes or until hot.

3. Pour the Italian sauce in a 2-quart saucepan over medium heat. Cook until hot and bubbling, stirring occasionally. Arrange the chicken on a serving platter. Serve with the sauce for dipping.

Tip: Substitute frozen fully cooked breaded chicken strips for the refrigerated chicken strips. Increase the bake time to 10 minutes.

Roasted Garlic & Herb Shrimp with Spaghetti

prep 20 minutes | **cook** 15 minutes | **makes** 4 servings

- 2 tablespoons olive oil
- 3 cloves garlic, crushed
- 3 cups Prego® Roasted Garlic & Herb Italian Sauce
- ½ teaspoon crushed red pepper
- 1 pound fresh **or** thawed frozen medium shrimp, peeled and deveined
- 1 package (10 ounces) Pepperidge Farm® Garlic Bread
- 1 package (16 ounces) spaghetti, cooked and drained (about 8 cups)
- 3 tablespoons minced fresh Italian parsley

1. Heat the oven to 400°F. for the bread.

2. Heat the oil in a 12-inch skillet over medium heat. Add the garlic and cook until it's golden.

3. Stir the Italian sauce and red pepper in the skillet and heat to a boil. Reduce the heat to low. Add the shrimp and cook for 5 minutes or until cooked through.

4. Meanwhile, bake the bread according to the package directions.

5. Toss the spaghetti with the shrimp mixture. Sprinkle with the parsley. Cut the bread into 2-inch diagonal slices. Serve the bread with the spaghetti mixture.

Quick & Easy Pumpkin Soup

prep 10 minutes | **cook** 15 minutes | **makes** 6 servings

- 2 **tablespoons butter**
- 2 **large onions, sliced (about 2 cups)**
- 2 **cups Swanson® Chicken Broth (Regular, Natural Goodness® or Certified Organic)**
- 1 **cup heavy cream**
- 1 **can (30 ounces) pumpkin pie mix (3¼ cups)**

1. Heat the butter in a 10-inch skillet over medium heat. Add the onions and cook until tender.

2. Spoon **half** of the onion mixture in an electric blender container. Add **half** of the broth, cream and pumpkin. Cover and blend until smooth. Pour into a 3-quart saucepan. Repeat with the remaining onions, broth, cream and pumpkin.

3. Heat the soup over medium heat until hot.

Cheesy Enchilada Stack

prep 20 minutes | **bake** 45 minutes | **makes** 8 servings

- 1 **pound ground beef**
- 2 **cups prepared enchilada sauce**
   Vegetable cooking spray
- 6 **flour tortillas (10-inch)**
- 8 **ounces shredded Cheddar cheese (about 2 cups)**
- 1 **can (about 16 ounces) refried beans**
- 2 **cans (4 ounces each) chopped green chiles, drained**
   Chopped green onions

1. Cook the beef in a 10-inch skillet over medium-high heat until well browned, stirring often to separate the meat. Pour off any fat. Stir ½ **cup** of the enchilada sauce in the skillet. Spray a baking sheet with the cooking spray.

2. Place **1** tortilla onto the baking sheet. Top with ⅓ of the beef mixture and ¼ **cup** cheese. Top with **1** tortilla, ½ of the refried beans, ½ **cup** enchilada sauce, **1 can** chiles and ¼ **cup** cheese. Repeat the layers. Top with **1** tortilla, remaining beef mixture and ¼ **cup** cheese. Top with the remaining tortilla. Cover the stack with aluminum foil.

3. Bake at 400°F. for 40 minutes or until the filling is hot. Uncover the stack. Top with the remaining enchilada sauce, cheese and onions. Bake for 5 minutes or until the cheese is melted. Cut the stack into **8** wedges.

Pumpkin Apple Mash

prep 10 minutes | **cook** 20 minutes | **makes** 4 servings

- 2 **tablespoons butter**
- 1 **small onion, chopped** (about ¼ cup)
- ¾ **cup Swanson® Chicken Broth** (Regular, Natural Goodness® **or** Certified Organic)
- 1 **tablespoon packed brown sugar**
- ¼ **teaspoon dried thyme leaves, crushed**
- ⅛ **teaspoon ground black pepper**
- 1 **pumpkin or calabaza squash** (about 2½ pounds), peeled, seeded and cut into 1-inch pieces (about 5 to 6 cups)
- 2 **medium McIntosh apples, peeled, cored and cut into** 1-inch pieces

1. Heat the butter in a 4-quart saucepan over medium-high heat. Add the onion and cook until the onion is tender-crisp.

2. Stir the broth, brown sugar, thyme, black pepper and pumpkin in the saucepan and heat to a boil. Reduce the heat to low. Cover and cook for 10 minutes or until the pumpkin is tender.

3. Stir the apples in the saucepan. Cook for 5 minutes or until the apples are tender. Mash the pumpkin mixture, adding additional broth, if needed, until desired consistency.

Savory Balsamic Herb Chicken

prep 10 minutes | **cook** 25 minutes | **makes** 6 servings

- 1½ **pounds skinless, boneless chicken thighs**
- 2 **tablespoons all-purpose flour**
- 1 **tablespoon olive oil**
- 1 **medium onion, chopped (about 1 cup)**
- 2 **cloves garlic, minced**
- 1 **cup Swanson® Chicken Stock**
- 2 **tablespoons balsamic vinegar**
- 1 **teaspoon dried thyme leaves, crushed**
    Hot cooked rice

1. Coat the chicken with the flour.

2. Heat the oil in a 10-inch skillet over medium-high heat. Add the chicken in 2 batches and cook until well browned on both sides. Remove the chicken from the skillet.

3. Add the onion and garlic to the skillet and cook until tender. Stir the stock, vinegar and thyme in the skillet and heat to a boil. Return the chicken to the skillet. Reduce the heat to low. Cover and cook for 5 minutes or until the chicken is cooked through. Serve with the rice.

Chicken Mozzarella

prep 5 minutes | **bake** 20 minutes | **stand** 5 minutes | **makes** 4 servings

- **4** skinless, boneless chicken breasts halves (about 1 pound)
- **1** can (10¾ ounces) Campbell's® Healthy Request® Condensed Tomato Soup
- **½** teaspoon dried Italian seasoning **or** dried oregano leaves
- **½** teaspoon garlic powder
- **¼** cup shredded mozzarella cheese
- **3** cups corkscrew-shaped pasta (rotini), cooked without salt and drained

1. Place the chicken into a 2-quart shallow baking dish. Stir the soup, Italian seasoning and garlic powder in a small bowl. Spoon the soup mixture over the chicken.

2. Bake at 400°F. for 20 minutes or until the chicken is cooked through. Sprinkle with the cheese. Let stand for 5 minutes. Serve the chicken and sauce with the pasta.

Maple Dijon Chicken

prep 10 minutes | **cook** 25 minutes | **makes** 4 servings

- 1 tablespoon olive oil
- 4 skinless, boneless chicken breast halves (about 1 pound)
- 2 shallots, chopped (about ½ cup)
- 2 cloves garlic, minced
- 1 cup Swanson® Chicken Stock
- ⅓ cup maple-flavored syrup
- 1 tablespoon Dijon-style mustard
- ⅛ teaspoon crushed red pepper

1. Heat the oil in a 12-inch skillet over medium-high heat. Add the chicken and cook for 15 minutes or until well browned on both sides and cooked through. Remove the chicken from the skillet.

2. Add the shallots and garlic to the skillet and cook until tender. Stir in the stock, syrup, mustard and pepper and heat to a boil. Reduce the heat to low. Cook for 10 minutes or until the stock mixture is slightly thickened and reduced to **about 1 cup**. Serve the stock mixture over the chicken.

Baked Chicken & Cheese Risotto

prep 10 minutes | **bake** 45 minutes | **stand** 5 minutes | **makes** 4 servings

- 1 can (10¾ ounces) Campbell's® Condensed Cream of Mushroom Soup (Regular **or** 98% Fat Free)
- 1¼ cups water
- ½ cup milk
- ¼ cup shredded part-skim mozzarella cheese
- 3 tablespoons grated Parmesan cheese
- 1½ cups frozen mixed vegetables
- 2 skinless, boneless chicken breast halves (about ½ pound), cut into cubes
- ¾ cup **uncooked** Arborio **or** regular long-grain white rice

1. Stir the soup, water, milk, mozzarella cheese, Parmesan cheese, vegetables, chicken and rice in a 3-quart shallow baking dish. Cover the baking dish.

2. Bake at 400°F. for 35 minutes. Stir the rice mixture. Cover the baking dish.

3. Bake for 10 minutes or until the chicken is cooked through and the rice is tender. Let stand, covered, for 5 minutes.

Orange Beef Steak

prep 10 minutes | **broil** 25 minutes | **makes** 6 servings

1   jar (12 ounces) Campbell's® Slow Roast Beef Gravy
1   tablespoon grated orange zest
2   tablespoons orange juice
½   teaspoon garlic powder **or** 2 cloves garlic, minced
1   boneless beef top round steak, 1½-inch thick (about
     1½ pounds)

1. Stir the gravy, orange zest, orange juice and garlic powder in a 1-quart saucepan.

2. Heat the broiler. Place the beef on a rack in a broiler pan. Broil 4 inches from the heat for 25 minutes for medium or to desired doneness, turning the beef over halfway through cooking and brushing often with the gravy mixture. Thinly slice the beef.

3. Heat the remaining gravy mixture over medium-high heat to a boil. Serve the gravy mixture with the beef.

October 21

Harvest Salad

prep 10 minutes | **makes** 8 servings

- 2 packages (about 7 ounces **each**) mixed salad greens (about 8 cups)
- 2 cups cut-up fresh vegetables (red onions, cucumbers **and** carrots)
- 1 can (10¾ ounces) Campbell's® Condensed Tomato Soup (Regular **or** Healthy Request®)
- ¼ cup vegetable oil
- ¼ cup red wine vinegar
- 1 tablespoon honey **or** sugar
- 1 package (0.7 ounce) Italian salad dressing mix
- 2 cups your favorite Pepperidge Farm® croutons
- ¼ cup shelled pumpkin **or** sunflower seeds

1. Place the salad greens and vegetables into a large bowl.

2. Beat the soup, oil, vinegar, honey and salad dressing mix in a small bowl with a fork or whisk. Pour ¾ **cup** soup mixture over the salad mixture and toss to coat.

3. Arrange the salad on a serving platter. Top with the croutons and pumpkin seeds. Serve the salad with the remaining soup mixture.

Quick Mushroom Chicken Bake

prep 15 minutes | **bake** 30 minutes | **makes** 4 servings

- 4 skinless, boneless chicken breast halves (about 1 pound)
  Lemon pepper seasoning
- 1 tablespoon vegetable oil
- 1 can (10¾ ounces) Campbell's Condensed Cream of Mushroom Soup (Regular **or** 98% Fat Free)
- 1 can (4 ounces) sliced mushrooms, drained
- ⅔ cup milk
- ½ cup grated Parmesan cheese
- 1 clove garlic, crushed
  Ground black pepper
  Mashed potatoes, hot cooked rice **or** pasta

1. Season the chicken with the lemon pepper seasoning. Heat the oil in a 10-inch skillet. Add the chicken and cook for 10 minutes or until well browned on both sides. Place the chicken into a 2-quart baking dish.

2. Stir the soup, mushrooms, milk, cheese and garlic in a small bowl. Season with the black pepper. Pour the soup mixture over the chicken.

3. Bake at 350°F. for 30 minutes or until the chicken is cooked through. Serve the chicken and sauce with the mashed potatoes.

Chicken Corn Chowder

prep 10 minutes | **cook** 5 minutes | **makes** 4 servings

- 1   **can (10¾ ounces) Campbell's® Condensed Cream of Celery Soup (Regular or 98% Fat Free)**
- 1   **soup can milk**
- ½   **cup Pace® Picante Sauce**
- 1   **can (about 8 ounces) whole kernel corn, drained**
- 1   **cup cubed cooked chicken or turkey**
- 4   **slices bacon, cooked and crumbled**
-      **Shredded Cheddar cheese**
-      **Sliced green onion**

1. Heat the soup, milk, picante sauce, corn, chicken and bacon in a 3-quart saucepan over medium heat until the mixture is hot and bubbling, stirring occasionally.

2. Sprinkle with the cheese and onion. Drizzle **each** serving with additional picante sauce.

Tip: Substitute Campbell's® Condensed Cream of Chicken Soup for the Cream of Celery.

Mushroom-Smothered Beef Burgers

prep 15 minutes | **cook** 25 minutes | **makes** 4 servings

- 1 can (10¾ ounces) Campbell's® Condensed Cream of Mushroom Soup (Regular **or** 98% Fat Free)
- 1 pound ground beef
- ⅓ cup Italian-seasoned dry bread crumbs
- 1 small onion, finely chopped (about ¼ cup)
- 1 egg, beaten
- 1 tablespoon vegetable oil
- 1 tablespoon Worcestershire sauce
- 2 tablespoons water
- 1½ cups sliced mushrooms (about 4 ounces)

1. Thoroughly mix ¼ **cup** soup, beef, bread crumbs, onion and egg in a large bowl. Shape the beef mixture **firmly** into **4** (½-inch-thick) burgers.

2. Heat the oil in a 10-inch skillet over medium-high heat. Add the burgers and cook until well browned on both sides. Pour off any fat.

3. Add the remaining soup, Worcestershire, water and mushrooms to the skillet and heat to a boil. Reduce the heat to low. Cover and cook for 10 minutes or until the burgers are cooked through.

Tip: You can substitute ground turkey for the ground beef in this recipe.

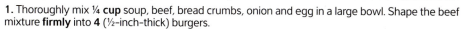

Golden Chicken & Autumn Vegetables

prep 10 minutes | **cook** 30 minutes | **makes** 4 servings

- 1 tablespoon vegetable oil
- 4 skinless, boneless chicken breast halves (about 1 pound)
- 1 cup Swanson® Chicken Stock
- 2 tablespoons minced garlic
- ½ teaspoon dried rosemary leaves, crushed
- ½ teaspoon dried thyme leaves, crushed
- ¼ teaspoon ground black pepper
- 2 large sweet potatoes, cut into ½-inch pieces
- 2 cups fresh **or** frozen whole green beans

1. Heat the oil in a 12-inch skillet over medium-high heat. Add the chicken and cook for 10 minutes or until well browned on both sides. Remove the chicken from the skillet.

2. Stir the stock, garlic, rosemary, thyme, black pepper, potatoes and green beans in the skillet and heat to a boil. Cook for 5 minutes.

3. Reduce the heat to low. Return the chicken to the skillet. Cover and cook for 10 minutes or until the chicken is cooked through and the potatoes are tender. Season as desired.

Herbed Chicken Dijon with Wine: Add ¼ cup white wine, **1 teaspoon** lemon juice and **2 tablespoons** Dijon-style mustard with the stock in step 2. Substitute Yukon Gold potatoes for the sweet potatoes.

Spaghetti Squash Alfredo

prep 10 minutes | **bake** 55 minutes | **makes** 5 servings

- 1 **medium spaghetti squash (about 3 pounds)**
- 1 **can (10¾ ounces) Campbell's® Condensed Cream of Celery Soup (Regular or 98% Fat Free)**
- ¾ **cup water**
- ¼ **cup milk**
- 1 **cup shredded lowfat Swiss cheese (about 4 ounces)**
- 2 **tablespoons grated Parmesan cheese**
  Chopped fresh parsley or chives

1. Pierce the squash with a fork.

2. Bake at 350°F. for 50 minutes or until the squash is fork-tender. Cut the squash in half and scoop out and discard the seeds. Scrape the flesh with a fork to separate the spaghetti-like strands.

3. Heat the soup, water and milk in a 3-quart saucepan over medium heat to a boil. Stir in the Swiss cheese. Add the squash and toss to coat. Sprinkle with the Parmesan cheese and parsley.

Honey Mustard Chicken Bites

prep 15 minutes | **bake** 15 minutes | **cook** 5 minutes | **makes** about 40 appetizers

- 1½ **pounds skinless, boneless chicken breast halves, cut into 1-inch pieces**
- 1 **jar (12 ounces) refrigerated honey mustard salad dressing**
- 2 **cups Pepperidge Farm® Herb Seasoned Stuffing, crushed**
- 2 **tablespoons orange juice**

1. Dip the chicken into ¾ **cup** of the dressing. Coat with the stuffing.

2. Put the chicken on a baking sheet. Bake at 400°F. for 15 minutes or until the chicken is cooked through.

3. Stir the remaining dressing and orange juice in a 1-quart saucepan over medium heat. Cook and stir until hot. Serve with the chicken for dipping.

Tip: To microwave dip, mix remaining dressing and orange juice in microwavable bowl. Microwave on HIGH 1 minute or until hot.

March 30

Crunchy Chicken and Gravy

prep 10 minutes | **bake** 20 minutes | **cook** 5 minutes | **makes** 4 servings

- 1 cup Pepperidge Farm® Herb Seasoned Stuffing, crushed
- 2 tablespoons grated Parmesan cheese
- 1 egg
- 4 skinless, boneless chicken breast halves (about 1 pound)
- 2 tablespoons butter, melted
- 1 jar (12 ounces) Campbell's® Slow Roast Chicken Gravy

1. Stir the stuffing and cheese on a plate. Beat the egg in a shallow dish with a fork or whisk. Dip the chicken into the egg. Coat the chicken with the stuffing mixture. Place the chicken onto a baking sheet. Drizzle with the butter.

2. Bake at 400°F. for 20 minutes or until the chicken is cooked through.

3. Heat the gravy in a 1-quart saucepan over medium heat until hot and bubbling. Serve the gravy with the chicken.

Beef Taco Skillet

prep 5 minutes | **cook** 20 minutes | **makes** 4 servings

- **1** pound ground beef
- **1** can (10¾ ounces) Campbell's® Condensed Tomato Soup (Regular **or** Healthy Request®)
- **½** cup Pace® Picante Sauce
- **½** cup water
- **6** flour tortillas (6-inch), cut into 1-inch pieces
- **½** cup shredded Cheddar cheese

1. Cook the beef in a 10-inch skillet over medium-high heat until well browned, stirring often to separate the meat. Pour off any fat.

2. Stir the soup, picante sauce, water and tortillas in the skillet and heat to a boil. Reduce the heat to low. Cook for 5 minutes. Stir the beef mixture. Top with the cheese.

Creamy Mexican Fiesta: Stir in ½ **cup** sour cream with the soup.

Ranchero Style: Use corn tortillas instead of flour tortillas and shredded Mexican cheese blend instead of Cheddar.

Double-Apricot Glazed Ham

prep 15 minutes | **bake** 2 hours | **makes** 32 servings

- 1 **cup dried apricots**
- 1 **cup Swanson® Chicken Stock**
- ½ **cup packed brown sugar**
- 1 **fully-cooked whole boneless ham (6 to 8 pounds)**
- 2 **tablespoons butter**
- ½ **cup finely chopped shallots**
- 2 **jars (12 ounces each) apricot preserves**
- ¼ **cup Dijon-style mustard**
- 2 **teaspoons grated orange zest**

1. Place the apricots and stock into a microwave-safe measuring cup. Microwave on HIGH for 2 minutes. Let the mixture cool. Remove the apricots and cut into strips. Reserve the stock. Stir the apricots, brown sugar and ¼ **cup** reserved stock in a small bowl.

2. Place the ham into a roasting pan. Bake at 325°F. for 2 hours or until heated through. Brush with the apricot mixture during the last 30 minutes of baking and baste frequently with pan drippings.

3. Heat the butter in a 10-inch skillet over medium heat. Add the shallots and cook until tender. Stir in the preserves, mustard, orange zest and remaining reserved stock and heat to a boil. Reduce the heat to low. Cook and stir for 10 minutes or until the stock mixture is slightly thickened.

4. Slice the ham and serve with the apricot sauce.

Skillet Chicken & Rice

prep 5 minutes | **cook** 35 minutes | **makes** 4 servings

- 1 pound skinless, boneless chicken breasts, cut into cubes
- 1¾ cups Swanson® Chicken Stock
- ½ teaspoon dried basil leaves, crushed
- ½ teaspoon garlic powder
- ¾ cup **uncooked** regular long-grain white rice
- 1 package (16 ounces) frozen vegetable combination (broccoli, cauliflower, carrots)

1. Cook the chicken in a 10-inch nonstick skillet over medium-high heat until well browned, stirring often. Remove the chicken from the skillet.

2. Stir in the stock, basil and garlic powder and heat to a boil. Stir in the rice. Reduce the heat to low. Cover and cook for 5 minutes.

3. Stir in the vegetables. Return the chicken to the skillet. Cover and cook for 15 minutes or until the chicken is cooked through and the rice is tender.

3-Cheese Pasta Bake

prep 20 minutes | **bake** 20 minutes | **makes** 4 servings

- **1** **can (10¾ ounces) Campbell's® Condensed Cream of Mushroom Soup (Regular or 98% Fat Free)**
- **1** **package (8 ounces) shredded two-cheese blend (about 2 cups)**
- **⅓** **cup grated Parmesan cheese**
- **1** **cup milk**
- **¼** **teaspoon ground black pepper**
- **3** **cups corkscrew-shaped pasta (rotini), cooked and drained**

1. Stir the soup, cheeses, milk and black pepper in a 1½-quart casserole. Stir in the pasta.

2. Bake at 400°F. for 20 minutes or until the mixture is hot and bubbling.

Tip: Substitute **2 cups** of your favorite shredded cheese for the two-cheese blend.

Bacon Horseradish Burgers

prep 5 minutes | **cook** 20 minutes | **makes** 6 servings

- 1½ **pounds ground beef**
- 1 **can (10¾ ounces) Campbell's® Condensed Bean with Bacon Soup**
- ½ **cup water**
- 1 **tablespoon horseradish**
- 6 **slices Cheddar cheese (about 6 ounces)**
- 6 **Pepperidge Farm® Classic Sandwich Buns with Sesame Seeds, split**

1. Shape the beef into **6** (½-inch-thick) burgers.

2. Cook the burgers in a 12-inch skillet over medium-high heat for 10 minutes or until well browned on both sides. Pour off any fat.

3. Stir the soup, water and horseradish in the skillet and heat to a boil. Reduce the heat to low. Cover and cook for 5 minutes or until the burgers are cooked through. Top the burgers with the cheese and cook until the cheese is melted. Serve the burgers and sauce on the buns.

Teriyaki Burgers

prep 10 minutes | **cook** 15 minutes | **makes** 6 servings

- 1½ **pounds ground beef**
- 1 **can (10½ ounces) Campbell's® Condensed Beef Broth**
- 1 **tablespoon soy sauce**
- 2 **teaspoons brown sugar**
- ¼ **teaspoon ground ginger**
- 6 **Pepperidge Farm® Classic Sandwich Buns with Sesame Seeds, split**

1. Shape the beef into **6** (½-inch thick) burgers.

2. Cook the burgers in a 12-inch skillet over medium-high heat until well browned on both sides. Pour off any fat.

3. Stir the broth, soy sauce, brown sugar and ginger in the skillet and heat to a boil. Reduce the heat to low. Cover and cook for 5 minutes for medium or to desired doneness. Serve the burgers and sauce on the buns.

Apple Strudel

thaw 40 minutes | **prep** 30 minutes | **bake** 35 minutes | **cool** 20 minutes | **makes** 6 servings

- 1 **egg**
- 1 **tablespoon water**
- 2 **tablespoons granulated sugar**
- 1 **tablespoon all-purpose flour**
- ¼ **teaspoon ground cinnamon**
- 2 **large Granny Smith apples, peeled, cored and thinly sliced**
- 2 **tablespoons raisins**
- ½ **of a 17.3-ounce package Pepperidge Farm® Puff Pastry Sheets (1 sheet), thawed**
  Confectioners' sugar (optional)

1. Heat the oven to 375°F. Beat the egg and water in a small bowl with a fork or whisk. Stir the granulated sugar, flour and cinnamon in a medium bowl. Add apples and raisins and toss to coat.

2. Unfold the pastry sheet on a lightly floured surface. Roll the pastry sheet into a 16×12-inch rectangle. With the short side facing you, spoon the apple mixture onto the bottom half of the pastry sheet to within 1 inch of the edge. Roll up like a jelly roll. Place seam-side down onto a baking sheet. Tuck the ends under to seal. Brush the pastry with the egg mixture. Cut several slits in the top of the pastry.

3. Bake for 35 minutes or until the strudel is golden brown. Let the strudel cool on the baking sheet on a wire rack for 20 minutes. Sprinkle with the confectioners' sugar, if desired.

Penne Bolognese-Style

prep 20 minutes | **cook** 30 minutes | **makes** 4 servings

1 **pound lean ground beef**
1 **large onion, minced (about 1 cup)**
3 **large carrots, shredded (about 2 cups)**
1 **jar (24 ounces) Prego® Veggie Smart® Smooth & Simple Italian Sauce**
½ **cup water**
3 **tablespoons fresh basil leaves, cut into very thin strips**
3 **cups penne pasta, cooked and drained (about 4½ cups)**
2 **tablespoons grated Parmesan cheese**

1. Cook the beef, onion and carrots in a 12-inch skillet over medium-high heat until the beef is well browned, stirring often to separate the meat. Pour off any fat.

2. Stir the Italian sauce and water in the skillet and heat to a boil. Reduce the heat to low. Cook for 15 minutes or until the vegetables are tender, stirring occasionally. Stir in additional water, if needed, until desired consistency.

3. Place the basil and penne into a large bowl. Add the beef mixture and toss to coat. Sprinkle with the cheese.

Sausage Walnut Stuffing

prep 10 minutes | **cook** 15 minutes | **makes** 12 servings

½ **pound bulk pork sausage**
¼ **cup (½ stick) butter**
2 **stalks celery, sliced (about 1 cup)**
1 **large onion, chopped (about 1 cup)**
1 **medium apple, cored and chopped**
1¾ **cups Swanson® Chicken Broth (Regular, Natural Goodness® or Certified Organic)**
1 **bag (14 ounces) Pepperidge Farm® Cubed Country Style Stuffing**
½ **cup chopped walnuts**

1. Cook the sausage in a 4–quart saucepot until well browned. Pour off any fat. Add the butter, celery, onion and apple and cook until tender.

2. Add the broth and heat to a boil. Remove the saucepot from the heat. Add the stuffing and walnuts. Mix lightly.

Good-for-You Stuffed Peppers

prep 20 minutes | **bake** 45 minutes | **stand** 5 minutes | **makes** 6 servings

- ½ cup **uncooked** quick-cooking brown rice
- 1 pound extra lean ground beef
- 3 cups Prego® Heart Smart Traditional Italian Sauce
- 6 medium green peppers
- 4 ounces shredded fat-free mozzarella cheese (about 1 cup)

1. Cook the rice without salt or butter according to the package directions.

2. Cook the beef in a 10-inch skillet over medium-high heat until it's well browned, stirring often to separate the meat. Pour off any fat. Stir **2 cups** of the Italian sauce and the rice in the skillet.

3. Cut **each** pepper in half lengthwise. Discard the seeds and white membranes. Place the pepper shells in a 17×11-inch roasting pan.

4. Spoon the beef mixture into the pepper shells. Pour the remaining sauce over the filled peppers. **Cover** the dish.

5. Bake at 400° F. for 45 minutes or until the peppers are tender. Top with the cheese. Let stand for 5 minutes or until the cheese is melted.

Hot Mulled Sipper

prep 5 minutes | **makes** 1 serving

- 1 **cup Diet V8 Splash® Tropical Blend Juice Drink**
- 1 **cinnamon stick**
  Dash ground nutmeg

Fill a microwave-safe mug **or** cup with the juice drink. Microwave on HIGH until hot. Serve with a cinnamon stick and nutmeg.

Broccoli and Pasta Bianco

prep 20 minutes | **bake** 25 minutes | **makes** 8 servings

- 6 cups **uncooked** penne pasta
- 4 cups fresh **or** frozen broccoli florets
- 1 can (10¾ ounces) Campbell's® Condensed Cream of Mushroom Soup (Regular **or** 98% Fat Free)
- 1½ cups milk
- ½ teaspoon ground black pepper
- 1½ cups shredded mozzarella cheese (about 6 ounces)
- ¼ cup shredded Parmesan cheese

1. Heat the oven to 350°F.

2. Cook the pasta according to the package directions. Add the broccoli for the last 4 minutes of cooking time. Drain the pasta mixture well in a colander.

3. Stir the soup, milk and black pepper in a 2-quart shallow baking dish. Stir in the pasta mixture, ¾ **cup** mozzarella cheese and **2 tablespoons** Parmesan cheese. Top with the remaining mozzarella and Parmesan cheeses.

4. Bake for 25 minutes or until the pasta mixture is hot and bubbling and the cheese is melted.

Tip: Creamy white pastas like this one taste great with the tang and heat of crushed red pepper flakes. Serve it on the side.

Quick & Easy Dinner Nachos Supreme

prep 10 minutes | **cook** 15 minutes | **makes** 4 servings

- 1 **pound ground beef**
- 1 **package (about 1 ounce) taco seasoning mix**
- 1 **can (10¾ ounces) Campbell's® Condensed Tomato Soup**
- 1½ **cups water**
- 1½ **cups uncooked instant white rice**
- **Pace® Chunky Salsa**
- **Shredded Cheddar cheese**
- **Shredded lettuce**
- **Tortilla chips**

1. Cook the beef and taco seasoning in a 10-inch skillet until the beef is well browned, stirring often to separate the meat. Pour off any fat.

2. Stir the soup, water and rice in the skillet and heat to a boil. Reduce the heat to low. Cover and cook for 5 minutes or until the rice is tender.

3. Top with the salsa, cheese and lettuce. Serve with the tortilla chips for dipping.

Breakfast Omelet Sandwiches

prep 25 minutes | **cook** 20 minutes | **makes** 2 servings

Vegetable cooking spray
- ½ **cup chopped fresh mushrooms**
- ¼ **cup chopped green pepper**
- ¼ **cup chopped tomato**
- 2 **tablespoons finely chopped onions**
- ½ **cup cholesterol-free egg substitute**
- 2 **teaspoons freshly grated Parmesan cheese**
- 4 **slices Pepperidge Farm® 100% Natural Nine Grain Bread**

1. Spray an 8-inch nonstick skillet with the cooking spray and heat over medium heat for 1 minute. Add the mushrooms, pepper, tomato and onions. Cover and cook until the vegetables are tender. Remove the vegetables from the skillet. Remove the skillet from the heat. Wipe out the skillet with a paper towel.

2. Spray the skillet with the cooking spray and heat over medium heat for 1 minute. Add ¼ **cup** egg substitute and top with **half** the cooked vegetables. Cook until the eggs are set but still moist on top, lifting the edges of the omelet with a spatula. Sprinkle with **half** of the cheese. Fold the omelet in half. Place the omelet on **1** bread slice and top with another bread slice. Repeat with the remaining ingredients.

Tip: Also delicious with Pepperidge Farm® Whole Grain 15 Grain Bread.

Crispy Italian Chicken

prep 15 minutes | **bake** 20 minutes | **makes** 4 servings

	Vegetable cooking spray
2	**cups Pepperidge Farm® Four Cheese and Garlic Croutons**
1	**egg**
4	**skinless, boneless chicken breast halves (about 1 pound)**
1	**cup Prego® Traditional Italian Sauce or Tomato Basil & Garlic Italian Sauce**
¼	**cup shredded mozzarella cheese**

1. Heat the oven to 375°F. Spray a baking sheet with the cooking spray. Place the croutons into a gallon size resealable plastic bag. Seal the bag and crush the croutons with a rolling pin.

2. Beat the egg in a shallow dish with a fork or whisk. Dip the chicken into the egg. Add the chicken to the bag. Seal the bag and shake to coat. Place the chicken onto the baking sheet. Spray the chicken with the cooking spray.

3. Bake for 20 minutes or until the chicken is cooked through. Spoon the Italian sauce over the chicken and sprinkle with the cheese.

Tip: You can substitute your favorite Pepperidge Farm® croutons for the Four Cheese and Garlic.

Sweet 'n' Spicy Barbecued Brisket Sandwich

prep 10 minutes | **marinate** 8 hours | **cook** 8 hours | **stand** 10 minutes | **makes** 10 servings

- 1   **trimmed beef brisket (about 5 pounds)**
-     **Ground black pepper**
- 1   **tablespoon garlic powder**
- 2   **cups Pace® Picante Sauce**
- ½   **cup packed brown sugar**
- ½   **cup Worcestershire sauce**
- 10   **sandwich rolls or hamburger rolls, split**
-     **Prepared coleslaw**

1. Season the beef with the black pepper and garlic powder and place into a 13×9×2-inch shallow baking dish.

2. Stir the picante sauce, brown sugar and Worcestershire in a small bowl. Spread the picante sauce mixture over the beef. Cover and refrigerate at least 8 hours or overnight.

3. Place the beef into a 7-quart slow cooker. Cover and cook on LOW for 8 to 9 hours* or until the beef is fork-tender. Remove the beef from the cooker to a cutting board and let stand for 10 minutes.

4. Thinly slice the beef across the grain, or, using 2 forks, shred the beef. Return the beef to the cooker. Divide the beef and juices among the rolls. Top the beef with the coleslaw.

*Or on HIGH for 4 to 5 hours.

Harvest Fruit Stuffing

prep 10 minutes | **cook** 10 minutes | **bake** 20 minutes | **makes** 8 servings

- 1¾ **cups Swanson® Chicken Broth (Regular, Natural Goodness® or Certified Organic)**
- ¼ **cup apple juice**
- 1 **cup cut-up mixed dried fruit**
- 1 **stalk celery, sliced (about ½ cup)**
- 1 **medium onion, chopped (about ½ cup)**
- 5 **cups Pepperidge Farm® Herb Seasoned Stuffing**

1. Heat the oven to 350°F.

2. Stir the broth, apple juice, dried fruit, celery and onion in a 3-quart saucepan. Heat to a boil over medium-high heat. Reduce the heat to low. Cover and cook for 5 minutes or until the vegetables are tender. Remove the saucepan from the heat. Add the stuffing and stir lightly to coat.

3. Spoon the stuffing into a 1½–quart casserole. Bake for 20 minutes or until hot.

April 8

7-Layer Meatless Tortilla Pie

prep 20 minutes | **bake** 40 minutes | **makes** 6 servings

- 2 **cans (about 15 ounces each)** pinto beans, rinsed and drained
- 1 cup Pace® Picante Sauce
- ¼ teaspoon garlic powder **or** 1 clove garlic, minced
- 2 tablespoons chopped fresh cilantro leaves
- 1 can (about 15 ounces) black beans, rinsed and drained
- 1 small tomato, chopped (about ½ cup)
- 7 flour tortillas (8-inch)
- 8 ounces shredded Cheddar cheese (about 2 cups)

1. Mash pinto beans in medium bowl with a fork. Stir in ¾ cup picante sauce and the garlic powder.

2. Stir the remaining picante sauce, cilantro, black beans and tomato in a medium bowl.

3. Place **1** tortilla onto a baking sheet. Spread ¾ cup pinto bean mixture over the tortilla to within ½ inch of the edge. Top with ¼ cup cheese. Top with **1** tortilla and ⅔ **cup** black bean mixture. Top with ¼ **cup** cheese. Repeat the layers twice more. Top with the remaining tortilla and spread with the remaining pinto bean mixture. Cover with aluminum foil.

4. Bake at 400°F. for 40 minutes or until the filling is hot. Uncover the pie. Top with the remaining cheese. Cut the pie into **6** wedges. Serve with additional picante sauce and sprinkle with additional cilantro, if desired.

Shortcut Stuffed Peppers

prep 10 minutes | **cook** 10 minutes | **makes** 4 servings

1½	**pounds ground beef**
1	**can (10¾ ounces) Campbell's® Condensed Tomato Soup**
1	**cup uncooked instant white rice**
2	**teaspoons garlic powder**
½	**teaspoon ground black pepper**
2	**large green peppers, cut in half lengthwise and seeded**

1. Mix the beef, soup, rice, garlic powder and black pepper in a large bowl.

2. Place the pepper halves, cut-side up, into an 8×8-inch microwavable baking dish. Divide the beef mixture among the pepper halves (the pepper halves will be very full).

3. Cover and microwave on HIGH for 10 minutes or until the beef mixture is cooked through.

Tip: The shortcut is in the cooking—arrange the peppers in the glass dish in a circle for the most effective cooking in the microwave.

Italian-Style Sloppy Joes

prep 10 minutes | **cook** 10 minutes | **makes** 6 servings

- 1 **pound ground beef**
- 1 **medium onion, chopped (about 1 cup)**
- 1½ **cups Prego® Traditional or Roasted Garlic & Herb Italian Sauce**
- 1 **tablespoon Worcestershire sauce**
- 6 **Pepperidge Farm® Classic Sandwich Buns with Sesame Seeds, split and toasted**

1. Cook the beef and onion in a 10-inch skillet over medium-high heat until browned, stirring often to separate the meat. Pour off any fat.

2. Stir the Italian sauce and Worcestershire in the skillet and cook until the mixture is hot and bubbling. Evenly divide the beef mixture among the rolls.

Oven–Roasted Root Vegetables

prep 35 minutes | **roast** 50 minutes | **makes** 8 servings

    Vegetable cooking spray
- 3 medium red potatoes (about 1 pound), cut into 1-inch pieces
- 2 cups fresh **or** frozen whole baby carrots
- 1 pound celery root (celeriac), peeled and cut into 1-inch pieces (about 2 cups)
- 1 rutabaga (about 3 pounds), peeled and cut into 1-inch pieces (about 6 cups)
- 2 medium red onions, cut into 8 wedges **each**
- 2 medium parsnips, peeled and cut into 1-inch pieces (about 1½ cups)
- 5 cloves garlic, cut into thin slices
- 1 tablespoon chopped fresh rosemary leaves **or** fresh thyme leaves
- 1 tablespoon olive oil
- 1 cup Swanson® Vegetable Broth (Regular **or** Certified Organic)

1. Heat the oven to 425°F. Spray a 17×11-inch roasting pan or shallow baking sheet with the cooking spray.

2. Stir the potatoes, carrots, celery root, rutabaga, onions, parsnips, garlic, rosemary and oil in the prepared pan. Roast the vegetables for 30 minutes. Pour the broth over the vegetables and stir.

3. Roast for 20 minutes or until the vegetables are fork-tender.

Mexi-Mac

prep 5 minutes | **cook** 20 minutes | **makes** 4 servings

- 1 **pound ground beef**
- 1 **cup Pace® Picante Sauce**
- 1 **tablespoon chili powder**
- 1 **can (14.5 ounces) whole peeled tomatoes, cut up**
- 1 **cup frozen whole kernel corn**
- 3 **cups cooked elbow macaroni**
- ½ **cup shredded Cheddar cheese**
  Sliced avocado
  Sour cream

1. Cook the beef in a 10-inch skillet over medium-high heat until well browned, stirring to separate the meat. Pour off any fat.

2. Stir the picante sauce, chili powder, tomatoes and corn in the skillet. Heat to a boil. Reduce the heat to low. Cook for 10 minutes. Add the macaroni. Sprinkle with the cheese. Cover and heat until the cheese melts. Garnish with avocado and sour cream.

Sausage-Stuffed Green Peppers

prep 20 minutes | **bake** 40 minutes | **makes** 8 servings

- 1 tablespoon vegetable oil
- 1 pound sweet Italian pork sausage, casing removed
- 1 medium onion, chopped (about ½ cup)
- 1 teaspoon dried oregano leaves, crushed
- 1 cup shredded part-skim mozzarella cheese (about 4 ounces)
- 4 medium green peppers, seeded and cut in half lengthwise
- 2 cups Prego® Traditional Italian Sauce **or** Tomato, Basil & Garlic Italian Sauce

1. Heat the oven to 400°F. Heat the oil in a 10-inch skillet over medium-high heat. Add the sausage and cook until well browned, stirring often to separate the meat. Add the onion and oregano and cook until the onion is tender. Pour off any fat. Stir in the cheese.

2. Arrange the peppers in a 3-quart shallow baking dish. Spoon the sausage mixture into the peppers. Pour the Italian sauce over the filled peppers. Cover the baking dish.

3. Bake for 40 minutes or until the peppers are tender.

Shortcut Paella

prep 15 minutes | **cook** 25 minutes | **makes** 8 servings

1	tablespoon vegetable oil
2	cups **uncooked** regular long-grain white rice
4	cups Swanson® Chicken Stock, heated
1	cup Pace® Picante Sauce
1	teaspoon ground turmeric
1	package (16 ounces) turkey kielbasa, sliced
12	small frozen peeled, deveined, cooked shrimp, thawed
1	package (about 10 ounces) refrigerated fully-cooked chicken breast strips

1. Heat the oil in a 12-inch skillet over medium heat. Add the rice and cook for 30 seconds, stirring constantly. Stir the stock, picante sauce and turmeric in the skillet and heat to a boil. Reduce the heat to low. Cover and cook for 15 minutes.

2. Stir the kielbasa, shrimp and chicken in the skillet. Cover and cook for 5 minutes or until the rice is tender.

Roasted Chicken with Stuffing & Gravy

prep 30 minutes | **roast** 3 hours | **stand** 10 minutes | **makes** 6 servings

- ¼ cup (½ stick) butter
- 1 stalk celery, sliced (about ½ cup)
- 1 medium onion, chopped (about ½ cup)
- 1¼ cups water
- 1 medium carrot, shredded (about ½ cup) (optional)
- 4 cups Pepperidge Farm® Herb Seasoned Stuffing
- 1 roasting chicken (5 to 7 pounds)
- 1 jar (12 ounces) Campbell's® Slow Roast Chicken Gravy

1. Heat butter in a 3-quart saucepan over medium heat. Add the celery and onion and cook until tender. Stir in water and carrot. Remove saucepan from the heat. Add the stuffing and mix lightly.

2. Remove the package of the giblets and neck from the chicken cavity. Rinse the chicken with cold water and pat dry with a paper towel. Spoon the stuffing lightly into the neck and body cavities. Fold the loose skin over the stuffing. Tie the ends of the drumsticks together.

3. Place the chicken, breast-side up, on a rack in a shallow roasting pan. Brush the chicken with vegetable oil. Insert a meat thermometer into the thickest part of the meat, not touching the bone.

4. Roast for 2½ to 3 hours or until the drumstick moves easily and the center of the stuffing reaches 165°F., basting occasionally with the pan drippings. Let the chicken stand for 10 minutes before slicing.

5. Heat the gravy in a 1-quart saucepan over medium-high heat until hot and bubbling. Serve the gravy with the chicken.

Broccoli & Garlic Penne Pasta

prep 20 minutes | **cook** 10 minutes | **makes** 4 servings

- 1 **cup Swanson® Chicken Broth (Regular, Natural Goodness® or Certified Organic)**
- ½ **teaspoon dried basil leaves, crushed**
- ⅛ **teaspoon ground black pepper**
- 2 **cloves garlic, minced**
- 3 **cups broccoli florets**
- 4½ **cups penne pasta, cooked and drained**
- 1 **tablespoon lemon juice**
- 2 **tablespoons grated Parmesan cheese**

1. Heat the broth, basil, black pepper, garlic and broccoli in a 10-inch skillet over medium heat to a boil. Reduce the heat to low. Cover and cook until the broccoli is tender-crisp.

2. Add the pasta and lemon juice and toss to coat. Sprinkle the pasta mixture with the cheese.

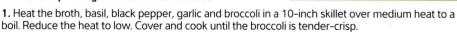

Quick and Easy Chocolate Fondue

prep 5 minutes | **cook** 5 minutes | **makes** 12 servings

- 2 **cups semi-sweet chocolate pieces**
- ½ **cup (1 stick) butter**
  Suggested Dippers: **Pepperidge Farm® Cinnamon Swirl Bread, toasted and cut into strips; Pepperidge Farm® Chessmen® Cookies; Pepperidge Farm® Gingerman Homestyle Cookies; Pepperidge Farm® Milano® Cookies**

1. Cook and stir the chocolate and butter in an 8-inch heavy skillet over low heat for 5 minutes or until the chocolate is melted and smooth.

2. Pour the chocolate mixture into a fondue pot or a decorative bowl. Serve warm with the *Dippers*.

Tip: You can also use this chocolate mixture to make festive chocolate and candy-coated puff pastry strips: Thaw **1** sheet Pepperidge Farm® Puff Pastry. Unfold the pastry sheet on a lightly floured surface and roll into a 12-inch square. Cut into **72** (4×½-inch) strips and place onto baking sheets. Bake at 400°F. for 20 minutes or until golden brown. Dip the pastry strips in the warm chocolate mixture and sprinkle with crushed candy canes. Place on wax paper-lined baking sheets. Refrigerate or let stand at room temperature until chocolate is set.

Chicken Balsamico

prep 10 minutes | **cook** 20 minutes | **makes** 4 servings

- 1 tablespoon olive oil
- 4 skinless, boneless chicken breast halves (about 1 pound)
- 1 clove garlic, minced
- 3 tablespoons balsamic vinegar
- ¾ cup water
- 1 can (10¾ ounces) Campbell's® Condensed Cream of Chicken Soup (Regular **or** 98% Fat Free)
- 1 cup diced plum tomatoes **or** ½ cup thinly sliced sun-dried tomatoes
- ½ cup sliced pitted kalamata olives (optional)
- ½ teaspoon dried oregano leaves, crushed
- ¼ cup crumbled feta cheese

  Hot cooked orzo pasta

1. Heat the oil in a 10-inch skillet over medium-high heat. Add the chicken and cook for 10 minutes or until well browned on both sides. Remove the chicken from the skillet.

2. Stir the garlic, vinegar and water in the skillet. Cook and stir for 1 minute. Stir in the soup, tomatoes, olives, if desired, and oregano and heat to a boil. Return the chicken to the skillet. Reduce the heat to low. Cook for 5 minutes or until the chicken is cooked through. Sprinkle with the cheese. Serve the chicken and sauce with the orzo.

Hearty Beef Stew

prep 15 minutes | **cook** 2 hours 15 minutes | **makes** 4 servings

- 1 **pound beef for stew, cut into 1-inch pieces**
- 3 **tablespoons all-purpose flour**
- 2 **tablespoons olive oil**
- 2 **cloves garlic, minced**
- 1¾ **cups Swanson® Beef Stock**
- 2 **medium onions, cut into quarters**
- 1 **bay leaf**
- ½ **teaspoon dried thyme leaves, crushed**
- ¼ **teaspoon ground black pepper**
- 2 **cups whole baby carrots**
- 2 **medium potatoes, cut into 2-inch pieces**
- ¼ **cup water**

1. Season the beef as desired. Coat with **1 tablespoon** flour. Heat the oil in a 6-quart saucepot over medium-high heat. Add the beef and cook until well browned, stirring often. Add the garlic to the saucepot and cook and stir for 1 minute.

2. Stir the stock, onions, bay leaf, thyme and black pepper in the saucepot and heat to a boil. Reduce the heat to low. Cover and cook for 1½ hours.

3. Add the carrots and potatoes to the saucepot. Cover and cook for 30 minutes or until the beef is fork-tender and the vegetables are tender. Remove and discard the bay leaf.

4. Stir the remaining flour and water in a small bowl until the mixture is smooth. Stir the flour mixture in the saucepot. Increase the heat to medium. Cook and stir until the mixture boils and thickens.

April 14

Beef Bourguignonne

prep 10 minutes | **cook** 8 hours | **makes** 6 servings

- 1 can (10¾ ounces) Campbell's® Condensed Golden Mushroom Soup
- 1 cup Burgundy **or** other dry red wine
- 2 cloves garlic, minced
- 1 teaspoon dried thyme leaves, crushed
- 2 cups small button mushrooms (about 6 ounces)
- 2 cups fresh **or** thawed frozen baby carrots
- 1 cup frozen small whole onions, thawed
- 1½ pounds beef top round steak, 1½-inches thick, cut into 1-inch pieces

1. Stir the soup, wine, garlic, thyme, mushrooms, carrots, onions and beef in a 3½-quart slow cooker.

2. Cover and cook on LOW for 8 to 9 hours* or until the beef is fork-tender.

Or on HIGH for 4 to 5 hours.

Quick & Easy Chicken Quesadillas

prep 15 minutes | **cook** 15 minutes | **bake** 5 minutes | **makes** 8 servings

- **4** skinless, boneless chicken breast halves (about 1 pound), cut into cubes
- **1** can (10¾ ounces) Campbell's® Condensed Cream of Chicken Soup (Regular **or** 98% Fat Free)
- ½ cup Pace® Picante Sauce
- ½ cup shredded Monterey Jack cheese
- **1** teaspoon chili powder
- **8** flour tortillas (8-inch), warmed

1. Heat the oven to 425°F.

2. Cook the chicken in a 10-inch nonstick skillet over medium-high heat until well browned and cooked through, stirring often. Stir in the soup, picante sauce, cheese and chili powder and cook until the mixture is hot and bubbling.

3. Place the tortillas onto **2** baking sheets. Spread **about** ⅓ **cup** chicken mixture on **half** of **each** tortilla to within ½ inch of the edge. Brush the edges of the tortillas with water. Fold the tortillas over the filling and press the edges to seal.

4. Bake for 5 minutes or until the filling is hot. Cut the quesadillas into wedges.

Simply Quick Macaroni & Cheese

prep 20 minutes | **cook** 10 minutes | **makes** 6 servings

- 1¾ cups Swanson® Chicken Broth (Regular, Natural Goodness® **or** Certified Organic)
- ¼ cup all-purpose flour
- ⅛ teaspoon ground black pepper
- ½ cup skim milk
- 5 slices process American cheese, cut up
- 3 cups elbow macaroni, cooked and drained

1. Stir the broth, flour, black pepper and milk in a 4-quart saucepan until the mixture is smooth. Cook and stir over medium heat until the mixture boils and thickens.

2. Stir the cheese in the saucepan. Cook and stir until cheese is melted. Add the macaroni and toss to coat.

October 1

2-Step Skillet Chicken Broccoli Divan

prep 10 minutes | **cook** 15 minutes | **makes** 4 servings

- 1 **tablespoon butter**
- 4 **skinless, boneless chicken breast halves (about 1 pound), cut into 1-inch pieces**
- 3 **cups fresh or frozen broccoli florets**
- 1 **can (10¾ ounces) Campbell's® Condensed Cream of Chicken Soup (Regular or 98% Fat Free)**
- ½ **cup milk**
- ½ **cup shredded Cheddar cheese**

1. Heat the butter in a 10-inch skillet over medium-high heat. Add the chicken and cook until well browned, stirring often.

2. Stir the broccoli, soup and milk in the skillet. Reduce the heat to low. Cover and cook for 5 minutes or until the chicken is cooked through. Sprinkle with the cheese.

Tip: Try this recipe with Campbell's® Cream of Mushroom Soup and shredded Swiss cheese.

Mediterranean Halibut with Couscous

prep 15 minutes | **cook** 15 minutes | **makes** 4 servings

- 4 **halibut steaks, about 1-inch thick**
- ¼ **cup all-purpose flour**
- 3 **tablespoons olive oil**
- 2 **shallots, chopped**
- 1 **cup Swanson® Chicken Stock**
- 2 **teaspoons dried oregano leaves, crushed**
- 1 **can (about 14.5 ounces) diced tomatoes, drained**
- ½ **cup kalamata olives, pitted and sliced**
  Hot cooked couscous*

*For the couscous: Prepare **1** package (10 ounces) couscous according to the package directions, substituting Swanson® Chicken Broth for the water.*

1. Coat the fish with the flour.

2. Heat **2 tablespoons** oil in a 12-inch skillet over medium-high heat. Add the fish and cook for 5 minutes or until well browned on both sides and cooked through. Remove the fish from the skillet and keep warm.

3. Heat the remaining oil in the skillet. Add the shallots and cook for 1 minute. Stir in the stock, oregano, tomatoes and olives and heat to a boil. Cook for 5 minutes or until the sauce is slightly thickened. Season to taste. Serve the sauce with the fish and couscous.

Tasty 2-Step Chicken

prep 5 minutes | **cook** 20 minutes | **makes** 4 servings

- 1 **tablespoon vegetable oil**
- 4 **skinless, boneless chicken breast halves (about 1 pound)**
- 1 **can (10¾ ounces) Campbell's® Condensed Cream of Mushroom Soup (Regular, 98% Fat Free or Healthy Request®)**
- ½ **cup water**

1. Heat the oil in a 10-inch skillet over medium-high heat. Add the chicken and cook for 10 minutes or until well browned on both sides. Remove the chicken from the skillet.

2. Stir the soup and water in the skillet and heat to a boil. Return the chicken to the skillet. Reduce the heat to low. Cover and cook for 5 minutes or until the chicken is cooked through.

Tip: This recipe is also delicious with Campbell's® Condensed Cream of Mushroom with Roasted Garlic Soup **or** Cream of Chicken with Herbs Soup.

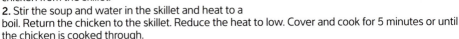

Broccoli & Noodles Supreme

prep 10 minutes | **cook** 25 minutes | **makes** 5 servings

- 3 cups **uncooked** medium egg noodles
- 2 cups fresh **or** frozen broccoli florets
- 1 can (10¾ ounces) Campbell's® Condensed Cream of Chicken Soup (Regular **or** 98% Fat Free)
- ½ cup sour cream
- ⅓ cup grated Parmesan cheese
- ⅛ teaspoon ground black pepper

1. Cook the noodles according to the package directions. Add the broccoli for the last 5 minutes of cooking time. Drain the noodle mixture well in a colander. Return the noodle mixture to the saucepan.

2. Stir the soup, sour cream, cheese and black pepper in the saucepan and cook over medium heat until the mixture is hot and bubbling, stirring often.

Jump Start Smoothie

prep 5 minutes | **makes** 4 servings

- **2** **cups V8 Splash® Mango Peach Juice Drink,** chilled
- **1** **cup low-fat vanilla yogurt**
- **2** **cups frozen whole strawberries or raspberries**

Put all the ingredients in a blender. Cover and blend until smooth. Serve immediately.

Layered Pasta, Veggie & Cheese Skillet

prep 20 minutes | **cook** 10 minutes | **makes** 4 servings

1 **jar (24 ounces) Prego® Veggie Smart® Chunky & Savory Italian Sauce**
1 **cup water**
1¼ **cups part skim ricotta cheese**
½ **cup grated Parmesan cheese**
1 **egg, beaten**
½ **of a 6-ounce package fresh baby spinach or arugula, coarsely chopped (about 4 cups)**
3 **cups trumpet-shaped pasta (campanelle), cooked and drained (about 4 cups)**

1. Stir the Italian sauce and water in a medium bowl. Stir the ricotta cheese, ⅓ **cup** Parmesan cheese, egg and spinach in a medium bowl.

2. Layer **1 cup** Italian sauce mixture, **half** the pasta and **half** the cheese mixture in a 12-inch skillet. Repeat the layers. Top with the remaining sauce mixture and the remaining Parmesan cheese. Cover the skillet.

3. Cook over medium heat for 10 minutes or until the mixture is hot.

Hamburger Pie

prep 15 minutes | **bake** 15 minutes | **makes** 6 servings

- 1½ **pounds ground beef**
- 1 **can (10¾ ounces) Campbell's® Condensed Cream of Mushroom Soup (Regular or 98% Fat Free)**
- 2 **packages (8 ounces each) refrigerated crescent rolls**
- 1 **cup of your favorite shredded cheese**

1. Cook the beef in a 10-inch skillet over medium-high heat until well browned, stirring often to separate the meat. Pour off any fat. Stir the soup in the skillet.

2. Unroll **1 package** crescent roll dough and press on the bottom and up the sides of a 9-inch pie plate. Press the seams to seal. Layer **half** the beef mixture and **half** the cheese in the pie plate. Repeat the layers. Unroll the remaining dough. Place the dough over the filling and press the edges to seal, if desired.

3. Bake at 350°F. for 15 minutes or until the crust is golden brown.

Cheese Steak Pockets

prep 10 minutes | **cook** 15 minutes | **makes** 8 servings

1 tablespoon vegetable oil
1 medium onion, cut in half and sliced (about ½ cup)
½ of a 24-ounce package frozen beef **or** frozen chicken
    sandwich steaks (8 steaks)
1 can (10¾ ounces) Campbell's® Condensed Cheddar
    Cheese Soup
1 jar (about 4½ ounces) sliced mushrooms, drained
4 pita breads (6-inch) cut in half, forming **8** pockets

1. Heat the oil in a 10-inch skillet over medium-high heat. Add the onion and cook until tender, stirring occasionally. Add the sandwich steaks in batches and cook until well browned on both sides. Pour off any fat.

2. Stir the soup and mushrooms in the skillet and cook until the mixture is hot and bubbling. Divide the sandwich steaks and soup mixture among the pita halves.

Tip: For a crispier pocket, heat whole pita in oven for 2 minutes.

Sicilian-Style Pizza

thaw 3 hours | **prep** 15 minutes | **bake** 25 minutes | **makes** 8 servings

Vegetable cooking spray
2 loaves (1 pound **each**) frozen white bread dough, thawed
1¾ cups Prego® Traditional Italian Sauce
2 cups shredded mozzarella cheese (about 8 ounces)

1. Heat the oven to 375°F. Spray a 15×10-inch jelly-roll pan with cooking spray.

2. Place the dough loaves into the pan. Press the dough from the center out until it covers the bottom of the pan. Pinch the edges of the dough to form a rim. Spread the sauce over the crust. Top with the cheese.

3. Bake for 25 minutes or until the cheese is melted and the crust is golden.

Pan-Seared Steaks with Mushroom Gravy

prep 5 minutes | **cook** 25 minutes | **makes** 4 servings

- 1 **boneless beef sirloin steak, cut into 4 pieces (about 1 pound)**
- 1 **tablespoon unsalted butter**
- 2 **cups sliced fresh mushrooms (about 6 ounces)**
- 1 **tablespoon all-purpose flour**
- 1 **cup Swanson® Beef Stock**

1. Season the steaks as desired. Cook the steaks in a 12-inch nonstick skillet over medium-high heat to desired doneness. Remove the steaks from the skillet. Do not pour off any fat.

2. Heat the butter in the skillet. Add the mushrooms and cook until tender. Stir in the flour and cook for 1 minute. Gradually stir in the stock. Cook and stir until the mixture boils and thickens. Serve the mushroom gravy with the steaks.

Broccoli con Queso

prep 10 minutes | **cook** 5 minutes | **makes** 6 servings

- 1 **cup Pace® Mexican Four Cheese Salsa con Queso**
- 1 **pound broccoli, cut into spears, cooked and drained**

In a 1-quart saucepan over low heat, heat the salsa. Serve over the broccoli.

Balsamic Glazed Salmon

prep 5 minutes | **bake** 15 minutes | **cook** 5 minutes | **makes** 8 servings

8	**fresh salmon fillets, ¾-inch thick (about 1½ pounds)**
	Freshly ground black pepper
3	**tablespoons olive oil**
4½	**teaspoons cornstarch**
1¾	**cups Swanson® Chicken Stock**
3	**tablespoons balsamic vinegar**
1	**tablespoon brown sugar**
1	**tablespoon orange juice**
1	**teaspoon grated orange zest**
	Orange slices for garnish

1. Place the salmon in an 11×8-inch (2-quart) shallow baking dish. Sprinkle with black pepper and drizzle with oil. Bake at 350°F. for 15 minutes or until the fish flakes easily when tested with a fork.

2. Stir the cornstarch, stock, vinegar, brown sugar, orange juice and orange zest in a 2-quart saucepan over high heat to a boil. Cook and stir until the mixture boils and thickens.

3. Place the salmon on a serving platter and serve with the sauce. Garnish with the orange slices.

Tip: When grating citrus fruits, you'll want to avoid rubbing too deeply into the peel. There's a white layer between the outer peel and the flesh, called the pith, which can be bitter.

Weekday Pot Roast & Vegetables

prep 15 minutes | **cook** 10 hours | **makes** 8 servings

- 1 boneless beef bottom round roast **or** chuck pot roast (2 to 2½ pounds)
- 1 teaspoon garlic powder
- 1 tablespoon vegetable oil
- 1 pound potatoes, cut into wedges
- 3 cups fresh **or** frozen whole baby carrots
- 1 medium onion, thickly sliced (about ¾ cup)
- 2 teaspoons dried basil leaves, crushed
- 2 cans (10¼ ounces **each**) Campbell's® Beef Gravy

1. Season the beef with the garlic powder. Heat the oil in a 10-inch skillet over medium-high heat. Add the beef and cook until well browned on all sides.

2. Place the potatoes, carrots and onion in a 3½-quart slow cooker. Sprinkle with the basil. Add the beef to the cooker. Pour the gravy over the beef and vegetables.

3. Cover and cook on LOW for 10 to 11 hours* or until the beef is fork-tender.

*Or on HIGH for 5 to 6 hours.

Mushroom Bacon Burgers

prep 10 minutes | **cook** 25 minutes | **makes** 6 servings

- 1½ **pounds ground beef**
- 1 **can (10¾ ounces) Campbell's® Condensed Cream of Mushroom Soup (Regular or 98% Fat Free)**
- ⅓ **cup water**
- 6 **slices Cheddar cheese**
- 6 **Pepperidge Farm® Classic Sandwich Buns with Sesame Seeds**
- 6 **slices bacon, cooked**
- 6 **red onion slices**

1. Shape the beef into **6** (½-inch thick) burgers.

2. Cook the burgers in a 12-inch skillet over medium-high heat until well browned on both sides. Pour off any fat.

3. Stir the soup and water in the skillet and heat to a boil. Reduce the heat to low. Cover and cook for 5 minutes or until desired doneness.

4. Top the burgers with the cheese and cook until the cheese is melted. Serve the burgers and sauce on the buns. Top with the bacon and onion.

Quick Skillet Chicken & Macaroni Parmesan

prep 15 minutes | **cook** 15 minutes | **stand** 5 minutes | **makes** 6 servings

- 1 jar (1 pound 10 ounces) Prego® Traditional Italian Sauce
- ¼ cup grated Parmesan cheese
- 3 cups cubed cooked chicken
- 1½ cups elbow macaroni, cooked and drained
- 1½ cups shredded part-skim mozzarella cheese (6 ounces)

1. Heat the Italian sauce, **3 tablespoons** of the Parmesan cheese, chicken and macaroni in a 10-inch skillet over medium-high heat to a boil. Reduce the heat to medium. Cover and cook for 10 minutes or until the mixture is hot and bubbling, stirring occasionally.

2. Sprinkle with the mozzarella cheese and remaining Parmesan cheese. Let stand for 5 minutes or until the cheese melts.

Tip: Use **1½ pounds** skinless, boneless chicken breasts, cut into cubes, for the cooked chicken. Heat **1 tablespoon** olive oil in a 12-inch skillet over medium-high heat. Add the chicken in 2 batches and cook until well browned, stirring often. Continue to cook, proceeding as directed in step 1 above.

Skillet Beef & Macaroni

prep 20 minutes | **cook** 15 minutes | **makes** 4 servings

1 **pound ground beef**
2 **stalks celery, diced (about 1 cup)**
½ **teaspoon dried oregano leaves, crushed**
1 **can (10¾ ounces) Campbell's® Condensed Cream of Mushroom Soup (Regular or 98% Fat Free)**
1 **cup Pace® Picante Sauce**
1 **can (about 8 ounces) whole kernel corn, drained**
1 **cup elbow macaroni, cooked and drained**
   Shredded Cheddar cheese

1. Cook the beef, celery and oregano in a 10-inch skillet over medium-high heat until the beef is well browned, stirring often to separate the meat. Pour off any fat.

2. Stir the soup, picante sauce, corn and macaroni in the skillet. Cook and stir until the mixture is hot and bubbling. Sprinkle with the cheese and cook until the cheese is melted.

Beef & Pasta

prep 5 minutes | **cook** 25 minutes | **makes** 4 servings

¾	**pound ground beef (85% lean)**
1¾	**cups Swanson® Vegetable Broth (Regular or Certified Organic)**
1	**tablespoon Worcestershire sauce**
½	**teaspoon dried oregano leaves, crushed**
½	**teaspoon garlic powder**
1	**can (about 8 ounces) stewed tomatoes**
1½	**cups uncooked medium tube-shaped (ziti) or corkscrew-shaped (rotini) pasta**

1. Cook the beef in a 10-inch skillet over medium-high heat until well browned, stirring often to separate the meat. Pour off any fat.

2. Stir the broth, Worcestershire, oregano, garlic powder and tomatoes in the skillet and heat to a boil. Stir in the pasta. Reduce the heat to low. Cover and cook for 10 minutes, stirring often. **Uncover.**

3. Cook for 5 minutes or until the pasta is tender.

Pasta e Fajioli

prep 15 minutes | **cook** 30 minutes | **makes** 4 servings

- 1 **tablespoon olive oil**
- 2 **stalks celery, finely chopped (about 1 cup)**
- 2 **medium carrots, finely chopped (about 1 cup)**
- 1 **medium onion, chopped (about ½ cup)**
- 2 **cloves garlic, minced**
- 2 **cups Swanson® Chicken Broth (Regular, Natural Goodness® or Certified Organic)**
- 1 **teaspoon Italian seasoning, crushed**
- 1 **can (14.5 ounces) diced tomatoes, undrained**
- ¾ **cup short tube–shaped ditalini pasta, cooked and drained**
- 1 **can (about 15 ounces) white kidney beans (cannellini), undrained**

1. Heat the oil in a 12-inch skillet over medium heat. Cook the celery, carrots, onion and garlic until tender.

2. Stir the broth, Italian seasoning and tomatoes in the skillet. Heat to a boil. Reduce the heat to low and cook for 15 minutes or until the vegetables are tender-crisp.

3. Add the pasta and beans and cook for 5 minutes.

4. Place **half** of the broth mixture into a blender or food processor. Cover and blend until smooth. Pour the puréed mixture into the skillet. Cook over medium heat until the mixture is hot.

Sideline Spicy Bean Spread

prep 10 minutes | **stand** 15 minutes | **makes** 16 servings (about 2 cups)

- 1 can (about 16 ounces) white kidney beans (cannellini), rinsed and drained
- 1½ cups Pace® Chunky Salsa
- 2 tablespoons chopped fresh cilantro leaves
- 1 tablespoon lime juice

Assorted crackers

Mash the beans lightly in a 1-quart bowl with a fork. Stir in the salsa, cilantro and lime juice. Let stand for 15 minutes. Serve with the crackers.

Tip: Recipes that can be made ahead are always a plus for entertaining. Make this spread the day before and cover and refrigerate it overnight so that the flavors will have more time to develop before serving.

Chicken Tortilla Soup

prep 15 minutes | **bake** 15 minutes | **cook** 10 minutes | **makes** 4 servings

- **4   corn tortillas (6-inch), cut into strips**
- **3½ cups Swanson® Chicken Broth (Regular, Natural Goodness® or Certified Organic)**
- **½   cup Pace® Picante Sauce**
- **1   teaspoon garlic powder**
- **1   can (14.5 ounces) whole peeled tomatoes, cut up**
- **2   medium carrots, shredded (about 1 cup)**
- **1½ cups chopped cooked chicken**

1. Heat the oven to 400°F. Place the tortilla strips on a baking sheet.

2. Bake for 15 minutes or until they're golden.

3. Heat the broth, picante sauce, garlic powder, tomatoes and carrots in a 2-quart saucepan. Heat over medium-high heat to a boil. Reduce the heat to low. Cook for 5 minutes.

4. Stir the chicken in the saucepan and cook until the mixture is hot and bubbling. Top with the tortilla strips before serving.

Tip: For 1½ **cups** chopped cooked chicken, heat **4 cups** water in a 2-quart saucepan over medium heat to a boil. Add **¾ pound** skinless, boneless chicken breast halves **or** thighs, cut into cubes, and cook for 5 minutes or until the chicken is cooked through. Drain the chicken well in a colander.

Fall Confetti Oven Baked Risotto

prep 5 minutes | **bake** 50 minutes | **makes** 6 servings

1 can (10¾ ounces) Campbell's® Condensed
    Cream of Chicken with Herbs Soup

3¼ cups water

1¼ cups **uncooked** regular long-grain white rice

1 small carrot, shredded (about ⅓ cup)

¼ cup frozen peas

⅓ cup grated Parmesan cheese

1. Stir the soup, water, rice, carrot and peas in a 2-quart casserole. **Cover.**

2. Bake at 375°F. for 50 minutes or until rice is tender. Stir in the cheese. (Risotto will absorb liquid as it stands.)

Broccoli & Cheese Stuffed Shells

prep 25 minutes | **bake** 25 minutes | **makes** 6 servings

- 1 container (15 ounces) ricotta cheese
- 1 package (10 ounces) frozen chopped broccoli, thawed and well drained
- 1 cup shredded mozzarella cheese (about 4 ounces)
- ⅓ cup grated Parmesan cheese
- ¼ teaspoon black pepper
- 18 jumbo shell–shaped pasta, cooked and drained
- 1 jar (24 ounces) Prego® Chunky Garden Combination Italian Sauce

1. Stir the ricotta cheese, broccoli, ½ **cup** of the mozzarella cheese, Parmesan cheese and black pepper in a medium bowl. Spoon **about 2 tablespoons** of the cheese mixture into **each** shell.

2. Spread **1 cup** of the Italian sauce in a 13×9×2-inch shallow baking dish. Place the filled shells on the sauce. Pour the remaining sauce over the shells. Sprinkle with the remaining mozzarella cheese.

3. Bake at 400°F. for 25 minutes or until hot and bubbling.

Tip: To save time, thaw the broccoli in the microwave on HIGH for 4 minutes.

Meatloaf with Roasted Garlic Potatoes

prep 20 minutes | **bake** 1 hour | **makes** 6 servings

- 1 cup Pace® Picante Sauce
- 1½ pounds ground beef
- 1 cup fresh bread crumbs
- 1 egg, beaten
- 2 tablespoons chopped fresh parsley **or** 2 teaspoons dried parsley flakes
- 1 tablespoon Worcestershire sauce
- 4 cloves garlic, minced **or** ½ teaspoon garlic powder
- 2 tablespoons vegetable oil
- 4 medium potatoes (about 1¼ pounds), **each** cut into **8** wedges
  Paprika

1. Thoroughly mix ½ **cup** picante sauce, beef, bread crumbs, egg, parsley, Worcestershire and ½ the garlic in a large bowl. Firmly shape into 8×4-inch loaf in a baking pan.

2. Mix the oil and remaining garlic. Toss the potatoes with the oil mixture until evenly coated. Sprinkle with the paprika. Arrange the potatoes around the meatloaf.

3. Bake at 350°F. for 1 hour or until meatloaf is cooked through. Pour the remaining picante sauce over the meatloaf before serving.

Mexican Chicken & Rice

prep 10 minutes | **cook** 30 minutes | **makes** 5 servings

- 1¾ **cups Swanson® Chicken Stock**
- ½ **teaspoon ground cumin**
- ⅛ **teaspoon ground black pepper**
- 1 **medium onion, chopped (about ½ cup)**
- 1 **small green pepper, chopped (about ½ cup)**
- ¾ **cup uncooked regular long-grain white rice**
- 1 **can (about 15 ounces) kidney beans, rinsed and drained**
- 2 **cans (4.5 ounces each) Swanson® Premium White Chunk Chicken Breast in Water, drained**

1. Heat the stock, cumin, black pepper, onion and green pepper in a 3-quart saucepan over medium heat to a boil.

2. Stir the rice in the saucepan. Reduce the heat to low. Cover and cook for 20 minutes or until the rice is tender.

3. Stir in the beans and chicken and cook until the mixture is heated through.

September 19

Easy Spaghetti & Meatballs

prep 10 minutes | **cook** 8 minutes | **makes** 4 servings

- 1 **pound ground beef**
- 2 **tablespoons water**
- ⅓ **cup seasoned dry bread crumbs**
- 1 **egg, beaten**
- 1 **jar (24 ounces) Prego® Traditional Italian Sauce**
- ½ **of a 16-ounce package spaghetti, cooked and drained (about 4 cups)**

1. Mix **thoroughly** ground beef, water, bread crumbs and egg. Shape **firmly** into **12** (2-inch) meatballs. Arrange the meatballs in a 2-quart microwavable baking dish.

2. Microwave on HIGH for 5 minutes or until cooked through. Pour off any fat. Stir the Italian sauce in the dish. **Cover**. Microwave for 3 minutes or until hot. Serve over the spaghetti.

Citrus Chicken and Rice

prep 5 minutes | **cook** 35 minutes | **makes** 4 servings

4	skinless, boneless chicken breast halves (about 1 pound)
1¾	cups Swanson® Chicken Stock
¾	cup orange juice
1	medium onion, chopped (about ½ cup)
1	cup **uncooked** regular long-grain white rice
3	tablespoons chopped fresh parsley

1. Cook the chicken in a 10-inch nonstick skillet over medium-high heat for 10 minutes or until well browned on both sides. Remove the chicken from the skillet.

2. Stir the stock, orange juice, onion and rice in the skillet and heat to a boil. Reduce the heat to low. Cover and cook for 10 minutes.

3. Return the chicken to the skillet. Cover and cook for 10 minutes or until the chicken is cooked through and the rice is tender. Stir in the parsley.

Tip: For a special touch, cook orange slices in a nonstick skillet over medium-high heat until lightly browned. Serve over the chicken.

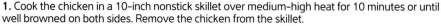

Baked Potatoes Olé

prep 5 minutes | **cook** 15 minutes | **makes** 4 servings

- 1 **pound ground beef**
- 1 **tablespoon chili powder**
- 1 **cup Pace® Picante Sauce**
- 4 **hot baked potatoes, split**
     Shredded Cheddar cheese

1. Cook the beef and chili powder in a 10-inch skillet over medium-high heat until the beef is well browned, stirring often to separate the meat. Pour off any fat.

2. Stir the picante sauce in the skillet. Reduce the heat to low. Cook until the mixture is hot and bubbling. Serve the beef mixture over the potatoes. Top with the cheese.

Tip: To bake the potatoes, pierce the potatoes with a fork. Bake at 400°F. for 1 hour or microwave on HIGH for 12 minutes or until fork-tender.

Saucy Baked Chicken & Broccoli

prep 15 minutes | **bake** 30 minutes | **makes** 8 servings

- 1 **pound broccoli, trimmed, cut into 1-inch pieces, cooked and drained**
- 8 **skinless, boneless chicken breast halves (about 2 pounds)**
- 1 **can (26 ounces) Campbell's® Condensed Cream of Mushroom Soup (Regular or 98% Fat Free)**
- ⅔ **cup milk**
- ¼ **teaspoon ground black pepper**
- 8 **cups hot cooked rice**

1. Place broccoli and chicken in 3-quart shallow baking dish. Mix soup, milk and black pepper and pour over all.

2. Bake at 400°F. for 30 minutes or until done. Stir sauce before serving. Serve with the rice.

Tip: Substitute **1 bag** (16 ounces) frozen broccoli cuts, thawed and drained for fresh. To thaw broccoli, microwave on HIGH 5 minutes.

Zesty Pork Chops

prep 5 minutes | **cook** 30 minutes | **makes** 4 servings

- 4 **bone-in pork chops (about 1¼ pounds)**
- **All-purpose flour**
- 1 **cup Pace® Picante Sauce**
- 2 **tablespoons packed brown sugar**
- 1 **apple, peeled, cored and cut into slices, ¼-inch thick**
- 2 **tablespoons olive oil**

1. Coat the pork with the flour. Stir the picante sauce, brown sugar and apple in a medium bowl.

2. Heat the oil in a 10-inch skillet over medium-high heat. Add the pork and cook until well browned on both sides. Pour off any fat.

3. Pour the picante sauce mixture over the pork. Reduce the heat to low. Cover and cook for 20 minutes or until the pork is cooked through.

Tip: You can really spice up this recipe by adding **1 teaspoon** hot pepper sauce to the picante sauce mixture.

Citrus Picante Roast Pork

prep 15 minutes | **bake** 35 minutes | **stand** 10 minutes | **makes** 8 servings

- 1 jar (11 ounces) Pace® Picante Sauce
- 1 can (11 ounces) Mandarin orange segments, drained
- 2 pork tenderloins (about 1 pound **each**)
- 1 teaspoon olive oil
- 2 tablespoons chopped fresh cilantro leaves
- 1 lime, cut into wedges

1. Heat the oven to 425°F. Stir the picante sauce and oranges in a small bowl.

2. Place the pork into a 3-quart shallow baking pan. Rub the pork with the oil. Pour the salsa mixture over the pork.

3. Bake for 35 minutes or until the pork is cooked through. Remove the pork from the pan and let stand for 10 minutes. Sprinkle with the cilantro and serve with the lime.

Tip: You can try canned diced peaches **or** pineapple in this recipe, if you like.

Souper Sloppy Joes

prep 5 minutes | **cook** 15 minutes | **makes** 6 servings

- 1   pound ground beef
- 1   can (10¾ ounces) Campbell's® Condensed Tomato Soup
- ¼   cup water
- 1   tablespoon prepared yellow mustard
- 6   Pepperidge Farm® Classic Sandwich Buns with Sesame Seeds

1. Cook the beef in a 10-inch skillet over medium-high heat until well browned, stirring often to separate the meat. Pour off any fat.

2. Stir the soup, water and mustard in the skillet and cook until the mixture is hot and bubbling. Spoon the beef mixture on the buns.

Broth Simmered Rice

prep 5 minutes | **cook** 25 minutes | **makes** 4 servings

- 1¾ **cups Swanson® Chicken Broth (Regular, Natural Goodness® or Certified Organic)**
- ¾ **cup uncooked regular long-grain white rice**

1. Heat the broth in a 2-quart saucepan over medium-high heat to a boil.

2. Stir in the rice. Reduce the heat to low. Cover and cook for 20 minutes or until the rice is tender.

Tip: This recipe will work with any variety of Swanson® Broth.

Florentine Simmered Rice: Add **1 teaspoon** dried Italian seasoning to broth. Add **1 cup** chopped spinach with rice. Stir in ½ **cup** grated Parmesan cheese before serving. Serve with additional cheese.

Touchdown Twists

thaw 40 minutes | prep 20 minutes | bake 10 minutes | makes 28 twists

- ½ of a 17.3-ounce package Pepperidge Farm® Puff Pastry Sheets (1 sheet)
- ¾ cup shredded Cheddar cheese
- 1 tablespoon butter, melted
- ¼ cup grated Parmesan cheese
- ¼ teaspoon ground black pepper

1. Heat the oven to 400°F. Lightly grease a baking sheet.

2. Unflold the pastry sheet on a lightly floured surface. Roll the sheet into a 14×10-inch rectangle. Cut the pastry in half lengthwise. Top **1** rectangle with the Cheddar cheese. Place the remaining rectangle over the cheese-topped rectangle. Roll gently with a rolling pin to seal.

3. Cut crosswise into **28** (½-inch) strips. Brush the strips with melted butter then sprinkle with the Parmesan cheese and black pepper. Twist the strips and place 2 inches apart on the baking sheet, pressing down the ends.

4. Bake for 10 minutes or until golden. Serve the twists warm or at room temperature. Store in an airtight container.

Pan-Grilled Veggie & Cheese Sandwiches

prep 5 minutes | **cook** 15 minutes | **makes** 4 servings

Vegetable cooking spray
2 portobello mushrooms, cut into ½-inch slices
1 medium red pepper, cut into strips (about 1½ cups)
2 slices onions, ½-inch thick **each**
8 slices eggplant, ¼-inch thick **each**
   Garlic powder (optional)
½ cup shredded fat-free mozzarella cheese
2 tablespoons balsamic vinegar
8 slices Pepperidge Farm® 100% Natural 100% Whole Wheat
   Bread

1. Spray a nonstick grill pan with the cooking spray and heat over medium heat for 1 minute.

2. Add the mushrooms, pepper and onions to one side of the pan. Add the eggplant to the other side. Sprinkle the garlic powder over all, if desired. Cook until the vegetables are tender. Sprinkle the eggplant with the cheese and cook until the cheese is melted.

3. Place the mushrooms, pepper and onions into a medium bowl. Add the vinegar and toss to coat. Divide the eggplant slices among **4** bread slices. Top with the mushroom mixture and remaining bread slices.

Tip: If you don't have a grill pan, this recipe can be made in a 12-inch nonstick skillet.

Classic Tuna Noodle Casserole

prep 10 minutes | **bake** 25 minutes | **makes** 4 servings

- 1 can (10¾ ounces) Campbell's® Condensed Cream of Celery Soup (Regular **or** 98% Fat Free)
- ½ cup milk
- 1 cup cooked peas
- 2 tablespoons chopped pimientos
- 2 cans (about 6 ounces **each**) tuna, drained and flaked
- 2 cups hot cooked medium egg noodles
- 2 tablespoons dry bread crumbs
- 1 tablespoon butter, melted

1. Heat the oven to 400°F. Stir the soup, milk, peas, pimientos, tuna and noodles in a 1½-quart baking dish. Stir the bread crumbs and butter in a small bowl.

2. Bake for 20 minutes or until the tuna mixture is hot and bubbling. Stir the tuna mixture. Sprinkle with the bread crumb mixture.

3. Bake for 5 minutes or until the bread crumbs are golden brown.

Tips: Substitute Campbell's® Condensed Cream of Mushroom Soup for the Cream of Celery Soup.

To melt the butter, remove the wrapper and place the butter in a microwavable cup. Cover and microwave on HIGH for 30 seconds.

Spicy Turkey, Corn and Zucchini Skillet

prep 15 minutes | **cook** 20 minutes | **makes** 4 servings

- 2 **teaspoons olive oil**
- 2 **cloves garlic, chopped**
- 1 **onion, finely chopped (about 1 cup)**
- 2 **medium zucchini, finely chopped (about 3 cups)**
- 1 **pound lean ground turkey**
- 2 **medium tomatoes, chopped (about 2 cups)**
- 1 **carton (18.3 ounces) Campbell's® V8® Southwest Corn Soup**
- 2 **cups baked tortilla chips (fat free)**
- 2 **ounces fat-free shredded Cheddar cheese (about ½ cup)**
-   **Chopped fresh cilantro leaves**

1. Heat the oil in a 10-inch nonstick skillet over medium-high heat. Add the garlic, onion and zucchini and cook for 5 minutes. Add the turkey and cook until well browned, stirring often to separate the meat. Stir the tomatoes in the skillet and cook for 2 minutes.

2. Stir the soup in the skillet and heat to a boil. Reduce the heat to low. Cook for 5 minutes or until the turkey mixture is hot and bubbling. Top with the tortilla chips and cheese. Garnish with the cilantro.

Slow Cooker Fall Harvest Pork Stew

prep 20 minutes | **cook** 7 hours | **makes** 8 servings

- 2 **pounds boneless pork shoulder, cut into 2-inch pieces**
- 1 **can (10¾ ounces) Campbell's® Condensed French Onion Soup**
- ½ **cup apple cider or apple juice**
- 3 **large Granny Smith apples, cut into thick slices (about 3 cups)**
- 3 **cups butternut squash peeled, seeded and cut into 2-inch pieces**
- 2 **medium parsnips, peeled and cut into 1-inch pieces (about 2 cups)**
- ½ **teaspoon dried thyme leaves, crushed**

1. Stir the pork, soup, cider, apples, squash, parsnips and thyme in a 6-quart slow cooker.

2. Cover and cook on LOW for 7 to 8 hours* or until the pork is fork-tender.

Or on HIGH for 4 to 5 hours.

Tip: For thicker gravy, stir ¼ **cup** all-purpose flour and ½ **cup** water in a small bowl until the mixture is smooth. Stir the flour mixture in the cooker. Cover and cook on HIGH for 10 minutes or until the mixture boils and thickens.

May 4

Puff Pastry-Wrapped Jumbo Shrimp

thaw 40 minutes | **prep** 30 minutes | **bake** 15 minutes | **makes** 18 servings

- 1 package (5.2 ounces) garlic & herb spreadable cheese, softened
- 1 tablespoon finely chopped fresh parsley
- 2 slices bacon, cooked and crumbled
- 18 fresh jumbo shrimp (about 1 pound), peeled with tail left on, deveined and butterflied
- ½ of a 17.3-ounce package Pepperidge Farm® Puff Pastry Sheets (1 sheet), thawed

1. Heat the oven to 400°F.

2. Stir the cheese, parsley and bacon in a medium bowl. Spoon about **2 teaspoons** cheese mixture down the center of **each** shrimp. Fold the sides of the shrimp over the filling.

3. Unfold the pastry sheet on a lightly floured surface. Cut the pastry sheet crosswise into **18** (½-inch-wide) strips. Starting at the top, wind **1** pastry strip around **1** shrimp, slightly overlapping the pastry and ending just before the tail. Repeat with remaining pastry strips and shrimp. Place the pastries onto a baking sheet.

4. Bake for 15 minutes or until the pastries are golden brown.

Family Spaghetti Pie

prep 25 minutes | **bake** 30 minutes | **stand** 5 minutes | **makes** 6 servings

- 1 **pound ground beef**
- 1 **cup Pace® Picante Sauce**
- 1 **cup Prego® Fresh Mushroom Italian Sauce**
- ⅓ **of a 16-ounce package spaghetti, cooked and drained (about 3 cups)**
- ⅓ **cup grated Parmesan cheese**
- 1 **egg, beaten**
- 1 **tablespoon butter, melted**
- 1 **cup ricotta cheese**
- 4 **ounces shredded mozzarella cheese (about 1 cup)**

1. Cook the beef in a 10-inch skillet over medium-high heat until meat is well browned, stirring often to separate the meat. Pour off any fat. Stir the picante sauce and Italian sauce into the skillet and cook until hot and bubbling.

2. Stir the spaghetti, Parmesan cheese, egg and butter in a medium bowl. Spread the mixture on the bottom and up the side of greased 10-inch pie plate. Spread the ricotta cheese in the spaghetti shell. Top with the beef mixture.

3. Bake at 350°F. for 30 minutes or until hot and bubbling. Sprinkle with the mozzarella cheese. Let stand for 5 minutes before serving. Cut into **6** wedges.

Chicken with Grape Tomatoes & Mushrooms

prep 15 minutes | **cook** 20 minutes | **makes** 4 servings

- 2 **tablespoons olive oil**
- 1¼ **pounds skinless, boneless chicken breast halves, cut into thin strips**
- 1 **package (8 ounces) sliced fresh mushrooms (about 2¼ cups)**
- 1 **clove garlic, minced**
- 1 **pint grape tomatoes (about 2½ cups)**
- 3 **green onions, cut into 1-inch pieces (about ⅓ cup)**
- 2 **packets Swanson® Flavor Boost™ Concentrated Chicken Broth**
- 2 **tablespoons water**

1. Heat **1 tablespoon** oil in a 12-inch skillet over medium-high heat. Add the chicken and cook until well browned, stirring often. Remove the chicken from the skillet.

2. Heat the remaining oil in the skillet over medium heat. Add the mushrooms and cook until tender, stirring occasionally.

3. Add the garlic, tomatoes and onions to the skillet and cook and stir for 1 minute. Return the chicken to the skillet. Stir in the concentrated broth and water and cook until the chicken is cooked through.

2-Bean Chili

prep 10 minutes | **cook** 15 minutes | **makes** 6 servings

- 1   **pound ground beef**
- 1   **large green pepper, chopped (about 1 cup)**
- 1   **large onion, chopped (about 1 cup)**
- 2   **tablespoons chili powder**
- ¼   **teaspoon ground black pepper**
- 3   **cups Campbell's® Tomato Juice**
- 1   **can (about 15 ounces) kidney beans, rinsed and drained**
- 1   **can (about 15 ounces) great Northern beans, rinsed and drained**
-    **Sour cream**
-    **Sliced green onions**
-    **Shredded Cheddar cheese**
-    **Chopped tomato**

1. Cook the beef, green pepper, onion, chili powder and black pepper in a 10-inch skillet until the beef is well browned, stirring often to separate the meat. Pour off any fat.

2. Stir the tomato juice and beans in the skillet and cook until the mixture is hot and bubbling. Top the beef mixture with the sour cream, green onions, cheese and tomato before serving.

Cheeseburger Pasta

prep 5 minutes | **cook** 20 minutes | **makes** 5 servings

- 1 **pound ground beef**
- 1 **can (10¾ ounces) Campbell's® Condensed Cheddar Cheese Soup**
- 1 **can (10¾ ounces) Campbell's® Condensed Tomato Soup (Regular or Healthy Request®)**
- 1½ **cups water**
- 2 **cups uncooked medium shell-shaped pasta**

1. Cook the beef in a 10-inch skillet over medium-high heat until well browned, stirring often to separate the meat. Pour off any fat.

2. Stir the soups, water and pasta in the skillet and heat to a boil. Reduce the heat to medium. Cook for 10 minutes or until the pasta is tender, stirring often.

Cheeseburger Chowder

prep 10 minutes | **cook** 20 minutes | **makes** 8 servings

- 1 **pound ground beef**
- 1 **large onion, chopped (about 1 cup)**
- 2 **cans (26 ounces each) Campbell's® Condensed Cream of Mushroom Soup (Regular or 98% Fat Free)**
- 2 **soup cans milk**
- 1 **cup finely shredded Cheddar cheese**
- 1 **cup Pepperidge Farm® Seasoned Croutons**

1. Cook the beef and onion in a 3-quart saucepan over medium-high heat until the beef is well browned, stirring often to separate the meat. Pour off any fat.

2. Stir the soup and milk in the saucepan. Cook until the mixture is hot and bubbling. Stir in ½ **cup** cheese. Cook and stir until the cheese is melted.

3. Divide the soup among 8 serving bowls. Top **each** bowl with 1 **tablespoon** remaining cheese and 2 **tablespoons** croutons.

Polynesian Burgers

prep 10 minutes | **cook** 20 minutes | **makes** 6 servings

1½	**pounds ground beef**
1	**can (8 ounces) pineapple slices in juice, undrained**
1	**can (10½ ounces) Campbell's® Condensed French Onion Soup**
2	**teaspoons packed brown sugar**
1	**tablespoon cider vinegar**
1	**loaf French bread, cut crosswise into 6 pieces**

1. Shape the beef into **6** (½-inch thick) burgers.

2. Cook the burgers in a 12-inch skillet over medium-high heat until well browned on both sides. Pour off any fat. Top **each** burger with **1** slice pineapple. Reserve the pineapple juice.

3. Stir the soup, reserved pineapple juice, brown sugar and vinegar in a small bowl. Add the soup mixture to the skillet and heat to a boil. Reduce the heat to low. Cover and cook for 5 minutes or until the burgers are cooked through.

4. Split the bread pieces. Serve the burgers and sauce on the bread.

Chicken Fajitas

prep 5 minutes | **marinate** 30 minutes | **grill** 15 minutes | **makes** 6 servings

- ¼ **cup Italian salad dressing**
- 6 **skinless, boneless chicken breast halves (about 1½ pounds)**
- 1 **can (10¾ ounces) Campbell's® Condensed Cheddar Cheese Soup**
- ½ **cup Pace® Picante Sauce**
- 12 **flour tortillas (8-inch), warmed**
- 4 **green onions, thinly sliced (about ½ cup)**
- 1 **small avocado, peeled, pitted and sliced (optional)**

1. Pour the dressing into a shallow nonmetallic dish or gallon-size resealable plastic bag. Add the chicken and turn to coat. Cover the dish or seal the bag and refrigerate for 30 minutes. Remove the chicken from the marinade. Discard the marinade.

2. Lightly oil the grill rack and heat the grill to medium. Grill the chicken for 15 minutes or until cooked through, turning it over once halfway through grilling.

3. Heat the soup and picante sauce in a 1-quart saucepan over medium-high heat until the mixture is hot and bubbling.

4. Cut the chicken into thin strips. Divide the chicken among the tortillas. Top with the soup mixture, onions and avocado, if desired. Fold the tortillas around the filling.

Hot Chicken & Potato Salad

prep 15 minutes | **bake** 25 minutes | **makes** 8 servings

1	can (6 ounces) French fried onions
⅓	cup chopped walnuts
4	cups diced cooked chicken
2	cups frozen peas and carrots, thawed
1	can (10¾ ounces) Campbell's® Condensed Cream of Mushroom Soup (Regular **or** 98% Fat Free)
1½	cups shredded Monterey Jack cheese **or** shredded Swiss cheese (about 6 ounces)
¾	cup plain yogurt
1	large potato, cut into cubes

1. Stir ½ **can** onions and walnuts in a medium bowl.

2. Stir the remaining onions, chicken, peas and carrots, soup, cheese, yogurt and potato in a large bowl. Pour the chicken mixture into a 2-quart baking dish.

3. Bake at 350°F. for 20 minutes or until the chicken mixture is hot and bubbling. Stir the chicken mixture. Sprinkle with the walnut mixture.

4. Bake for 5 minutes or until the walnut mixture is golden brown.

Game-Winning Drumsticks

prep 10 minutes | **marinate** 4 hours | **bake** 1 hour | **makes** 6 servings

- **15 chicken drumsticks (about 4 pounds)**
- **1¾ cups Swanson® Chicken Stock**
- **½ cup Dijon-style mustard**
- **⅓ cup Italian-seasoned dry bread crumbs**

1. Place the chicken in a single layer into a 15×10-inch disposable foil pan.

2. Stir the stock and mustard in a small bowl. Pour the stock mixture over the chicken and turn to coat. Sprinkle the bread crumbs over the chicken. Cover the pan and refrigerate for 4 hours.

3. Bake at 375°F. for 1 hour or until the chicken is cooked through. Serve hot or at room temperature.

Tip: Keep disposable foil pans on hand for convenience to tote casseroles to friends' parties or covered-dish suppers. As a safety reminder, be sure to support the bottom of the filled pan when handling them in and out of the oven.

Chicken & Roasted Garlic Risotto

prep 5 minutes | **cook** 20 minutes | **stand** 5 minutes | **makes** 4 servings

- 1 tablespoon butter
- 4 skinless, boneless chicken breast halves (about 1 pound)
- 1 can (10¾ ounces) Campbell's® Condensed Cream of Chicken Soup (Regular **or** 98% Fat Free)
- 1 can (10¾ ounces) Campbell's® Condensed Cream of Mushroom with Roasted Garlic Soup
- 2 cups water
- 2 cups **uncooked** instant white rice
- 1 cup frozen peas and carrots

1. Heat the butter in a 10-inch skillet over medium-high heat. Add the chicken and cook for 10 minutes or until well browned on both sides. Remove the chicken from the skillet.

2. Stir the soups and water in the skillet and heat to a boil. Stir in the rice and vegetables. Return the chicken to the skillet. Reduce the heat to low. Cover and cook for 5 minutes or until the chicken is cooked through. Remove the skillet from the heat. Let stand for 5 minutes.

Tip: Traditionally, risotto is made by sautéing rice in butter then stirring broth into the rice a little at a time—very labor-intensive. This dish gives you the same creamy texture with a lot less work!

Harvest Fruit Compote

prep 10 minutes | **cook** 4 hours | **makes** 10 servings

- **1** **lemon**
- **2** **packages (12 ounces each) prunes (about 4 cups)**
- **1** **package (7 ounces) mixed dried fruit (about 1½ cups)**
- **1** **package (about 6 ounces) dried apricots (about 1½ cups)**
- **½** **cup dried cranberries**
- **⅓** **cup raisins**
- **4** **cups V8 V-Fusion® Pomegranate Blueberry Juice**
- **1** **cup white Zinfandel wine**
- **1** **teaspoon vanilla extract**

1. Grate **1 teaspoon** zest from the lemon.

2. Stir the prunes, mixed fruit, apricots, cranberries, raisins, juice, wine, lemon zest and vanilla extract in a 6-quart slow cooker.

3. Cover and cook on HIGH for 4 to 5 hours*.

Or on LOW for 7 to 8 hours.

Tip: The compote can be served warm or cold. Try it warm spooned over vanilla ice cream or pound cake. Try it warm or cold as an accompaniment to roast pork loin.

Tuna & Pasta Cheddar Melt

prep 10 minutes | **cook** 15 minutes | **makes** 4 servings

- 1 **can (10½ ounces) Campbell's® Condensed Chicken Broth**
- 1 **soup can water**
- 3 **cups uncooked corkscrew-shaped pasta (rotini)**
- 1 **can (10¾ ounces) Campbell's® Condensed Cream of Mushroom Soup (Regular or 98% Fat Free)**
- 1 **cup milk**
- 1 **can (about 6 ounces) tuna, drained and flaked**
- 1 **cup shredded Cheddar cheese (about 4 ounces)**
- 2 **tablespoons Italian-seasoned dry bread crumbs**
- 2 **teaspoons butter, melted**

1. Heat the broth and water in a 12-inch skillet over medium-high heat to a boil. Stir in the pasta. Reduce the heat to medium. Cook until the pasta is tender, stirring often. Do not drain.

2. Stir the soup, milk and tuna in the skillet. Top with the cheese. Stir the bread crumbs and butter in a small bowl. Sprinkle over the tuna mixture. Cook until the cheese is melted.

Beef Taco Bake

prep 10 minutes | **bake** 30 minutes | **makes** 4 servings

- 1 **pound ground beef**
- 1 **can (10¾ ounces) Campbell's® Condensed Tomato Soup**
- 1 **cup Pace® Picante Sauce**
- ½ **cup milk**
- 6 **flour tortillas (8-inch) or corn tortillas (6-inch), cut into 1-inch pieces**
- 1 **cup shredded Cheddar cheese (about 4 ounces)**

1. Cook the beef in a 10-inch skillet over medium-high heat until well browned, stirring often. Pour off any fat.

2. Stir the soup, picante sauce, milk, tortillas and **half** the cheese in the skillet. Spoon the beef mixture into a 2-quart shallow baking dish. Cover the baking dish.

3. Bake at 400°F. for 30 minutes or until the beef mixture is hot and bubbling. Sprinkle with the remaining cheese.

Cheddar Broccoli Frittata

prep 10 minutes | **cook** 15 minutes | **makes** 4 servings

- **6 eggs**
- **1 can (10¾ ounces) Campbell's® Condensed Broccoli Cheese Soup (Regular or 98% Fat Free)**
- **¼ cup milk**
- **⅛ teaspoon ground black pepper**
- **1 tablespoon butter**
- **2 cups sliced mushrooms (about 6 ounces)**
- **1 large onion, chopped (about 1 cup)**
- **1 small zucchini, sliced (about 1 cup)**
- **¼ cup shredded Cheddar cheese**
- **1 green onion, chopped (about 2 tablespoons)**

1. Beat the eggs, soup, milk and black pepper in a medium bowl with a fork or whisk.

2. Heat the butter in a 12-inch ovenproof nonstick skillet over medium heat. Add the mushrooms, onion and zucchini and cook until tender. Stir in the egg mixture. Reduce the heat to low. Cook for 5 minutes or until the eggs are set but still moist.

3. Heat the broiler. Sprinkle the cheese over the egg mixture. Broil the frittata with the top 4 inches from the heat for 2 minutes or until the top is golden brown. Sprinkle with the green onion.

Holiday Brisket with Savory Onion Jus

prep 15 minutes | **cook** 3 hours 15 minutes | **stand** 10 minutes | **makes** 8 servings

- 2 tablespoons olive **or** vegetable oil
- 6 medium onions, cut into quarters (about 6 cups)
- 1 medium butternut squash (about 3 pounds), peeled, seeded and cut into 1½-inch cubes (about 6 cups)
  3-pound boneless beef brisket
- 1¾ cups Swanson® Beef Stock
- ½ cup orange juice
- ½ cup dry red wine
- ½ cup packed brown sugar
- 1 can (about 28 ounces) whole peeled tomatoes

1. Heat the oil in an 8-quart saucepot over medium-high heat. Add the onions and squash and cook over medium heat until tender-crisp. Remove the vegetables from the saucepot.

2. Season the beef as desired. Increase the heat to medium-high. Add the beef to the saucepot and cook until well browned on both sides. Remove the beef from the saucepot. Pour off any fat.

3. Add the stock, orange juice, wine, brown sugar and tomatoes to the saucepot and heat to a boil. Reduce the heat to low. Return the beef to the saucepot. Cover and cook for 2 hours.

4. Return the vegetables to the saucepot. Cover and cook for 1 hour or until the beef is fork-tender.

5. Remove the beef to a cutting board. Let stand for 10 minutes. Serve the beef with the vegetables and sauce.

Easy Pasta Primavera

prep 20 minutes | **cook** 15 minutes | **makes** 4 servings

- 2 **tablespoons cornstarch**
- 1¾ **cups Swanson® Natural Goodness® Chicken Broth**
- 1 **teaspoon dried oregano leaves, crushed**
- ¼ **teaspoon garlic powder or 2 garlic cloves, minced**
- 2 **cups broccoli florets**
- 2 **medium carrots, sliced (about 1 cup)**
- 1 **medium onion, cut into wedges**
- 1 **medium tomato, diced (about 1 cup)**
- ½ **of a 1-pound package thin spaghetti, cooked and drained (about 4 cups)**
- 3 **tablespoons grated Parmesan cheese**

1. Stir the cornstarch and ¾ **cup** broth in a small bowl until the mixture is smooth.

2. Heat the remaining broth, oregano, garlic powder, broccoli, carrots and onion in a 4-quart saucepan over medium heat to a boil. Reduce the heat to low. Cover and cook for 5 minutes or until the vegetables are tender-crisp.

3. Stir the cornstarch mixture in the saucepan. Cook and stir until the mixture boils and thickens. Stir in the tomato. Add the spaghetti and toss to coat. Sprinkle with the cheese.

Hearty Chicken Tortilla Soup

prep 10 minutes | **cook** 30 minutes | **makes** 6 servings

Vegetable cooking spray
4   skinless, boneless chicken breasts, cut into 1-inch pieces
3½ cups Swanson® Chicken Broth (Regular, Natural Goodness®
      or Certified Organic)
1   teaspoon ground cumin
½   cup **uncooked** regular long-grain white rice
1   can (11 ounces) whole kernel corn with red and green
      peppers, drained
1   cup Pace® Picante Sauce
1   tablespoon chopped fresh cilantro leaves
2   tablespoons fresh lime juice
    Crisp Tortilla Strips

1. Spray a 6-quart saucepot with the cooking spray. Heat over medium-high heat for 1 minute. Add the chicken to the saucepot. Cook until browned, stirring often.

2. Stir the broth, cumin and rice in the saucepot. Heat to a boil. Reduce the heat to low. Cover and cook for 20 minutes.

3. Stir the corn, picante sauce, cilantro and lime juice in the saucepot. Cook until the rice is tender. Top **each** serving of soup with *Crisp Tortilla Strips*.

Crisp Tortilla Strips: Heat the oven to 425°F. Cut **4** corn tortillas into thin strips and place them on a baking sheet. Spray with the cooking spray. Bake for 10 minutes or until golden.

Chicken Crunch

prep 10 minutes | **bake** 20 minutes | **cook** 5 minutes | **makes** 4 servings

- **1** **can (10¾ ounces) Campbell's® Condensed Cream of Chicken Soup (Regular or 98% Fat Free)**
- **½** **cup milk**
- **4** **skinless, boneless chicken breast halves (about 1 pound)**
- **2** **tablespoons all-purpose flour**
- **1½** **cups Pepperidge Farm® Herb Seasoned Stuffing, finely crushed**
- **2** **tablespoons butter, melted**

1. Heat the oven to 400°F. Stir ⅓ **cup** soup and ¼ **cup** milk in a shallow dish. Coat the chicken with the flour. Dip the chicken in the soup mixture. Coat the chicken with the stuffing. Place the chicken onto a baking sheet. Drizzle with the butter.

2. Bake for 20 minutes or until the chicken is cooked through.

3. Heat the remaining soup and milk in a 1-quart saucepan over medium-high heat until the mixture is hot and bubbling. Serve the sauce with the chicken.

Easy Chicken Pot Pie

prep 10 minutes | **bake** 30 minutes | **makes** 4 servings

- 1 can (10¾ ounces) Campbell's® Condensed Cream of Chicken Soup (Regular **or** 98% Fat Free)
- 1 package (9 ounces) frozen mixed vegetables, thawed
- 1 cup cubed cooked chicken **or** turkey
- ½ cup milk
- 1 egg
- 1 cup all-purpose baking mix

1. Heat the oven to 400°F. Stir the soup, vegetables and chicken in a 9-inch pie plate.
2. Stir the milk, egg and baking mix in a small bowl. Spread the batter over the chicken mixture.
3. Bake for 30 minutes or until the topping is golden brown.

Tips: You can easily substitute Campbell's® Condensed Cream of Chicken with Herbs Soup for the Cream of Chicken.
Substitute reduced-fat all-purpose baking mix for the regular baking mix.

Sun-Dried Tomato Bow Tie Pasta

prep 10 minutes | **cook** 20 minutes | **makes** 4 servings

- 1 **tablespoon olive oil**
- 1 **large onion, finely chopped (about 1 cup)**
- ⅓ **cup sun-dried tomatoes, cut into thin strips**
- 2 **cloves garlic, minced**
- 1 **can (10¾ ounces) Campbell's® Condensed Cream of Chicken Soup (Regular or 98% Fat Free)**
- 1 **cup milk**
- 2 **tablespoons thinly sliced fresh basil leaves**
- 1 **package (1 pound) bow tie pasta (farfalle) (about 6 cups), cooked and drained**
- 2 **tablespoons grated Parmesan cheese**
  Freshly ground black pepper

1. Heat the oil in a 10-inch skillet over medium heat. Add the onion and cook until tender.

2. Add the tomatoes and garlic and cook for 1 minute. Stir the soup, milk and basil in the skillet. Cook until the mixture is hot and bubbling, stirring occasionally.

3. Place the pasta into a large serving bowl. Pour the soup mixture over the pasta and toss to coat. Sprinkle with the cheese. Season with the black pepper, if desired.

Tip: For a thinner sauce, reserve ¼ **cup** of the pasta cooking water and add it to the skillet with the soup and milk.

Bistro Onion Burgers

prep 5 minutes | **cook** 10 minutes | **makes** 6 servings

- 1½ **pounds ground beef**
- 1 **envelope (about 1 ounce) dry onion soup and recipe mix**
- 3 **tablespoons water**
- 6 **Pepperidge Farm® Classic Sandwich Buns with Sesame Seeds, split and toasted**
  Lettuce leaves
  Tomato slices

1. Thoroughly mix the beef, soup mix and water. Shape the beef mixture into **6** (½-inch-thick) burgers.

2. Cook the burgers in batches in a 10-inch skillet over medium-high heat until well browned on both sides, 10 minutes for medium or to desired doneness.

3. Serve the burgers on the buns. Top with the lettuce and tomato.

Monterey Chicken Tortilla Casserole

prep 15 minutes | **bake** 40 minutes | **makes** 4 servings

- 1 cup coarsely crumbled tortilla chips
- 2 cups cubed cooked chicken **or** turkey
- 1 can (about 15 ounces) cream-style corn
- ¾ cup Pace® Picante Sauce
- ½ cup sliced pitted ripe olives
- 2 ounces shredded Cheddar cheese (about ½ cup)
  Chopped green **or** red pepper
  Tortilla chips

1. Layer the crumbled chips, chicken, corn and picante sauce in a 1-quart casserole. Top with the olives and cheese.

2. Bake at 350°F. for 40 minutes or until the mixture is hot and bubbling. Top with the pepper. Serve with the chips.

French Toast Casserole

prep 10 minutes | **chill** 1 hour | **bake** 50 minutes | **makes** 8 servings

- **1** **loaf (16 ounces) Pepperidge Farm® Cinnamon Swirl Bread, cut into cubes (about 8 cups)**
- **6** **eggs**
- **3** **cups milk**
- **2** **teaspoons vanilla extract**
   Confectioners' sugar
   Maple-flavored syrup (optional)

1. Place the bread cubes into a greased 3-quart shallow baking dish. Beat the eggs, milk and vanilla extract in a medium bowl with a fork or whisk. Pour the milk mixture over the bread cubes. Stir and press the bread cubes into the milk mixture to coat. Cover and refrigerate for 1 hour or overnight.

2. Heat the oven to 350°F. Uncover the baking dish.

3. Bake for 50 minutes or until a knife inserted in the center comes out clean. Sprinkle with the confectioners' sugar. Serve with the syrup, if desired.

Tip: This recipe will work with any of the Pepperidge Farm® Swirl Breads (Cinnamon, Raisin Cinnamon **or** Brown Sugar Cinnamon)

Creamy Pork Marsala with Fettuccine

prep 5 minutes | **cook** 25 minutes | **makes** 4 servings

- 1 **tablespoon olive oil**
- 4 **boneless pork chops, ¾-inch thick (about 1 pound)**
- 1 **cup sliced mushrooms (about 3 ounces)**
- 1 **clove garlic, minced**
- 1 **can (10¾ ounces) Campbell's® Condensed Cream of Mushroom Soup (Regular or 98% Fat Free)**
- ½ **cup milk**
- 2 **tablespoons dry Marsala wine**
- 8 **ounces spinach fettuccine, cooked and drained**

1. Heat the oil in a 10-inch skillet over medium-high heat. Add the pork and cook until well browned on both sides.

2. Reduce the heat to medium. Add the mushrooms and garlic to the skillet and cook until the mushrooms are tender.

3. Stir the soup, milk and wine in the skillet and heat to a boil. Reduce the heat to low. Cover and cook for 5 minutes or until the pork is cooked through. Serve the pork and sauce with the pasta.

Tip: Marsalas can range from dry to sweet, so be sure to use a dry one for this recipe.

Best-of-the-West Bean Salad

prep 10 minutes | **chill** 2 hours | **makes** 8 servings

- ¾ cup Pace® Picante Sauce
- 2 tablespoons chopped fresh cilantro leaves
- 2 tablespoons red wine vinegar
- 1 tablespoon vegetable oil
- 1 large green pepper, diced (about 1 cup)
- 1 medium red onion, very thinly sliced (about ½ cup)
- 1 can (about 15 ounces) kidney beans, rinsed and drained
- 1 can (about 15 ounces) pinto beans, rinsed and drained

Stir the picante sauce, cilantro, vinegar, oil, pepper, onion, kidney beans and pinto beans in a medium bowl. Cover and refrigerate for 2 hours, stirring occasionally during chilling time. Garnish with additional cilantro.

Chicken & Stir-Fry Vegetable Pizza

prep 5 minutes | **cook** 5 minutes | **bake** 10 minutes | **makes** 4 servings

- 1 can (10¾ ounces) Campbell's® Condensed Cream of Mushroom Soup (Regular **or** 98% Fat Free)
- 1 prepared pizza crust (12-inch)
- 1 tablespoon vegetable oil
- 3 cups frozen vegetables
- ⅛ teaspoon garlic powder
- 1 package (about 10 ounces) refrigerated cooked chicken strips
- 1 cup shredded Cheddar cheese (about 4 ounces)
  Dried oregano leaves **or** crushed red pepper

1. Spread the soup on the crust to within ¼ inch of the edge. Bake at 450°F. for 5 minutes.

2. Heat the oil in a 10-inch skillet over medium heat. Add the vegetables and garlic powder and cook until the vegetables are tender-crisp, stirring occasionally.

3. Spoon the vegetables on the pizza. Top with the chicken and cheese. Sprinkle with the oregano, if desired.

4. Bake for 5 minutes or until the cheese is melted.

Turkey & Avocado Sandwiches

prep 10 minutes | **makes** 4 servings

- 4   **leaves lettuce**
- 8   **thin slices deli turkey breast (about 8 ounces)**
- ½   **peeled pitted avocado, cut into 8 slices**
- 8   **slices Pepperidge Farm® Whole Grain 15 Grain Bread, toasted**
- 2   **tablespoons Pace® Chunky Salsa**

Divide the lettuce, turkey and avocado among **4** bread slices. Top **each** with **1½ teaspoons** salsa and the remaining bread slices.

Halibut with Beans and Spinach

prep 10 minutes | **cook** 15 minutes | **makes** 4 servings

- 2 tablespoons olive oil
- 1 teaspoon minced garlic
- 4 fresh halibut fillets (6 ounces **each**)
- 1¾ cups Swanson® Chicken Stock
- 2 tablespoons lemon juice
- 2 cups frozen cut leaf spinach
- 1 can (about 15 ounces) Great Northern beans, rinsed and drained
  Generous dash crushed red pepper

1. Stir **1 tablespoon** of the oil and garlic in a shallow dish. Add the halibut and turn to coat.

2. Heat the remaining oil in a 10-inch skillet over medium-high heat. Add the fish and cook for about 4 minutes, turning halfway through cooking. Remove the fish with a spatula.

3. Stir the stock and lemon juice into the skillet. Heat to a boil. Add the spinach, beans and red pepper. Return the fish to the skillet. Reduce the heat to low. Cover and cook for 2 minutes or until the fish flakes easily when tested with a fork and the mixture is hot and bubbling.

Tomato Soup Spice Cupcakes

prep 10 minutes | **bake** 20 minutes | **cool** 20 minutes |
makes 24 servings

- 1 box (about 18 ounces) spice cake mix
- 1 can (10¾ ounces) Campbell's® Condensed Tomato Soup (Regular **or** Healthy Request®)
- ½ cup water
- 2 eggs
  Store-bought **or** homemade cream cheese frosting

1. Heat the oven to 350°F. Place liners into **24** (2½-inch) muffin-pan cups.

2. Combine the cake mix, soup, water and eggs in a large bowl and mix according to the package directions. Spoon the batter into the muffin-pan cups.

3. Bake for 20 minutes or until a toothpick inserted in the center of a cupcake comes out clean.

4. Let the cupcakes cool in the pans on wire racks for 10 minutes. Remove the cupcakes from the pans and let cool completely.

5. Frost with your favorite cream cheese frosting.

Tip: After frosting, you can sprinkle the cupcakes with toasted chopped pecans **or** walnuts.

Oven-Roasted Chicken with Artichokes, Lemon and Tomato Sauce

prep 15 minutes | **roast** 35 minutes | **makes** 6 servings

- 6 **skinless, boneless chicken breast halves (about 1½ pounds)**
- 1 **package (8 ounces) frozen artichoke hearts, cut into quarters**
- 3 **cups Prego® Heart Smart Roasted Red Pepper & Garlic Italian Sauce**
- 1 **tablespoon lemon juice**
- 1 **teaspoon grated lemon zest**
- 3 **cups hot cooked couscous**

1. Heat the oven to 400°F.

2. Place the chicken and artichoke hearts into a 17×11-inch shallow roasting pan. Stir the Italian sauce, lemon juice and lemon zest in a medium bowl. Pour the sauce mixture over the chicken and artichoke hearts.

3. Roast for 35 minutes or until the chicken is cooked through. Serve the chicken mixture over the couscous.

Tip: Try sprinkling the finished dish with some chopped pitted kalamata olives.

August 28

Frosty Fruit Cooler

prep 10 minutes | **makes** 2 servings

1	cup V8 Splash® Mango Peach Juice Drink
¼	cup vanilla yogurt
½	cup cut-up strawberries **or** raspberries
½	cup ice cubes

Put all of the ingredients in a blender. Cover and blend until smooth. Serve immediately.

Tip: Place in an insulated thermos, so kids can take it with them on-the-go. Recipe may be doubled.

Creamy 3-Cheese Pasta

prep 20 minutes | **bake** 20 minutes | **makes** 4 servings

- 1 **can (10¾ ounces) Campbell's® Condensed Cream of Mushroom Soup (Regular or 98% Fat Free)**
- 1 **package (8 ounces) shredded two-cheese blend (about 2 cups)**
- ⅓ **cup grated Parmesan cheese**
- 1 **cup milk**
- ¼ **teaspoon ground black pepper**
- 3 **cups corkscrew-shaped pasta (rotini), cooked and drained**

1. Stir the soup, cheeses, milk and black pepper in a 1½-quart casserole. Stir in the pasta.

2. Bake at 400°F. for 20 minutes or until the pasta mixture is hot and bubbling.

Spring Salmon Salad Sandwiches

prep 10 minutes | **makes** 2 servings

- 2 tablespoons reduced-fat sour cream
- 2 tablespoons mayonnaise
- 2 teaspoons lemon juice
- 1 tablespoon chopped fresh dill weed **or** dried dill weed
- 1 can (6 ounces) chunk salmon packed in water, drained

  Freshly ground black pepper

  Red leaf lettuce leaves
- 4 slices Pepperidge Farm® Whole Grain 100% Whole Wheat Bread
- 12 thin cucumbers slices

1. Stir the sour cream, mayonnaise, lemon juice and dill in a medium bowl. Add the salmon and toss to coat. Season with the black pepper.

2. Divide the lettuce and salmon mixture between 2 bread slices. Top with the cucumber and remaining bread slices.

Salsa Onion Dip

prep 5 minutes | **chill** 2 hours | **makes** 24 servings (about 3 cups)

- 1 **envelope (about 1 ounce) dry onion soup and recipe mix**
- 1 **container (16 ounces) sour cream**
- 1 **cup Pace® Chunky Salsa**
  Sliced green onion
  Tortilla chips or fresh vegetables

Stir the soup mix, sour cream and salsa in a medium bowl. Cover and refrigerate for 2 hours. Sprinkle with the onion. Serve with the tortilla chips for dipping.

Dilled Tuna & Egg Sandwiches

prep 10 minutes | **makes** 3 servings

- 1 can (6 ounces) low-sodium chunk white tuna in water, drained
- 2 hard-cooked egg whites, chopped
- ⅓ cup nonfat sour cream
- 2 tablespoons chopped green onions
- 2 teaspoons Dijon-style mustard
- 2 teaspoons chopped fresh dill weed (optional)
- 6 slices Pepperidge Farm® 100% Natural Nine Grain Bread, toasted

  Romaine lettuce leaves

1. Stir the tuna, egg whites, sour cream, green onions, mustard and dill weed, if desired, in a medium bowl.

2. Divide the tuna mixture among **3** bread slices. Top with the lettuce and remaining bread slices.

Mini Tacos

prep 20 minutes | **bake** 5 minutes | **makes** 24 servings

- 24 **wonton wrappers**
- 1 **pound lean ground beef**
- 1 **package (about 1 ounce) taco seasoning mix**
- 2 **tablespoons Pace® Picante Sauce**
- ½ **cup Pace® Chunky Salsa**
- 4 **ounces shredded Mexican cheese blend (about 1 cup)**
  Sour cream (optional)
  Sliced pitted ripe olives (optional)

1. Heat the oven to 425°F. Press the wonton wrappers into **24** (1½-inch) mini muffin-pan cups.

2. Cook the beef in a 10-inch skillet over medium-high heat until well browned, stirring often to separate the meat. Pour off any fat. Stir in the taco seasoning mix and picante sauce.

3. Spoon the beef mixture into the wonton cups. Top with the salsa and cheese.

4. Bake for 5 minutes or until the wontons are golden brown and the cheese is melted.

5. Garnish with sour cream and olives, if desired. Serve immediately with additional salsa.

Crispy Chicken with Asparagus Sauce

prep 10 minutes | **cook** 20 minutes | **makes** 4 servings

- 1 **egg**
- 4 **skinless, boneless chicken breast halves (about 1 pound)**
- ½ **cup dry bread crumbs**
- 2 **tablespoons vegetable oil**
- 1 **can (10¾ ounces) Campbell's® Condensed Cream of Asparagus Soup**
- ⅓ **cup milk**
- ⅓ **cup water**
- 4 **cups hot cooked rice**
  Grated Parmesan cheese

1. Beat the egg in a shallow dish with a fork or whisk. Dip the chicken into the egg. Coat the chicken with the bread crumbs.

2. Heat the oil in a 10-inch skillet over medium-high heat. Add the chicken and cook for 15 minutes or until well browned on both sides and cooked through. Remove the chicken from the skillet and keep warm.

3. Stir the soup, milk and water in the skillet and heat over medium heat until the mixture is hot and bubbling. Serve the chicken and sauce with the rice. Sprinkle with the cheese.

Curried Chicken Spread

prep 10 minutes | **makes** 10 servings (1¼ cups)

- **3** tablespoons nonfat mayonnaise
- **3** tablespoons chopped chutney
- **¼** teaspoon curry powder
- **1** can (4.5 ounces) Swanson® Premium Chunk Chicken Breast in Water, drained
- **½** cup chopped Granny Smith apple
- **1** tablespoon chopped, unsalted dry roasted peanuts

Stir the mayonnaise, chutney, curry powder, chicken, apple and peanuts in a small bowl.

Citrus Cooler

prep 5 minutes | **makes** 6 servings

- 3 **cups V8® 100% Vegetable Juice**
- 1½ **cups orange juice**
- 1½ **cups seltzer water or club soda**
- ¼ **cup lime juice**
- **Orange and lime slice for garnish**

Stir the vegetable juice, orange juice, seltzer and lime juice in a large pitcher. Serve over ice. Garnish with orange and lime slices.

Oven-Fried Chicken Chimichangas

prep 20 minutes | **bake** 25 minutes | **makes** 6 servings

- ⅔ **cup Pace® Picante Sauce**
- 1 **teaspoon ground cumin**
- ½ **teaspoon dried oregano leaves, crushed**
- 1½ **cups chopped cooked chicken**
- 4 **ounces shredded Cheddar cheese (about 1 cup)**
- 2 **green onions, chopped (about ¼ cup)**
- 6 **flour tortillas (8-inch)**
- 2 **tablespoons butter, melted**
  Fresh cilantro leaves

1. Stir the picante sauce, cumin, oregano, chicken, cheese and onions in a medium bowl.

2. Place **about ½ cup** of the chicken mixture in the center of **each** tortilla. Fold the opposite sides over the filling. Roll up from the bottom and place seam-side down on a baking sheet. Brush with butter.

3. Bake at 400°F. for 25 minutes or until golden brown. Garnish with cilantro. Serve with additional picante sauce.

Tip: For 1½ **cups** chopped chicken, in a 2-quart saucepan over medium heat, in **4 cups** boiling water, cook ¾ **pound** boneless chicken breasts **or** thighs, cubed, for 5 minutes or until the chicken is cooked through. Drain and chop the chicken.

Punchy Piña Colada

prep 10 minutes | **makes** 10 servings

- **1 can (about 20 ounces) pineapple chunks in juice**
- **1 can (about 15 ounces) cream of coconut**
- **2 bottles (16 ounces each) V8 Splash® Tropical Blend Juice Drink (4 cups)**
- **3 cups ice cubes**
- **½ cup light rum (optional)**

1. Put the pineapple with juice and cream of coconut in a blender. Cover and blend until the mixture is smooth. Pour the mixture into a 3-quart pitcher.

2. Put the juice drink and ice cubes into the blender. Cover and blend until the mixture is smooth. Add to the pineapple mixture and stir in the rum, if desired. Serve immediately.

Sizzling Fajitas

prep 10 minutes | **cook** 15 minutes | **makes** 4 servings

- 2 **tablespoons vegetable oil**
- 1 **pound skinless, boneless chicken breast or beef sirloin steak, cut into strips**
- 1 **medium green or red pepper, cut into 2-inch-long strips (about 1½ cups)**
- 1 **medium onion, sliced (about ½ cup)**
- 1½ **cups Pace® Picante Sauce**
- 8 **flour tortillas (8-inch), warmed**
  Guacamole (optional)

1. Heat the oil in a 12-inch skillet over medium-high heat. Add the chicken and cook until well browned, stirring often.

2. Stir the pepper and onion in the skillet and cook until tender-crisp. Stir the picante sauce in the skillet and cook until the mixture is hot and bubbling.

3. Spoon **about ½ cup** chicken mixture down the center of **each** tortilla. Top with additional picante sauce. Fold the tortillas around the filling. Serve with the guacamole, if desired.

Chocolate Goldfish® Pretzel Clusters

prep 5 minutes | **cook** 1 minute | **chill** 30 minutes | **makes** 24 servings

1	package (12 ounces) semi-sweet chocolate pieces (about 2 cups)
2½	cups Pepperidge Farm® Pretzel Goldfish® Crackers
1	container (4 ounces) multi-colored nonpareils

1. Line a baking sheet with wax paper.

2. Place the chocolate into a microwavable bowl. Microwave on MEDIUM for 30 seconds. Stir. Repeat until the chocolate is melted and smooth. Add the Goldfish® crackers and stir to coat.

3. Drop the chocolate mixture by tablespoonfuls onto the baking sheet. Sprinkle the clusters with the nonpareils.

4. Refrigerate for 30 minutes or until the clusters are firm. Keep refrigerated until ready to serve.

Tip: To wrap for gift-giving, arrange the clusters in a small box lined with colored plastic wrap.

Sweet & Spicy Chicken Wings

prep 10 minutes | **bake** 55 minutes | **makes** 24 appetizers

- 1 cup **Pace® Picante Sauce**
- ¼ cup **honey**
- ½ teaspoon **ground ginger**
- 12 **chicken wings or chicken drummettes**

1. Stir the picante sauce, honey and ginger in a small bowl.

2. Cut the chicken wings at the joints into **24** pieces. Discard the tips or save them for another use. Put the wings in a small bowl. Add the picante sauce mixture and toss to coat. Put the wings on a foil-lined shallow baking pan.

3. Bake at 400°F. for 55 minutes or until the wings are glazed and cooked through, turning and brushing often with sauce during the last 30 minutes of cooking.

Spinach Onion Dip

prep 10 minutes | **chill** 2 hours | **makes** 20 servings (about 2½ cups)

- 1 envelope (about 1 ounce) dry onion soup and recipe mix
- 1 container (16 ounces) sour cream
- 1 package (about 10 ounces) frozen chopped spinach, thawed and well drained
- ⅓ cup chopped toasted almonds (optional)
  Assorted Pepperidge Farm® Crackers, chips **or** fresh vegetables

Stir the soup mix, sour cream, spinach and almonds, if desired, in a medium bowl. Cover and refrigerate for 2 hours. Serve with the crackers for dipping.

Tip: To thaw the spinach, microwave on HIGH for 3 minutes, breaking apart with a fork halfway through heating.

White Tomato Herb Pizza

thaw 40 minutes | prep 15 minutes | bake 20 minutes | makes 2 servings

- ½ **of a 17.3-ounce package Pepperidge Farm® Puff Pastry Sheets (1 sheet), thawed**
- 2 **tablespoons olive oil**
- ¼ **cup grated Parmesan cheese**
- ⅔ **cup ricotta cheese**
- 2 **medium plum tomatoes, sliced**
- 2 **tablespoons chopped fresh basil leaves**

1. Heat the oven to 375°F. Line a baking sheet with parchment paper or spray with vegetable cooking spray.

2. Unfold the pastry on a lightly floured surface. Roll into a 9 × 13-inch rectangle. Cut the rectangle into **2** (4½ × 12-inch) rectangles. Roll in the edges to form a rim. Place the pastry rectangles on the baking sheet. Drizzle **each** with **1 tablespoon** olive oil.

3. Stir **2 tablespoons** Parmesan cheese and ricotta cheese in a small bowl.

4. Top **each** pastry rectangle with **half** the ricotta cheese mixture, **half** the tomatoes, **half** the basil and **half** the remaining Parmesan cheese.

5. Bake for 20 minutes or until the crust is golden.

August 20

Mediterranean Chop Salad

prep 25 minutes | **makes** 8 servings

- 3   stalks celery, sliced (about 1½ cups) **or** 1 cup sliced fennel
- 1   cup chopped roasted red **or** yellow pepper
- 1   large seedless cucumber, peeled and chopped (about 1⅔ cups)
- ½   cup chopped pitted ripe olives
- ½   cup prepared balsamic vinaigrette salad dressing
- 1   package (12 ounces) hearts of romaine, chopped (about 8 cups)
- 1   box (5.5 ounces) Pepperidge Farm® Seasoned Croutons (your favorite variety)
-   Freshly ground black pepper
-   Parmesan cheese shavings

1. Stir the celery, pepper, cucumber, olives and dressing in a large serving bowl. Cover and refrigerate until serving time.

2. Add the lettuce and croutons to the dressing mixture just before serving and toss to coat. Season with the black pepper. Top with the cheese.

Panhandle Pepperoni Chicken

prep 10 minutes | **cook** 20 minutes | **makes** 4 servings

- 1 tablespoon olive oil **or** vegetable oil
- 4 skinless, boneless chicken breasts halves (about 1 pound)
- 1 cup Pace® Picante Sauce
- 1 teaspoon Italian seasoning, crushed
- 1 medium green pepper, cut into 1-inch pieces (about 1 cup)
- ⅓ cup chopped pepperoni
  Shredded mozzarella cheese for garnish
- 4 cups hot cooked rice

1. Heat the oil in a 10-inch skillet over medium-high heat. Add the chicken and cook for 10 minutes or until well browned on both sides. Remove the chicken and set aside. Pour off any fat.

2. Stir the picante sauce, Italian seasoning, green pepper and pepperoni into the skillet. Heat to a boil. Return chicken to the pan. Reduce heat to low. Cover and cook for 5 minutes or until the chicken is cooked through. Garnish with the cheese. Serve with the rice.

Tuna Melts

prep 10 minutes | **broil** 3 minutes | **makes** 2 servings

- 1 **can (about 6 ounces) tuna, drained and flaked**
- ¼ **cup chopped celery**
- 2 **tablespoons mayonnaise**
- 4 **slices Pepperidge Farm® Farmhouse® Soft Hearty White Bread, toasted**
- 4 **slices Cheddar cheese or process American cheese (about 4 ounces)**

1. Stir the tuna, celery and mayonnaise in a medium bowl.

2. Place the toast on a rack in a broiler pan. Divide the tuna mixture evenly among the toast and spread to the edges. Top the tuna mixture with the cheese.

3. Heat the broiler. Broil 4 inches from heat for 3 minutes or until the cheese is melted.

Tip: In the second step, place the toast on a microwave-safe plate. Divide the tuna mixture evenly among the toast. Top with the cheese. Microwave on HIGH for 1½ minutes or until the cheese is melted.

Simple Creamy Chicken Risotto

prep 10 minutes | **cook** 35 minutes | **makes** 4 servings

- **1** tablespoon vegetable oil
- **4** skinless, boneless chicken breast halves (about 1 pound), cut into 1-inch pieces
- **1** can (10¾ ounces) Campbell's® Condensed Cream of Mushroom with Roasted Garlic Soup
- **1** can (10½ ounces) Campbell's® Condensed Chicken Broth
- **¾** cup water
- **1** small carrot, shredded (about ¼ cup)
- **2** green onions, sliced (about ¼ cup)
- **1** tablespoon grated Parmesan cheese
- **1** cup **uncooked** regular long-grain white rice

1. Heat the oil in a 10-inch skillet over medium-high heat. Add the chicken and cook until well browned, stirring often.

2. Stir the soup, broth, water, carrot, green onions and cheese in the skillet and heat to a boil. Stir in the rice. Reduce the heat to low. Cover and cook for 25 minutes or until the chicken is cooked through and the rice is tender.

Grilled Swordfish Steaks with Citrus Salsa

prep 20 minutes | **grill** 10 minutes | **makes** 4 servings

- ¾ **cup Pace® Picante Sauce**
- 1 **teaspoon grated orange zest**
- 2 **tablespoons orange juice**
- 1 **tablespoon chopped fresh cilantro leaves**
- 1 **cup coarsely chopped orange**
- 1 **medium tomato, chopped (about 1 cup)**
- 2 **green onions, sliced (about ¼ cup)**
- 4 **swordfish steaks, 1-inch thick (about 1½ pounds)**

1. Stir the picante sauce, orange zest, orange juice and cilantro in a medium bowl. Reserve ½ **cup** to baste the fish. For the salsa, add the orange, tomato and onions to the remaining picante sauce mixture. Set the salsa aside.

2. Lightly oil the grill rack and heat the grill to medium. Grill the fish for 10 minutes or until cooked through, turning the fish over once during grilling and brushing often with the reserved picante sauce mixture. Discard the remaining picante sauce mixture.

3. Serve the fish with the citrus salsa.

Spinach and Feta Mini-Calzones

thaw 40 minutes | **prep** 30 minutes | **bake** 15 minutes | **cool** 10 minutes | **makes** 16 servings

- ½ **of a 17.3-ounce package Pepperidge Farm® Puff Pastry Sheets (1 sheet), thawed**
- 1 **tablespoon olive oil**
- 1 **small onion, chopped (about ¼ cup)**
- 1 **package (10 ounces) frozen chopped spinach, thawed and well drained**
- ½ **cup crumbled feta cheese (plain or flavored)**
- ¼ **teaspoon ground black pepper**

1. Heat the oven to 400°F.

2. Heat the oil in a 10-inch skillet over medium heat. Add the onion and cook until tender. Add the spinach and cook for 3 minutes. Remove the skillet from the heat. Stir in the cheese and black pepper. Let the mixture cool to room temperature.

3. Unfold the pastry sheet on a lightly floured surface. Roll the pastry sheet into a 12-inch square. Cut into **16** (3-inch) squares. Brush edges of the squares with water. Place **about 1 tablespoon** spinach mixture in the center of each square. Fold the pastry over the filling to form triangles. Press the edges to seal. Place the filled pastries onto a baking sheet.

4. Bake for 15 minutes or until the pastries are golden brown. Remove the pastries from the baking sheet and let cool on wire racks for 10 minutes.

Tropical Champagne Ice

prep 15 minutes | **freeze** 3 hours | **makes** 18 servings

- 6 **cups V8 Splash® Tropical Blend Juice Drink, chilled**
- 1 **bottle (750 ml) champagne or other sparkling wine, chilled**
- 1 **teaspoon grated orange zest (optional)**
- 4½ **cups cut-up fresh fruit (mango, papaya or pineapple)**

1. Stir the juice drink, champagne and orange zest, if desired, in a 13×9×2-inch metal baking pan.

2. Cover the pan and freeze it for 3 hours, stirring with a fork every hour.

3. Scoop **about ½ cup** of the champagne ice into a stemmed glass or dessert glass. Top with the fruit. Serve immediately.

Tip: If you have any leftover ice, wrap the pan with plastic wrap and store in the freezer. When you want to serve it, remove it from the freezer about 5 minutes before serving to allow it to soften a bit before scooping.

Quick Chicken Mozzarella Sandwiches

prep 5 minutes | **cook** 15 minutes | **makes** 4 servings

1½ **cups Prego® Three Cheese Italian Sauce**
4 **refrigerated or thawed frozen cooked breaded chicken cutlets**
4 **slices mozzarella cheese**
4 **round hard rolls**

1. Heat the Italian sauce in a 10-inch skillet over medium heat to a boil. Place the chicken in the sauce. Reduce the heat to low. Cover and cook for 5 minutes or until the chicken is heated through.

2. Top the chicken with the cheese. Cover and cook until the cheese is melted. Serve on the rolls.

Cheesy Chicken Enchiladas Verde

prep 15 minutes | **bake** 20 minutes | **makes** 4 servings

- 1 jar (16 ounces) Pace® Salsa Verde
- 1½ cups shredded cooked chicken
- ½ cup sour cream
- 6 ounces shredded Cheddar Jack cheese (about 1½ cups)
- 8 corn tortillas **or** flour tortillas (6-inch), warmed

1. Heat the oven to 375°F. Spread ½ **cup** salsa verde in a 2-quart shallow baking dish.

2. Stir ¼ **cup** salsa verde, chicken, sour cream and ½ **cup** cheese in a medium bowl. Spoon **about 3 tablespoons** of the chicken mixture down the center of **each** tortilla. Roll up and place seam-side down in the baking dish. Top with the remaining salsa verde.

3. Bake for 15 minutes. Top with the remaining cheese and bake for 5 minutes or until the cheese is melted.

Buffalo Burgers

prep 10 minutes | **grill** 10 minutes | **cook** 10 minutes | **makes** 4 servings

1	**pound ground beef**
1	**can (10¾ ounces) Campbell's® Condensed Tomato Soup (Regular or Healthy Request®)**
½	**teaspoon Louisiana-style hot sauce**
½	**cup crumbled blue cheese or 4 slices blue cheese**
4	**Pepperidge Farm® Hamburger Buns, split**
	Lettuce leaves, red onion slices, tomato slices (optional)

1. Shape the beef into **4** (½-inch-thick) burgers.

2. Lightly oil the grill rack and heat the grill to medium. Grill the burgers for 10 minutes for medium or to desired doneness, turning the burgers over once halfway through the grilling time.

3. Heat the soup and hot sauce in a 1-quart saucepan over medium heat to a boil. Reduce the heat to low. Cover and cook for 5 minutes. Top the burgers with the soup mixture. Sprinkle with the cheese. Serve the burgers on the buns with the lettuce, onion and tomato, if desired.

Tip: Any leftover soup mixture can also be a great dipping sauce for French fries.

Black and White Bean Salad

prep 15 minutes | **chill** 2 hours | **makes** 4 servings

- 1 cup V8® 100% Vegetable Juice*
- 1 tablespoon vegetable oil
- ¼ teaspoon garlic powder **or** 1 clove garlic, minced
- 1 can (about 15 ounces) black beans, rinsed and drained
- 1 can (about 15 ounces) small white beans, rinsed and drained
- 1 can (about 8 ounces) whole kernel corn, drained
- 1 large green **or** red pepper, chopped (about 1 cup)
- 1 medium onion, chopped (about ½ cup)

*Also delicious with Low Sodium V8®, Calcium Enriched V8® **or** Essential Antioxidants V8® .*

Stir the vegetable juice, oil, garlic powder, black beans, white beans, corn, pepper and onion in a large bowl until evenly coated. Refrigerate for at least 2 hours.

Company Buffet Layered Salad

prep 35 minutes | **chill** 4 hours | **makes** 12 servings

- 1 can (10¾ ounces) Campbell's® Condensed Cream of Mushroom Soup (Regular **or** 98% Fat Free)
- 1 cup sour cream, plain yogurt **or** mayonnaise
- ¼ cup grated Parmesan Cheese
- 1 tablespoon grated onion
- 6 cups mixed salad greens, torn into bite-sized pieces
- 2 medium carrots, zucchini **or** cucumbers, thinly sliced
- 2 cups sliced mushrooms (about 6 ounces)
- 2 medium tomatoes, diced (about 2 cups)
- 4 green onions, sliced (about ½ cup)
  Sliced pitted ripe olives, parsley **or** chopped hard-cooked egg

1. Stir the soup, sour cream, cheese and onion in a small bowl.

2. Layer the salad greens, carrots, mushrooms and tomatoes in a clear 4-quart serving bowl. Spread the soup mixture over the salad. Cover and refrigerate for 4 hours. Sprinkle with the green onions and olives before serving.

Tip: Substitute Campbell's® Condensed Cream of Celery **or** Cream of Chicken Soup for the Cream of Mushroom Soup.

Whole Wheat Chicken Salad Sandwiches

prep 10 minutes | **makes** 4 servings

- 2 cans (4.5 ounces **each**) Swanson® Premium White Chunk Chicken Breast in Water, drained
- ¼ cup chopped celery
- 1 tablespoon finely chopped onion
- 2 tablespoons nonfat mayonnaise
- 2 tablespoons nonfat plain yogurt
- ⅛ teaspoon ground black pepper
- 8 slices Pepperidge Farm® Whole Grain 100% Whole Wheat Bread
- 8 tomato slices
- 4 lettuce leaves

1. Stir the chicken, celery, onion, mayonnaise, yogurt and black pepper in a small bowl.

2. Divide the chicken mixture among **4** bread slices. Top **each** with **2** slices tomato, **1** leaf lettuce and **1** remaining bread slice.

Creamy Vegetable Penne

prep 10 minutes | **cook** 20 minutes | **makes** 4 servings

2	tablespoons olive oil
1	bag (16 ounces) frozen vegetable combination (broccoli, cauliflower, carrots), thawed
3	cloves garlic, minced
1	can (10¾ ounces) Campbell's® Condensed Cream of Mushroom Soup (Regular **or** 98% Fat Free)
1	teaspoon dried basil leaves, crushed
1	can (about 14.5 ounces) diced tomatoes, undrained
½	of a 1-pound package medium tube-shaped pasta (penne) (about 2½ cups), cooked and drained
	Grated Parmesan cheese

1. Heat the oil in a 12-inch skillet over medium-high heat. Add the vegetables and garlic and cook for 2 minutes.

2. Stir the soup, basil and tomatoes in the skillet and heat to a boil. Reduce the heat to low. Cover and cook for 10 minutes, or until the vegetables are tender.

3. Place the pasta into a large serving bowl. Add the vegetable mixture and toss to coat. Sprinkle with the Parmesan cheese.

Cool & Creamy Fruit Smoothies

prep 10 minutes | **makes** 2 servings

- 1 **cup V8 Splash® Smoothies Strawberry Banana**
- ½ **cup peach sorbet or your favorite flavor**
- ½ **cup vanilla low-fat yogurt**
- ½ **cup fresh strawberries, cut into quarters**

Put all of the ingredients in a blender. Cover and blend until smooth. Serve immediately.

Goldfish Pizzas

prep 15 minutes | **bake** 10 minutes | **makes** 4 servings

- 2 **pieces Pepperidge Farm® Goldfish™ 100% Whole Wheat Sandwich Bread, split**
- ¼ **cup Prego® Traditional Italian Sauce**
- ½ **cup shredded part–skim mozzarella cheese Pitted ripe olives (optional)**

1. Heat the oven to 350°F. Place the bread pieces, split-side up, onto a baking sheet.

2. Spread **1 tablespoon** Italian sauce on **each** bread piece. Top **each** with **2 tablespoons** cheese.

3. Bake for 10 minutes or until the cheese is melted. Decorate the faces of the goldfish with the olives, if desired.

Tip: For a more crispy crust, split and toast the bread pieces before topping with the sauce and cheese.

Barbecued Chicken Sandwiches

prep 10 minutes | **cook** 15 minutes | **makes** 4 servings

- 1 tablespoon butter
- 1 small green pepper, chopped (about ½ cup) (optional)
- 1 small onion, chopped (about ¼ cup)
- ¼ cup chopped celery
- ½ cup barbecue sauce
- 2 cans (4.5 ounces **each**) Swanson® Premium White Chunk Chicken Breast in Water, drained
- 4 Pepperidge Farm® Classic Sandwich Buns with Sesame Seeds, split and toasted

1. Heat the butter in a 2-quart saucepan over medium heat. Stir the pepper, onion and celery in the saucepan and cook until tender.

2. Stir the barbecue sauce and chicken in the saucepan. Heat until the mixture is hot and bubbling. Divide the chicken mixture among the buns.

June 5

Mediterranean Tuna Salad

prep 10 minutes | **makes** 2 servings

- 1 small head romaine lettuce, torn into bite-sized pieces (about 5 cups)
- 1 can (about 6 ounces) tuna packed in water, drained and flaked
- 2 hard-cooked eggs, cut into wedges (optional)
- 2 tablespoons sliced pitted ripe olives
- 1 small red onion, sliced (about ¼ cup)
- ½ cup Pepperidge Farm® Seasoned Croutons
- ¼ cup prepared Italian salad dressing

Arrange the lettuce, tuna, eggs, if desired, olives, onion and croutons on **2** plates. Drizzle with the dressing.

Grilled Fish Steaks with Chunky Tomato Sauce

prep 15 minutes | **cook** 10 minutes | **grill** 10 minutes | **makes** 6 servings

- ½ **cup chopped celery (about 1 stalk)**
- ½ **cup chopped green pepper (about 1 small)**
- ½ **cup chopped onion (about 1 medium)**
- ½ **teaspoon dried thyme leaves, crushed**
- ¼ **teaspoon garlic powder or 2 cloves garlic, minced**
- 1 **can (10¾ ounces) Campbell's® Healthy Request® Condensed Tomato Soup**
- 2 **tablespoons lemon juice**
- ⅛ **teaspoon hot pepper sauce (optional)**
- 6 **swordfish steaks, 1-inch thick**

1. Spray a 2-quart saucepan with cooking spray. Heat over medium heat for 1 minute. Add the celery, pepper, onion, thyme and garlic powder and cook until tender, stirring often.

2. Stir the soup, lemon juice and hot pepper sauce, if desired, in the saucepan and cook until the mixture is hot and bubbling.

3. Lightly oil the grill rack and heat the grill to medium. Grill the fish for 10 minutes or until the fish flakes easily when tested with a fork, turning once during grilling. Serve the soup mixture over the fish.

Range-Top Margherita-Style Pizza

prep 15 minutes | **cook** 5 minutes | **makes** 2 servings

- **2   slices Pepperidge Farm® 100% Natural Nine Grain Bread**
- **Vegetable cooking spray**
- **½   teaspoon dried oregano leaves, crushed**
- **2   medium plum tomatoes, thinly sliced**
- **2   ounces mozzarella cheese, cut up**
- **6   fresh basil leaves, thinly sliced**

1. Spray the top of **each** bread slice with the cooking spray and sprinkle with the oregano.

2. Heat a 10-inch nonstick skillet over medium heat for 1 minute. Add the bread slices, oregano-side down, and cook until lightly browned. Turn the bread slices over.

3. Top the bread slices with the tomatoes and cheese. Cover and cook until the cheese is melted. Sprinkle with the basil.

Tip: Also delicious with Pepperidge Farm® Whole Grain 15 Grain Bread.

Chicken with Picante Peach Salsa

prep 10 minutes | **grill** 15 minutes | **makes** 6 servings

⅔ cup Pace® Picante Sauce

2 tablespoons lime juice

1 can (about 15 ounces) peach halves in heavy syrup, drained and diced

⅓ cup chopped green **or** red pepper

2 green onions, sliced (about ¼ cup)

½ teaspoon ground cumin

½ teaspoon chili powder

6 skinless, boneless chicken breast halves

½ cup peach preserves **or** apricot preserves

1. Stir ⅓ **cup** picante sauce, lime juice, peaches, pepper and onions in a medium bowl. Reserve the mixture to serve with the chicken.

2. Stir the cumin and chili powder in a small bowl. Season the chicken with the cumin mixture. Stir the remaining picante sauce and preserves in a small bowl.

3. Lightly oil the grill rack and heat the grill to medium. Grill the chicken for 15 minutes or until cooked through, turning and brushing often with the preserve mixture. Discard the remaining preserve mixture.

4. Serve the chicken with the peach salsa mixture.

Garden Vegetable Pizza

thaw 4 hours | **prep** 20 minutes | **bake** 25 minutes | **makes** 8 servings

- 2 tablespoons olive oil
- 1 medium onion, sliced (about ½ cup)
- 1 clove garlic, minced
- 1 small eggplant, cubed (about 1½ cups)
- ½ cup red pepper, cut into 1-inch pieces
- ½ cup sliced zucchini
- 1 jar (24 ounces) Prego® Chunky Garden Mushroom Supreme Italian Sauce with Baby Portobello
- 2 loaves (1 pound **each**) frozen white bread dough, thawed
- 6 ounces shredded mozzarella cheese (about 1½ cups)

1. Heat the oven to 375°F. Heat the oil in a 12-inch skillet over medium heat. Stir the onion, garlic, eggplant, pepper and zucchini in the skillet and cook until tender-crisp. Stir the Italian sauce in the skillet.

2. Place the bread dough on a greased 15×10-inch baking pan. Pat the dough to cover the bottom of the pan, forming a single large crust. Pinch up the edges to form a rim. Top the dough with the vegetable mixture and spread it to within 1 inch of the edges. Sprinkle with the cheese.

3. Bake for 25 minutes or until the crust is golden brown.

August 9

Sunset Dip

prep 5 minutes | **cook** 2 minutes | **makes** 12 servings (about 1½ cups)

- **1 package (8 ounces) cream cheese, softened**
- **4 ounces shredded Cheddar cheese (about 1 cup)**
- **1 cup Pace® Picante Sauce or Chunky Salsa**
- **Tortilla chips**

1. Spread the cream cheese in a 9-inch microwavable pie plate. Sprinkle with the Cheddar cheese.

2. Microwave on HIGH for 2 minutes or until the Cheddar cheese is melted. Top with the picante sauce. Serve with the tortilla chips.

Salsa-Ranch Dip

prep 5 minutes | **chill** 1 hour | **makes** 20 servings (2½ cups)

- ¾ cup Pace® Chunky Salsa
- 1 container (16 ounces) sour cream
- 1 package (1.0 ounce) ranch dip mix
  Tortilla chips **or** assorted cut-up fresh vegetables

Stir the salsa, sour cream and dip mix in a small bowl. Cover and refrigerate for 1 hour or until the mixture is chilled. Serve with the tortilla chips or vegetables for dipping.

Picante Glazed Chicken Wings

prep 45 minutes | **bake** 40 minutes | **makes** 12 servings

- 12 **chicken wings** (about 2 pounds)
- 1 **jar (16 ounces) Pace® Picante Sauce**
- ⅓ **cup orange marmalade**
- 2 **teaspoons Dijon-style mustard**
- 1 **tablespoon sesame seeds, toasted**

1. Heat the oven to 425°F. Line a rimmed baking sheet with aluminum foil. Cut off the chicken wing tips and discard. Cut the chicken wings in half at the joint.

2. Heat 1½ **cups** picante sauce, marmalade and mustard in a 2-quart saucepan over medium heat to a boil. Reduce the heat to medium-low. Cook for 40 minutes or until the mixture is reduced to ¾ **cup**, stirring occasionally.

3. Place the chicken into a large bowl. Add the remaining picante sauce and toss to coat. Place the chicken onto the baking sheet.

4. Bake for 40 minutes or until the chicken is cooked through, turning the chicken over once halfway through the bake time. Baste the chicken with the picante-mustard mixture during the last 10 minutes of the bake time. Sprinkle with the sesame seeds, if desired.

Tip: You can substitute **24** chicken drumettes (about 2 pounds) for the **12** chicken wings in this recipe.

Light Ice Cream Soda

prep 5 minutes | **makes** 1 serving

- ½ **cup chilled Diet V8 Splash® Tropical Blend Juice Drink**
- ½ **cup chilled unflavored seltzer water or diet lemon-lime soda**
- ¼ **cup vanilla no-sugar-added ice cream**

Fill a glass with the juice drink and seltzer. Top with the ice cream.

Rainbow Splash Soda: Use Diet V8 Splash® and seltzer **or** sparkling mineral water. Top with small scoops of lime, raspberry **or** lemon sorbet.

August 7

Flank Steak with Mushroom Sauce

prep 20 minutes | **cook** 20 minutes | **makes** 4 servings

    2   **tablespoons olive oil**
    1   **beef flank steak or beef skirt steak (about 1 pound)**
    2   **tablespoons butter**
    8   **ounces mushrooms, sliced (about 3 cups)**
    1   **shallot, diced**
    1   **clove garlic, minced**
    1   **tablespoon chopped fresh rosemary leaves**
    2   **packets Swanson® Flavor Boost™ Concentrated Beef Broth**
    ¼   **cup water**

1. Heat **1 tablespoon** oil in a 10-inch skillet over medium heat. Add the beef and cook until well browned on both sides and until desired doneness, about 10 minutes for medium-rare. Remove the beef from the skillet.

2. Heat **1 tablespoon** butter and the remaining oil in the skillet. Add the mushrooms and cook for 5 minutes or until tender, stirring occasionally. Add the shallot, garlic and rosemary and cook and stir for 30 seconds. Stir in the concentrated broth, water and remaining butter and cool until the butter is melted.

3. Cut the beef diagonally against the grain into thin slices. Serve the mushroom mixture with the beef.

Awesome Grilled Cheese Sandwiches

prep 10 minutes | **cook** 5 minutes | **makes** 3 servings

- 1 **package (11.25 ounces) Pepperidge Farm® Garlic Texas Toast**
- 6 **slices fontina cheese or mozzarella cheese**
- 6 **thin slices deli smoked turkey**
- 3 **thin slices prosciutto**
- 1 **jar (12 ounces) sliced roasted red pepper, drained**

1. Heat a panini or sandwich press according to the manufacturer's directions until hot. (Or, use a cast-iron skillet or ridged grill pan.)

2. Top **3** of the bread slices with **half** of the cheese, turkey, prosciutto, peppers and remaining cheese. Top with the remaining bread slices.

3. Put the sandwiches on the press, closing the lid onto the sandwiches. Cook the sandwiches for 5 minutes (if cooking in a skillet or grill pan, press with a spatula occasionally or weigh down with another cast-iron skillet/foil-covered brick), until lightly browned and the bread is crisp and the cheese melts.

Tip: For a spicier flavor, add a dash of crushed red pepper flakes on the cheese when assembling the sandwiches.

Roasted Red Pepper & White Bean Spread

prep 10 minutes | **makes** 16 servings

- 1 cup roasted red peppers
- 1 can (about 15 ounces) small white beans, rinsed and drained
- 2 tablespoons olive oil
- ¼ teaspoon ground black pepper
- ¼ cup crumbled feta cheese
- 1 tablespoon chopped fresh Italian (flat-leaf) parsley
  Pepperidge Farm® Baked Naturals® Multigrain Wheat Crisps with a Touch of Honey

1. Place the roasted peppers, beans, oil, black pepper and **3 tablespoons** cheese into a food processor. Cover and process until the mixture is smooth.

2. Spoon the roasted pepper mixture into a serving bowl and sprinkle with the remaining cheese and the parsley. Serve with the wheat crisps.

Goldfish® Checkerboard Sandwich

prep 5 minutes | **makes** 1 serving

- 1 **slice Pepperidge Farm® White Sandwich Bread**
- 2 **tablespoons crunchy or smooth peanut butter**
- 1 **slice Pepperidge Farm® Whole Grain 100% Whole Wheat Bread**
- 2 **tablespoons grape jelly or your favorite jam**
- 4 **Pepperidge Farm® Goldfish® Cheddar Crackers**

1. Spread the white bread with the peanut butter. Spread the whole wheat bread with the jelly and place the **2** slices together with the filling inside.

2. Cut the sandwich into quarters. Turn over **2** quarters and place them back together on plate to resemble a checkerboard. Top **each** quarter with **1** Goldfish® cracker.

French Onion Burgers

prep 5 minutes | **cook** 20 minutes | **makes** 4 servings

- 1 **pound ground beef**
- 1 **can (10½ ounces) Campbell's® Condensed French Onion Soup**
- 4 **slices cheese**
- 4 **Pepperidge Farm® Sandwich Buns with Sesame Seeds, split**

1. Shape the beef into **4** (½-inch-thick) burgers.

2. Heat a 10-inch skillet over medium-high heat. Add the burgers and cook until well browned on both sides. Remove the burgers from the skillet. Pour off any fat.

3. Stir the soup in the skillet and heat to a boil. Return the burgers to the skillet. Reduce the heat to low. Cover and cook for 5 minutes or until desired doneness. Top the burgers with the cheese and cook until the cheese is melted. Serve the burgers on the buns with the soup mixture for dipping.

Tip: You can also serve these burgers in a bowl atop a mound of hot mashed potatoes with some of the soup mixture poured over.

Savory Vegetable Stir-Fry

prep 10 minutes | **cook** 10 minutes | **makes** 6 servings

- 1   **tablespoon olive oil**
- 2   **medium yellow squash, sliced (about 2 cups)**
- 2   **medium zucchini, sliced**
- ½   **of a 16-ounce package baby-cut carrots (about 2 cups)**
- 1   **medium red onion, cut in half and thickly sliced (about 1 cup)**
- 2   **packets Swanson® Flavor Boost™ Concentrated Vegetable Broth**

1. Heat the oil in a 12-inch skillet over medium-high heat. Add the yellow squash, zucchini, carrots and onion and stir-fry until the vegetables are tender-crisp.

2. Stir the concentrated broth in the skillet and cook until the mixture is hot.

Bourbon Orange Chocolate Lady Dessert

prep 15 minutes | **freeze** 45 minutes | **makes** 4 servings

- **2** ounces (4 tablespoons) bourbon **or** orange juice
- **1** bag (7 ounces) Pepperidge Farm® Orange Milano® Distinctive Cookies
- **1** pint dark chocolate ice cream, softened
  Orange slices
  Orange peel

1. Heat the bourbon in a 1-quart saucepan over high heat to a boil. Reduce the heat to low. Cook for 3 minutes. Remove from heat and let cool. Crush **3** of the cookies.

2. Stir the bourbon, ice cream and crushed cookies in a small bowl.

3. Freeze for 45 minutes or until the mixture is firm. Scoop into dessert dishes. Garnish with orange slices, orange peel, and remaining whole cookies, if desired.

Tip: Recipe may be doubled.

Cool, Cool Gazpacho

prep 30 minutes | **chill** 1 hour | **makes** 6 servings

6	medium tomatoes, peeled, seeded and chopped (about 6 cups)
1½	cups V8® 100% Vegetable Juice
1	medium cucumber, peeled, seeded and diced (about 1⅓ cups)
1	medium onion, finely diced (about ½ cup)
1	small green pepper, finely diced (about ⅓ cup)
2	cloves garlic, minced
¼	cup olive oil
2	tablespoons vinegar
⅛	teaspoon freshly ground black pepper
	Hot pepper sauce to taste

Stir the tomatoes, vegetable juice, cucumber, onion, green pepper, garlic, oil, vinegar, black pepper and hot pepper sauce in a large mixing bowl. Cover the bowl and refrigerate for at least 1 hour or until ready to serve.

Chicken with Peas & Quinoa

prep 10 minutes | **cook** 30 minutes | **makes** 4 servings

- 1 **tablespoon olive oil**
- 1 **pound skinless, boneless chicken tenders**
- 1 **teaspoon smoked paprika**
- 1 **cup uncooked quinoa, rinsed**
- 1½ **cups Swanson® Chicken Broth or Swanson® Chicken Stock**
- 1 **jar (24 ounces) Prego® Veggie Smart® Smooth & Simple Italian Sauce**
- 1 **package (10 ounces) frozen peas, thawed**

1. Heat the oil in a 12-inch skillet over medium-high heat. Add the chicken and cook for 10 minutes or until well browned on both sides. Remove the chicken from the skillet, cover and keep warm.

2. Add the paprika and quinoa to the skillet and stir to coat. Stir in the broth and Italian sauce and heat to a boil. Reduce the heat to medium. Cover and cook for 15 minutes or until the quinoa is tender. Stir in the peas. Return the chicken to the skillet. Cook until the chicken is cooked through.

Cookies 'n' Yogurt

prep 5 minutes | **makes** 1 serving

1 container (6- to 8-ounce) fruit-flavored yogurt
Pepperidge Farm® Nantucket™ Dark Chocolate Chunk
Cookies (1 cookie), any variety, crumbled
Fresh blueberries, cut-up strawberries **or** raspberries

1. Spoon **half** the yogurt into a glass. Top with **half** the crumbled cookie and **half** the berries.

2. Top with the remaining yogurt and berries. Sprinkle with the remaining crumbled cookie.

Nachos Grande

prep 10 minutes | **cook** 15 minutes | **makes** 8 servings

- 1 **can (10¾ ounces) Campbell's® Condensed Cheddar Cheese Soup**
- ½ **cup Pace® Chunky Salsa**
- 1 **pound ground beef**
- 1 **small onion, chopped (about ¼ cup)**
- 5 **cups tortilla chips**
- 1 **medium tomato, chopped (about 1 cup)**
- 1 **jalapeño pepper, sliced (optional)**

1. Stir the soup and salsa in a 2-quart saucepan.

2. Cook the beef and onion in a 10-inch skillet over medium-high heat until the beef is well browned, stirring often to separate the meat. Pour off any fat. Stir ½ **cup** soup mixture in the skillet and cook until the beef mixture is hot and bubbling.

3. Heat the remaining soup mixture over medium heat until hot and bubbling.

4. Place the chips onto a serving platter and top with the beef mixture. Spoon the soup mixture over the beef mixture. Top with the tomato and jalapeño pepper, if desired.

Tip: You can also substitute **1 can** Campbell's® Condensed Fiesta Nacho Cheese Soup for the Cheddar cheese soup and salsa in this recipe.

Oven Glazed Chicken Wings

prep 15 minutes | **bake** 45 minutes | **makes** 24 appetizers

1	cup V8® 100% Vegetable Juice
2	tablespoons honey
2	tablespoons soy sauce
1	teaspoon ground ginger
12	chicken wings (about 2 pounds)

1. Stir the vegetable juice, honey, soy sauce and ginger in a large bowl.

2. Cut the tips off the wings and discard or save for another use. Cut the wings in half at the joints to make **24** pieces. Add the wings to the juice mixture and toss to coat. Place the chicken mixture in a foil-lined shallow baking pan.

3. Bake at 400°F. for 45 minutes or until glazed and the chicken is cooked through, turning and brushing with the sauce during the last 15 minutes of baking time.

Fantastic Cookie Bars

thaw 40 minutes | **prep** 15 minutes | **bake** 30 minutes | **cool** 30 minutes | **makes** 48 pieces

- 1 **package (17.3 ounces) Pepperidge Farm® Puff Pastry Sheets, thawed**
- 1½ **cups chopped pecans**
- 1 **cup sweetened flaked coconut**
- 1 **bag (12 ounces) semi-sweet chocolate pieces (about 2 cups)**
- 1 **can (14 ounces) sweetened condensed milk**

1. Heat the oven to 400°F.

2. Unfold **1** pastry sheet on a lightly floured surface. Roll the pastry sheet into a 12-inch square. Place the pastry sheet onto a baking sheet. Brush the edges with water. Fold over the edges ½ inch on all sides, pressing firmly to form a rim. Prick the center of the pastry thoroughly with a fork. Repeat with the remaining pastry sheet.

3. Bake for 15 minutes, rotating the baking sheets between the top and bottom oven racks halfway through the baking time. Divide the pecans, coconut and chocolate between the pastry crusts. Drizzle **half** the condensed milk over **each**.

4. Bake for 15 minutes or until the pastries are golden brown, rotating the baking sheets between the top and bottom oven racks halfway through the baking time.

5. Let the pastries cool on the baking sheets on wire racks for 30 minutes. Cut **each** pastry into **24** bars.

Milano® Cookie Caramel Ice Cream Cake

prep 20 minutes | **freeze** 6 hours | **makes** 8 servings

- 1 package (6 ounces) Pepperidge Farm® Milano® Cookies
- 3 cups vanilla **or** chocolate ice cream, softened
- ⅓ cup prepared caramel topping

1. Line an 8-inch round cake pan with plastic wrap.

2. Cut the cookies in half crosswise and arrange around the edge of the pan. Place the remaining cookies into the bottom of the pan.

3. Spread **1½ cups** ice cream over the cookies. Drizzle with the caramel topping. Spread the remaining ice cream over the caramel topping. Cover and freeze for 6 hours or until the ice cream is firm.

4. Uncover the pan and invert the cake onto a serving plate. Serve with additional caramel topping.

Tip: Substitute chocolate topping for the caramel topping.

Grilled Chicken Salad

prep 15 minutes | **grill** 15 minutes | **makes** 4 servings

- ¾ cup prepared Italian salad dressing
- 4 skinless, boneless chicken breast halves (about 1 pound)
- 6 cups mixed salad greens torn into bite-size pieces
- 1 medium tomato, coarsely chopped (about 1 cup)
- 1½ cups Pepperidge Farm® Zesty Italian Croutons
- ½ cup grated Parmesan cheese
  Real bacon bits

1. Reserve ½ **cup** dressing.

2. Lightly oil the grill rack and heat the grill to medium. Grill the chicken for 15 minutes or until cooked through, turning and brushing often with the remaining dressing. Remove the chicken to a cutting board. Cut the chicken into thin strips.

3. Place the greens, tomato, chicken, croutons and cheese into a large bowl. Add the reserved dressing and toss to coat. Top with the bacon bits.

June 17

BLT Salad Toss

prep 20 minutes | **makes** 6 servings

- ½ **cup Pace® Picante Sauce**
- ¼ **cup prepared Italian salad dressing**
- 6 **cups romaine lettuce, torn into bite-sized pieces**
- 2 **medium tomatoes, cut into thin wedges**
- ⅔ **cup sliced pitted ripe olives**
- 2 **cups corn chips**
- 2 **ounces shredded Cheddar cheese (about ½ cup)**
- 3 **slices bacon, cooked and crumbled**

1. Stir the picante sauce and dressing in a large bowl.
2. Add the lettuce, tomatoes, olives and chips and toss to coat. Top with the cheese and bacon. Serve immediately.

Bulgur Salad

prep 10 minutes | **cook** 5 minutes | **stand** 20 minutes | **makes** 6 servings

- 1¼ **cups water**
- 1 **cup uncooked bulgur wheat**
- 1 **cup Pace® Pico De Gallo or Pace® Picante Sauce**
- 1 **cup rinsed, drained canned black beans**
- 1 **cup drained canned whole kernel corn**
- ¼ **cup chopped fresh cilantro leaves**

1. Heat the water in a 2-quart saucepan over medium-high heat to a boil. Stir the bulgur into the saucepan. Remove the saucepan from the heat. Let stand for 20 minutes.

2. Stir the bulgur, pico de gallo, beans, corn and cilantro in a medium bowl. Serve immediately or cover and refrigerate until ready to serve.

Tip: For a twist, stir in a squeeze of fresh lime juice.

Italian Dipping Sauce

prep 5 minutes | **cook** 5 minutes | **makes** 8 servings

- 1 **cup Prego® Traditional Italian Sauce or** Tomato, **Basil & Garlic Italian Sauce**
- 2 **tablespoons grated Parmesan cheese**
  Assorted fresh vegetables for dipping

Heat the sauce and cheese in a 1-quart saucepan over medium heat until the mixture is hot and bubbling. Serve with the vegetables.

Tip: This sauce is also delicious served with chicken nuggets, mozzarella sticks **or** fish sticks for dipping.

Roasted Tomato & Eggplant Bisque

prep 20 minutes | **roast** 25 minutes | **cook** 10 minutes | **makes** 6 servings

- 1 **medium eggplant, peeled and diced (about 4 cups)**
- 4 **large plum tomatoes, cut into quarters**
- 2 **cloves garlic, sliced**
- 1 **tablespoon olive oil**
- 4 **cups Swanson® Vegetable Broth (Regular or Certified Organic)**
- ½ **cup crumbled feta cheese**
- 2 **tablespoons light cream**
- 1 **tablespoon thinly sliced fresh basil leaves**

1. Heat the oven to 425°F. Arrange the eggplant, tomatoes and garlic in a 13×9-inch roasting pan. Pour the oil over the vegetables and toss to coat. Roast for 25 minutes.

2. Place the vegetable mixture in an electric blender or food processor container with **1 cup** of the broth and ¼ **cup** of the cheese. Cover and blend until smooth. Pour the puréed mixture into a 3-quart saucepan and add the remaining broth. Heat to a boil. Reduce the heat to low. Stir in the cream and basil. Cook for 5 minutes.

3. Divide the soup among **6** serving bowls. Garnish **each** serving of soup with about **2 teaspoons** of the remaining cheese.

Mini Pizzas

prep 5 minutes | **cook** 1 minute | **makes** 2 servings

- ½ cup Prego® Italian Sausage & Garlic Italian Sauce
- 4 slices Italian bread, ½-inch thick, toasted
- 1 ounce shredded mozzarella cheese (about ¼ cup)

1. Spread **about 2 tablespoons** Italian sauce on **each** bread slice. Top with the cheese. Place the pizzas on a microwavable plate.

2. Microwave on HIGH for 1 minute or until the cheese is melted.

Grilled Skewered Shrimp

prep 20 minutes | **grill** 10 minutes | **makes** 6 servings

- ⅔ **cup Pace® Picante Sauce**
- 1   **can (about 8 ounces) tomato sauce**
- 3   **tablespoons packed brown sugar**
- 2   **tablespoons lemon juice**
- 1½ **pounds large shrimp, peeled and deveined**

1. Stir the picante sauce, tomato sauce, brown sugar and lemon juice in a large bowl. Add the shrimp and toss to coat.

2. Thread the shrimp on **12** skewers.

3. Lightly oil the grill rack and heat the grill to medium. Grill the shrimp for 10 minutes or until cooked through, turning and brushing often with the picante sauce mixture. Discard any remaining picante sauce mixture.

Tip: For even easier preparation, you can buy frozen large shrimp already peeled and deveined. Just thaw and use instead of the fresh shrimp.

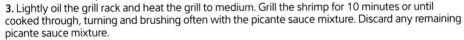

Spring Garden Vegetable Sandwiches

prep 15 minutes | **makes** 2 servings

- 4 tablespoons Neufchâtel cheese, softened
- 4 slices Pepperidge Farm® 100% Natural Honey Flax Bread, toasted
- 1 medium cucumber, peeled and thinly sliced (about 1⅔ cups)
- 2 medium carrots, shredded (about 1 cup)
- 1 cup spring salad mix
- 1 green onion, thinly sliced (about 2 tablespoons)
- 3 tablespoons fat-free sun-dried tomato salad dressing

1. Spread the cheese on the bread slices.

2. Arrange the cucumber on **2** bread slices. Place the carrots, spring mix and onions in a medium bowl. Add the dressing and toss to coat. Top the cucumber with the carrot mixture and the remaining bread slices.

Picnic Celery & Potato Salad

prep 15 minutes | **cook** 15 minutes | **chill** 2 hours | **makes** 12 servings

10	medium red potatoes, cut into 1-inch pieces (about 10 cups)
1	can (10¾ ounces) Campbell's® Condensed Cream of Celery Soup (Regular **or** 98% Fat Free)
2	tablespoons prepared mustard
2	tablespoons lemon juice
1	tablespoon cider vinegar
¼	teaspoon prepared horseradish
4	stalks celery, chopped (about 2 cups)
1	small onion, chopped (about ¼ cup)
	Ground black pepper

1. Place the potatoes into a 6-quart saucepot and add water to cover. Heat over medium-high heat to a boil. Reduce the heat to low. Cook for 10 minutes or until the potatoes are tender. Drain the potatoes well in a colander.

2. Stir the soup, mustard, lemon juice, vinegar and horseradish in a large bowl. Add the potatoes, celery and onion and toss to coat. Season with the black pepper. Cover and refrigerate for 2 hours.

Chilled Summer Vegetable Soup

prep 15 minutes | **cook** 10 minutes | **chill** 4 hours | **makes** 6 servings

- 1 **tablespoon vegetable oil**
- 1 **medium zucchini, coarsely chopped (about 1½ cups)**
- 1 **medium carrot, chopped (about ⅓ cup)**
- 2 **green onions, sliced (about ¼ cup)**
- ½ **teaspoon dried basil leaves, crushed**
- ¼ **teaspoon garlic powder or 1 clove garlic, minced**
- 3 **cups V8® 100% Vegetable Juice**
- 1 **can (about 8 ounces) whole kernel corn, drained**
- 1 **large tomato, chopped (about 1½ cups)**

1. Heat the oil in a 3-quart saucepan over medium heat. Add the zucchini, carrot, onions, basil and garlic powder and cook until the vegetables are tender-crisp.

2. Remove the saucepan from the heat. Stir in the vegetable juice, corn and tomato. Pour the mixture into a serving bowl. Cover the bowl and refrigerate for at least 4 hours.

Pasta with the Works

prep 15 minutes | **cook** 10 minutes | **makes** 8 servings

- 1   package (1 pound) corkscrew-shaped pasta (rotini), cooked and drained (about 6 cups)
- 7½ cups Prego® Traditional **or** Roasted Garlic & Herb Italian Sauce
- 1   cup thinly sliced pepperoni, cut in half
- 2   medium green peppers, chopped (about 1½ cups)
- 1   cup large pitted ripe olives, cut in half
- 2   cups shredded mozzarella cheese (about 8 ounces)
     Grated Parmesan cheese

1. Heat the pasta, Italian sauce, pepperoni, peppers, olives and mozzarella cheese in a 6-quart saucepot over medium heat until the mixture is hot and bubbling, stirring often.

2. Serve with the Parmesan cheese.

Mulled Raspberry Mosas

prep 10 minutes | **makes** 4 servings

   16   fresh **or** thawed frozen raspberries
   1⅓ cups V8 Splash® Tropical Blend Juice, chilled
    1   cup champagne **or** seltzer water, chilled

1. Place **4** raspberries in **each** of the **4** fluted champagne glasses. Mash them lightly with a fork.

2. Pour ⅓ **cup** juice and ¼ **cup** champagne into **each** glass. Stir. Serve immediately.

Berry Bordeaux Desserts

prep 20 minutes | **chill** 3 hours | **makes** 12 servings

- 24 **Pepperidge Farm® Bordeaux® Cookies**
- 1 **cup heavy cream**
- ¼ **cup sugar**
- 1 **teaspoon vanilla extract**
- 3 **cups mixed berries***
  Mint leaves (optional)

Use a combination of sliced strawberries, raspberries, blackberries and blueberries.

1. Place **12** cookies into a 2-quart shallow baking dish.

2. Beat the heavy cream, **2 tablespoons** sugar and vanilla extract in a medium bowl with an electric mixer on high speed until stiff peaks form.

3. Spoon the whipped cream in the baking dish. Top with the remaining cookies. Cover and refrigerate for 3 hours or until the cookies are soft.

4. Stir the berries with the remaining sugar in a medium bowl. Spoon the berry mixture over the cookie mixture. Garnish with the mint, if desired.

Power Breakfast Sandwiches

prep 5 minutes | **makes** 2 servings

- ¼ **cup peanut butter**
- 4 **slices Pepperidge Farm® Stone Ground 100% Whole Wheat**
- ¼ **cup raisins**
- 1 **medium banana, sliced**

Spread the peanut butter on **4** bread slices. Divide the raisins and banana between **2** bread slices. Top with the remaining bread slices, peanut butter-side down. Cut the sandwiches in half.

Tip: You can substitute **1** large apple, cored and sliced, for the raisins and banana.

Campbell's
Swanson · Pace · Prego · PEPPERIDGE FARM · V8

Miami Chicken Salad Sandwiches

prep 15 minutes | **makes** 2 servings

- 2 tablespoons light mayonnaise
- 2 tablespoons reduced-fat sour cream
- 1 teaspoon dried tarragon leaves, crushed
- 1 can (4.5 ounces) Swanson® Premium White Chunk Chicken Breast in Water, drained
- ¼ cup slivered almonds, toasted
- ¼ cup chopped jicama **or** celery
- 4 slices Pepperidge Farm® Whole Grain Soft Honey Oat Bread, toasted*
- 1 mango, pitted, peeled and sliced Green leaf lettuce leaves

Also delicious with Pepperidge Farm® 100% Natural Honey Flax Bread.

1. Stir the mayonnaise, sour cream and tarragon in a medium bowl. Stir in the chicken, almonds and jicama.

2. Divide the chicken mixture between **2** bread slices. Top with the mango, lettuce and remaining bread slices.

Broccoli & Cheese Casserole

prep 10 minutes | **bake** 30 minutes | **makes** 6 servings

- 1 can (10¾ ounces) Campbell's® Condensed Cream of Mushroom Soup (Regular **or** 98% Fat Free)
- ½ cup milk
- 2 teaspoons yellow mustard
- 1 bag (16 ounces) frozen broccoli florets, thawed
- 1 cup shredded Cheddar cheese (4 ounces)
- ⅓ cup dry bread crumbs
- 2 teaspoons butter, melted

1. Stir the soup, milk, mustard, broccoli and cheese in a 1½-quart casserole.

2. Stir the bread crumbs and butter in a small bowl. Sprinkle the crumb mixture over the broccoli mixture.

3. Bake at 350°F. for 30 minutes or until the mixture is hot and bubbling.

Rice Is Nice: Add **2 cups** cooked white rice to the broccoli mixture before baking.

Cheese Change–Up: Substitute mozzarella cheese for the Cheddar.

Bandito Baked Beans

prep 5 minutes | **cook** 15 minutes | **makes** 6 servings

- 1 **tablespoon vegetable oil**
- ½ **cup chopped onion**
- 1 **cup Pace® Picante Sauce**
- ¼ **cup molasses**
- 1 **tablespoon spicy-brown mustard**
- 1 **can (about 15 ounces) pork and beans**
- 1 **can (about 15 ounces) black beans, rinsed and drained**

1. Heat the oil in a 2-quart saucepan over medium heat. Add the onion and cook until tender.

2. Stir the picante sauce, molasses, mustard, pork and beans and black beans in the saucepan and heat to a boil. Reduce the heat to low. Cook for 5 minutes or until the mixture is hot and bubbling.

Meatball Mini Bites

thaw 40 minutes | **prep** 10 minutes | **bake** 15 minutes | **cool** 5 minutes | **makes** 32 servings

- 1 package (17.3 ounces) Pepperidge Farm® Puff Pastry Sheets, thawed
- 32 (½ ounce **each**) frozen fully cooked meatballs
- ¾ cup prepared pasta sauce, basil pesto **or** sun-dried tomato pesto
- 2 cups baby arugula
  Shredded mozzarella **or** Asiago cheese

1. Heat the oven to 400°F. Unfold the pastry sheets on a lightly floured surface. Cut **each** pastry sheet into **16** (2½-inch) squares. Place the pastry squares onto 2 baking sheets.

2. Bake for 15 minutes or until pastries are golden brown. Let cool on the baking sheets for 5 minutes. Split **each** pastry into **2** layers, making **64** layers in all.

3. Heat the meatballs according to the package directions. Spread **about 1 teaspoon** pasta sauce on **each** bottom pastry layer. Top **each** with **1 tablespoon** arugula and **1** meatball. Top with the cheese, if desired, and the top pastry layers.

Chef's Salad

prep 25 minutes | **makes** 2 servings

- 1 small head romaine lettuce, torn into bite-size pieces (about 5 cups)
- 2 ounces cooked ham, cut into strips (about ½ cup)
- 2 ounces cooked turkey breast, cut into strips (about ½ cup)
- 2 ounces Swiss cheese, cut into cubes (about ½ cup)
- 1 hard-cooked egg, sliced (optional)
- 1 medium tomato, cut into wedges
- ½ cup Pepperidge Farm® Zesty Italian Croutons
  Prepared Italian salad dressing

Divide the lettuce between **2** plates. Top with the ham, turkey, cheese, egg, tomato and croutons. Drizzle with the dressing.

Mozzarella Cheese Bread Sticks

prep 15 minutes | **bake** 10 minutes | **makes** 24 servings

- 1 loaf (11¾ ounces) Pepperidge Farm® Mozzarella Garlic Bread
- 1½ cups Prego® Traditional Italian Sauce **or** Prego® Tomato Basil & Garlic Italian Sauce

1. Heat the oven to 400°F. Remove the bread from the bag. Carefully separate the bread halves with a fork. Place the **2** bread halves, cut-side up, onto a baking sheet.

2. Bake for 10 minutes or until the bread is heated through. Cut **each** bread half into **12** (1-inch) slices, making **24** in all. Serve with the Italian sauce for dipping.

Breakfast Pizza

prep 20 minutes | **cook** 10 minutes | **bake** 5 minutes | **makes** 6 servings

1	tablespoon butter
¼	cup chopped onion
¼	cup chopped green pepper
¼	cup chopped Canadian bacon
1	(12-inch) prepared pizza crust
8	eggs, beaten
¼	teaspoon ground black pepper
¾	cup Pace® Picante Sauce
2	ounces shredded Cheddar cheese (about ½ cup)
2	tablespoons chopped fresh cilantro leaves

1. Heat the oven to 400°F.
2. Heat the butter in a 10-inch skillet over medium heat. Add the onion, green pepper and bacon and cook until the vegetables are tender.
3. Place the pizza crust onto a pizza pan or baking sheet. Place in the oven to warm.
4. Stir the eggs and black pepper in the skillet. Cook and stir until the eggs are set. Spoon the egg mixture onto the pizza crust. Top with the picante sauce. Sprinkle with the cheese.
5. Bake for 5 minutes or until the cheese is melted. Sprinkle with the cilantro. Cut the pizza into 6 slices.

Lightened Up Beef & Vegetable Stir-Fry

prep 25 minutes | **cook** 25 minutes | **makes** 4 servings

Vegetable cooking spray
1 pound boneless beef sirloin steak, ¾-inch thick (about 1 pound), sliced into very thin strips
2 cups broccoli florets
6 ounces sliced mushrooms (about 2 cups)
2 medium onions, cut into wedges
½ teaspoon garlic powder **or** 2 cloves garlic, minced
1 can (10¾ ounces) Campbell's® Healthy Request® Condensed Cream of Mushroom Soup
½ cup water
1 tablespoon low-sodium soy sauce
1 cup regular long-grain white rice, cooked without salt (about 3 cups)

1. Spray a 12-inch skillet with cooking spray and heat over medium-high heat for 1 minute. Add the beef and cook until well browned, stirring often. Remove the beef from the skillet and set aside.

2. Remove the skillet from the heat and spray with the cooking spray. Add the broccoli, mushrooms, onions and garlic powder and cook until the vegetables are tender-crisp, stirring often.

3. Stir the soup, water and soy sauce in the skillet and heat to a boil. Return the beef to the skillet and cook until cooked through. Serve the beef mixture over the rice.

Campbell's

Bellini Splash

prep 5 minutes | **makes** 2 servings

- ½ cup V8 Splash® Mango Peach Juice Drink, chilled
- ¼ cup peach nectar, chilled
- 1 cup champagne, sparkling wine **or** sparkling cider, chilled

1. Stir the juice drink and nectar in a **1 cup** measure.

2. Divide the mixture between **2** fluted champagne glasses. Pour in the champagne.

3. Serve immediately.

Chicken Pasta Salad Italiano

prep 20 minutes | **chill** 30 minutes | **makes** 4 servings

- **3 cups corkscrew-shaped pasta (rotini), cooked and drained**
- **2 cans (4.5 ounces each) Swanson® Premium White Chunk Chicken Breast in Water, drained**
- **1 small cucumber, cut in half lengthwise and sliced**
- **1 medium tomato, chopped (about ½ cup)**
- **½ cup frozen peas, thawed**
- **¾ cup fat-free Italian salad dressing or reduced-fat creamy Italian salad dressing**

Place the pasta, chicken, cucumber, tomato and peas in a large bowl. Add the dressing and toss to coat. Cover and refrigerate for 30 minutes.

Tip: This simple salad lends itself to variation…it's a great way to use the leftover veggies in your fridge.

Campbell's

Corn and Black-Eyed Pea Salad

prep 15 minutes | **chill** 4 hours | **makes** 8 servings

- 1 bag (16 ounces) frozen whole kernel corn, thawed (about 3 cups)
- 1 can (about 15 ounces) black-eyed peas, rinsed and drained
- 1 large green pepper, chopped (about 1 cup)
- 1 medium onion, chopped (about ½ cup)
- ½ cup chopped fresh cilantro leaves
- 1 jar (16 ounces) Pace® Picante Sauce

1. Stir the corn, peas, green pepper, onion and cilantro in a medium bowl. Add the picante sauce and stir to coat.

2. Cover and refrigerate for 4 hours. Stir before serving.

Tip: Prepare the salad as directed. Cover and refrigerate overnight. Stir the salad before serving.

Tropical Mojitos

prep 10 minutes | **makes** 8 servings

- 1 **cup fresh mint leaves**
     Ice cubes
- 3 **bottles (16 ounces each) V8 Splash® Tropical Blend**
     Juice Drink (6 cups), chilled
- 1 **cup rum**

1. Divide the mint leaves among **8** tall glasses. Mash them lightly with the back of a spoon. Fill the glasses with ice.

2. Stir the juice drink and rum in a 2-quart pitcher and pour into the ice-filled glasses.

Tip: Recipe may be doubled.

Spicy Onion Burgers

prep 10 minutes | **grill** 10 minutes | **makes** 6 servings

- 1½ **pounds ground beef**
- ½ **cup Pace® Picante Sauce**
- 1 **envelope (about 1 ounce) dry onion soup and recipe mix**
- 6 **Pepperidge Farm® Classic Sandwich Buns with Sesame Seeds**
- **Lettuce leaves**
- **Tomato slices**
- **Avocado slices**

1. Mix **thoroughly** the beef, picante sauce and soup mix. Shape **firmly** into **6** burgers, ½-inch thick **each**.

2. Lightly oil the grill rack and heat the grill to medium. Grill the burgers for 10 minutes or until desired doneness, turning the burgers over halfway through grilling.

3. Serve on buns with lettuce, tomato, avocado and additional picante sauce.

Mexican Pizza

thaw 40 minutes | **prep** 20 minutes | **bake** 15 minutes | **makes** 4 servings

- ½ **of a 17.3–ounce package Pepperidge Farm® Puff Pastry Sheets (1 sheet), thawed**
- ¾ **cup Prego® Traditional Italian Sauce**
- ¼ **cup Pace® Picante Sauce**
- ¾ **cup shredded mozzarella cheese**
- ¾ **cup shredded Cheddar cheese**
- ¼ **cup sliced pitted ripe olives**

1. Heat the oven to 400°F.

2. Unfold the pastry sheet on a lightly floured surface. Roll the pastry sheet into a 15×10-inch rectangle. Place the pastry onto a baking sheet. Prick the pastry thoroughly with a fork. Bake for 10 minutes or until the pastry is golden brown.

3. Stir the Italian sauce and picante sauce in a small bowl. Spread the sauce mixture on the pastry to within ½ inch of the edge. Top with the cheeses and sprinkle with the olives. Bake for 5 minutes or until the cheese is melted.

Campbell's

Lemon Broccoli Chicken

prep 5 minutes | **cook** 20 minutes | **makes** 4 servings

- 1 **lemon**
- 1 **tablespoon vegetable oil**
- 4 **skinless, boneless chicken breast halves (about 1 pound)**
- 1 **can (10¾ ounces) Campbell's® Condensed Cream of Broccoli Soup (Regular or 98% Fat Free)**
- ¼ **cup milk**
- ⅛ **teaspoon ground black pepper**

1. Cut **4** thin slices of the lemon. Squeeze **2 teaspoons** juice from the remaining lemon.

2. Heat the oil in a 10-inch skillet over medium-high heat. Add the chicken and cook for 10 minutes or until well browned on both sides.

3. Stir the soup, milk, lemon juice and black pepper in the skillet and heat to a boil. Top the chicken with the lemon slices. Reduce the heat to low. Cover and cook for 5 minutes or until the chicken is cooked through.

Crunchy Potato Salad

prep 25 minutes | **cook** 15 minutes | **chill** 3 hours |
makes 4 servings

- 9   medium potatoes, cut into cubes (about 9 cups)
- 1   can (10¾ ounces) Campbell's® Condensed Cream of Celery Soup (Regular **or** 98% Fat Free)
- ¾   cup mayonnaise
- ¼   cup vinegar
- ½   teaspoon ground black pepper
- 2   stalks celery, chopped (about 1 cup)
- 1   small green pepper, chopped (about ½ cup)
- 2   medium green onions, chopped (about ¼ cup)
- 2   hard-cooked eggs, chopped

1. Place the potatoes into a 3-quart saucepan and add water to cover. Heat over medium-high heat to a boil. Reduce the heat to low. Cook for 10 minutes or until the potatoes are tender. Drain the potatoes well in a colander.

2. Stir the soup, mayonnaise, vinegar and black pepper in a large bowl. Add the potatoes, celery, green pepper, onions and eggs and toss to coat. Cover and refrigerate for 3 hours or overnight.

Skinny Funsicles

prep 10 minutes | **freeze** 4 hours | **makes** 6 servings

1   cup no-sugar-added vanilla ice cream
6   (3-ounce) plastic cups
6   craft sticks
1½ cups Diet V8 Splash® Tropical Blend, Berry Blend **or** Strawberry Kiwi Juice Drink

1. Place **2 heaping tablespoons** ice cream into each plastic cup. Insert a craft stick into the ice cream.

2. Fill the cups almost to the top with the juice drink. Freeze them until firm.

Tip: To remove Funsicles easily from cups, let them stand at room temperature for a few minutes or place them under cold running water for a few seconds.

For Fruity Diet V8 Splash® Funsicles: Add frozen **or** fresh blueberries to the cups before freezing.

Campbell's

Picnic Chicken Salad Sandwiches

prep 15 minutes | **chill** 2 hours | **makes** 6 servings

- 1 can (10¾ ounces) Campbell's® Condensed Cream of Celery Soup (Regular **or** 98% Fat Free)
- 2 tablespoons mayonnaise
- ¼ teaspoon ground black pepper
- 2 cups chopped cooked chicken
- 2 stalks celery, sliced (about 1 cup)
- 1 small onion, finely chopped (about ¼ cup)
- 6 Pepperidge Farm® Classic Sandwich Buns with Sesame Seeds, split
  Lettuce leaves
  Tomato slices

1. Stir the soup, mayonnaise and black pepper in a large bowl. Add the chicken, celery and onion and toss to coat. Cover and refrigerate for 2 hours.

2. Place the lettuce and tomato on the buns. Divide the chicken mixture among the buns.

Tomato Soup & Grilled Cheese Sandwich

prep 5 minutes | **cook** 5 minutes | **makes** 4 servings

- 2 **cans** (10¾ ounces **each**) Campbell's® Condensed Tomato Soup
- 2 **cans** water
- 8 **teaspoons** butter, softened
- 8 **slices** Pepperidge Farm® White Sandwich Bread
- 8 **slices** process American cheese

1. Heat the soup and water in a 1-quart saucepan over medium heat until the mixture is hot and bubbling, stirring occasionally.

2. Spread the butter on the bread slices.

3. Place **4** bread slices, butter-side down, into a 12-inch skillet. Top with the cheese slices and remaining bread slices, butter-side up. Cook over medium heat until the sandwiches are lightly browned on both sides and the cheese is melted.

Tropical Freeze

prep 10 minutes | **makes** 4 servings

- 1 **bottle (16 ounces) V8 Splash® Tropical Blend Juice Drink, chilled**
- 1 **pint orange or mango sherbet or vanilla ice cream**
- 1 **cup crushed ice**
- 2 **medium bananas, sliced**

1. Put the juice drink, sherbet, ice and ½ of the bananas in a blender.

2. Cover and blend until the mixture is smooth. Garnish with the remaining banana slices. Serve immediately.

Frosted Citrus Green Tea

prep 15 minutes | **freeze** 1 hour 30 minutes | **chill** 1 hour 30 minutes | **makes** 6 servings

- **4** cups Diet V8 Splash® Tropical Blend Juice Drink, chilled
- **4** cups strong brewed green tea
  Fresh mint sprigs (optional)
  Lemon slices (optional)

1. Pour **2 cups** of the juice drink into **1** ice cube tray. Freeze for 1 hour 30 minutes or until frozen.

2. Stir the remaining juice drink and tea in a pitcher and refrigerate for at least 1 hour 30 minutes.

3. Unmold the cubes and place **3 to 4** cubes in each of **6** glasses. Pour the tea mixture into **each** glass. Serve with mint and lemon, if desired.

Summer Bruschetta

prep 15 minutes | **makes** 4 servings

- 1   tablespoon balsamic vinegar
- 1   tablespoon olive oil
- ¼   cup fresh basil leaves, cut into thin strips
- 1   tablespoon minced garlic
- 8   plum tomatoes, seeded and chopped
- 8   slices Pepperidge Farm® 100% Natural 100% Whole Wheat Bread, toasted **or** grilled and cut diagonally into quarters
- ¼   cup shredded Parmesan cheese

1. Beat the vinegar, oil, basil and garlic in a small bowl with a fork or whisk. Stir in the tomatoes.
2. Divide the tomato mixture among the bread quarters. Top the with cheese.

Honey-Barbecued Ribs

prep 10 minutes | **cook** 40 minutes | **grill** 20 minutes | **makes** 4 servings

- 1 rack pork spareribs (about 4 pounds)
- 1 can (10½ ounces) Campbell's® Condensed French Onion Soup
- ¾ cup ketchup
- ⅓ cup honey
- ½ teaspoon garlic powder
- ½ teaspoon ground black pepper

1. Place the ribs into a 6-quart saucepot and add water to cover. Heat over medium-high heat to a boil. Reduce the heat to low. Cover and cook for 30 minutes or until the meat is tender. Drain the ribs well in a colander.

2. Heat the soup, ketchup, honey, garlic powder and black pepper in a 2-quart saucepan over medium-high heat to a boil. Reduce the heat to low. Cook for 5 minutes.

3. Lightly oil the grill rack and heat the grill to medium. Grill the ribs for 20 minutes or until well glazed, turning and brushing often with the soup mixture. Cut the ribs into serving-size pieces.

Chilled Picante Gazpacho

prep 15 minutes | **chill** 2 hours | **makes** 4 servings

- 1 **can (28 ounces) whole peeled tomatoes**
- ¾ **cup Pace® Picante Sauce**
- 2 **tablespoons lemon juice**
- 1 **tablespoon chopped fresh cilantro leaves**
- ¼ **teaspoon garlic powder or 1 clove garlic, minced**
- 1 **cup thickly sliced cucumber**
- 1 **stalk celery, cut into 1-inch pieces**
- 1 **slice firm Pepperidge Farm® White Sandwich Bread**
- ¼ **cup chopped cucumber**
  Sliced green onions

1. Place the tomatoes, picante sauce, lemon juice, cilantro, garlic powder, sliced cucumber, celery and bread into a blender or food processor. Cover and blend until smooth. Refrigerate for at least 2 hours.

2. Top with the chopped cucumber. Garnish with the onions.

Campbell's

Bruschetta Salad

prep 20 minutes | **makes** 6 servings

- ½   cup olive oil
- 2   tablespoons red wine vinegar
- 2   medium tomatoes, cut into 1-inch pieces (about 2 cups)
- ½   cup thinly sliced cucumber
- 1   medium red onion, thinly sliced (about ½ cup)
- ¼   cup chopped fresh basil leaves
- 1   tablespoon drained capers
- 2   cups Pepperidge Farm® Whole Grain Seasoned Croutons

1. Beat the oil and vinegar in a large bowl with a fork or whisk. Add the tomatoes, cucumbers, onion, basil and capers and toss to coat.

2. Add the croutons just before serving and toss to coat. Serve immediately.

Tip: It's important to serve this salad immediately so that the croutons will stay crisp.

Grilled Maui Burgers

prep 15 minutes | **grill** 15 minutes | **makes** 4 servings

- 1 **can (8 ounces) pineapple slices in juice, drained (4 slices)**
- 1 **cup Pace® Picante Sauce**
- 1 **pound lean ground beef**
- 4 **slices deli Monterey Jack cheese (about 3 ounces)**
- 4 **Pepperidge Farm® Hamburger Buns, split and toasted**
- ½ **avocado, peeled, pitted and cut into 4 slices**

1. Lightly oil the grill rack and heat the grill to medium. Grill the pineapple for 5 minutes or until tender, turning it over once halfway through the grill time. Remove the pineapple to a cutting board. Dice the pineapple. Stir the pineapple and ⅔ **cup** picante sauce in a medium bowl.

2. Thoroughly mix the beef and the remaining picante sauce in a large bowl. Shape the beef mixture into **4** (½-inch-thick) burgers.

3. Grill the burgers for 10 minutes for medium or until desired doneness, turning the burgers over once halfway through the grill time. Top the burgers with the cheese.

4. Serve the burgers on the buns. Top with the pineapple-picante mixture and the avocado.

Tomato Mac 'n' Cheese

prep 20 minutes | **cook** 5 minutes | **makes** 5 servings

- 1 **can (10¾ ounces) Campbell's® Condensed Cheddar Cheese Soup**
- 1 **cup Prego® Traditional Italian Sauce**
- ⅓ **cup milk**
- 2 **cups elbow macaroni, cooked and drained Grated Parmesan cheese**

1. Heat the soup, Italian sauce, milk and macaroni in a 3-quart saucepan over medium heat until the mixture is hot and bubbling, stirring occasionally.

2. Serve with the cheese.

Layered Tex-Mex Salad

prep 20 minutes | **makes** 8 servings

½	cup Pace® Picante Sauce
½	cup mayonnaise
¼	cup sour cream **or** plain yogurt
3	cups coarsely shredded lettuce
2	medium tomatoes, chopped (about 2 cups)
1	small cucumber, cut in half lengthwise and sliced (about 1½ cups)
1	medium red onion, sliced
1	large avocado, peeled, pitted and thinly sliced (about 1 cup)
¼	cup sliced pitted ripe olives

1. Stir the picante sauce, mayonnaise and sour cream in a small bowl.

2. Layer the lettuce, tomatoes, cucumber, onion and avocado in a large clear glass bowl. Spoon the picante sauce mixture over the top. Sprinkle with the olives. Serve immediately.

Mango Milk Shakes

prep 5 minutes | **makes** 2 servings

- 2 cups V8 V-Fusion® Peach Mango Juice **or** V8 Splash® Tropical Blend Juice Drink
- 1 cup vanilla ice cream

Put the juice and ice cream in a blender. Cover and blend until the mixture is smooth. Serve immediately.

Campbell's

Lentil Rice Salad

prep 10 minutes | **cook** 20 minutes | **stand** 5 minutes |
chill 2 hours | **makes** 6 servings

- 1¾ cups Swanson® Chicken Broth (Regular, Natural Goodness® **or** Certified Organic)
- ½ cup **uncooked** regular long-grain white rice
- ⅓ cup dried lentils
- 2 tablespoons chopped fresh parsley
  Generous dash ground red pepper
- 1 stalk celery, sliced (about ½ cup)
- 1 medium red onion, chopped
- ½ cup diced green **or** red pepper
- ½ cup fat-free Italian vinaigrette
  Lettuce leaves

1. Heat the broth to a boil in a 2-quart saucepan over medium-high heat. Stir in the rice and lentils. Reduce the heat to low. Cover and cook for 20 minutes or until done. Let stand for 5 minutes or until the liquid is absorbed.

2. Toss the lentil mixture, parsley, ground red pepper, celery, onion, green pepper and vinaigrette in a large bowl until evenly coated. Cover and refrigerate for at least 2 hours or overnight. Serve on the lettuce.

German Potato Salad

prep 15 minutes | **cook** 30 minutes | **makes** 12 servings

- 10 **medium potatoes**
- 1¾ **cups Swanson® Beef Broth (Regular, Lower Sodium or Certified Organic)**
- ¼ **cup cider vinegar**
- ¼ **cup all-purpose flour**
- 3 **tablespoons sugar**
- ½ **teaspoon celery seed**
- ⅛ **teaspoon ground black pepper**
- 1 **medium onion, chopped (about ½ cup)**
- 3 **tablespoons chopped fresh parsley**

1. Place the potatoes into a 4-quart saucepan. Add water to cover. Heat over high heat to a boil. Reduce the heat to low. Cook for 20 minutes or until the potatoes are tender. Drain. Let cool and cut in cubes. Place the potatoes into a large bowl.

2. Stir the broth, vinegar, flour, sugar, celery seed and black pepper in the saucepan. Stir in the onion. Cook and stir over medium-high heat until the mixture boils and thickens. Reduce the heat to low. Cook for 5 minutes or until the onion is tender.

3. Add the parsley and broth mixture to the potatoes and stir to coat. Serve warm.

Tip: You can let this dish stand for a few minutes before serving. The dressing will soak into the warm potatoes—delicious!